THE MIRACLE, THE MESSAGE, THE STORY

THE MIRACLE,
THE MESSAGE,
THE STORY

Jean Vanier and l'Arche

Kathryn Spink

HiddenSpring

Designed by Sandie Boccacci

This edition published by arrangement with
Darton, Longman and Todd, Ltd
1 Spencer Court
140-142 Wandsworth High Street
London SW18 4JJ

ISBN 1-58768-038-6

Library of Congress Control Number: 2005938037

Published in 2006 by
HiddenSpring
An imprint of Paulist Press
997 Macarthur Boulevard
Mahwah, New Jersey 07430

www.hiddenspringbooks.com

Printed and bound in Great Britain

CONTENTS

LIST OF ILLUSTRATIONS

ACKNOWLEDGEMENTS

IT WOULD BE IMPOSSIBLE TO mention individually all those people who have contributed in many and various ways to the writing of this book, but I would like to express my particular thanks to all those members of the l'Arche communities in Trosly-Breuil, Toronto, Erie, Tegucigalpa, Choluteca, London, Kolkata and elsewhere who gave so generously of their hospitality and their insight. My thanks too to Gerry Arbuckle, Teresa de Bertodano, Caroline Weldon, to my long-suffering family, and to Barbara Swanekamp who came to Trosly-Breuil in 1965 with the intention of staying for three months and has been 'filling in the holes' ever since. She has been an invaluable if hidden source of information, support and tea ever since first I visited Trosly in 1988. A special debt of gratitude is also due to Thérèse Vanier and to Jean for trusting and for sharing so much.

ONE

READING THE MIRACLE

Jesus is in Jerusalem.
He does not go first to places of learning and power
But to the local asylum,
Where there was a multitude of people with disabilities: lame,
blind and paralyzed. (John 5:3)

Lying around, living in *dis-grace*.
They were no doubt dirty and ugly,
According to the values of the world, shunned and despised:
Neither beauty nor comeliness in them.
Yet it is to them that Jesus goes first.[1]

IN 1964, SOME 40 YEARS prior to writing these words, in the
scarcely definable but sure conviction that this was what Jesus
wanted of him, Jean Vanier bought an unassuming stone house in
Trosly-Breuil, an often cloud-hung village on the edge of the
Compiègne forest just north of Paris. He then invited three
broken, rejected people to leave the institution where they had
been living 'in dis-grace' and make their home with him. This
naïve but irreversible step was one born, by his own account, of
a desire to 'be good' and 'do good' to people with disabilities. He
had no idea at that time that those people would 'do good' to
him. Yet what began as an act of compassion towards the suffering that had profoundly moved him led to the very concrete
discovery of the riches of the biblically poor. It was an invitation
which enabled him and l'Arche (the Ark), the community that

grew out of it, to touch in a special way upon the mystery of the person with disabilities and so to enter more deeply into relationship with Jesus.

The desire simply to live together, not as 'educators' and people with disabilities, but as sharers in a life of communion, highlighted by contrast the great gulf more often fixed in our divided world between the strong and the weak, the powerful and the vulnerable, the clever and the disabled, between those with a voice in human affairs and those with none. The 'rich' have work, possessions, status, Jean Vanier was to maintain, but often lack what is essential: the capacity to love, to live relationships of communion without fear, without hiding behind the many trappings of success, power and defence. They look upon the 'poor' and weak as problems to be resolved according to their own vision, refusing to enter into a dialogue of trust with those who are oppressed and in distress. They will not listen to them. Sometimes they even want to prevent their very existence. To them it is inconceivable that the despised and pitied might hold in their hearts the solutions to the very problems they allegedly represent. In each one of us there is a strong resistance to the change to which dialogue with the poor inevitably calls us. The cry of the person in need inconveniences those who are comfortable and satisfied with themselves and their lot. The anguish of people with disabilities reveals our own anguish, their shadows are our shadows, and so we turn away.

And yet the small community begun in 1964 in Trosly-Breuil soon increased in number, not only of people with disabilities but also of 'assistants' prepared not to turn away but to seek instead to share their lives. Other communities in France and elsewhere followed rapidly in its wake, all born of a desire to create homes – not institutions but *foyers*, with all the associations of family life gathered about a shared hearth that the French word conveys – where people with disabilities and assistants could experience together the joy and the difficulties of a community life inspired by the Beatitudes. Inevitably they varied in their outer expression. By 1995, in excess of 400 people were living together in the original community, made up of more than 20 houses scattered throughout Trosly-Breuil and its neighbouring villages, despite the fact that in 1981 the Compiègne community, originally for those less disabled, many of whom could work in local industry, had become a separate entity. L'Arche 'Trosly-Breuil' had in fact become so large that the need was felt to split it into three. More recent communities may be composed of no more than a dozen people. By 2005 there were in excess of 125 l'Arche communities spread across the continents. As in France, l'Arche in India, North America, Britain, the Ivory Coast, Honduras, Burkino Faso, Australia or Poland sought to integrate with and so express itself in terms of the local culture. Some communities were set in the heart of capital cities; others in rural areas. Some had their own workshops; in others the people with disabilities went out to work elsewhere. Some welcomed severely mentally disabled people; some welcomed children; some had not felt called or were not equipped to do so.

Religious belief was not an obligatory part of life in l'Arche. Some communities did not set aside a specific place in which to pray. L'Arche in Trosly-Breuil had an oratory and two chapels, one of which was a converted barn, the stone walls and beams of which were still exposed. Chapels in communities elsewhere might be even simpler and more improvised; a tiny room with rush matting on the floor, a candle, an icon, a tabernacle where the Blessed Sacrament was reserved, an unoccupied bedroom or the corner of an attic. The prayer room in l'Arche or 'Asha Niketan' (Home of Hope) in Kolkata preserved in a series of niches in the wall seven books representing the seven major religions in India. The books were rotated so that no one religion was given precedence. In countries where the local people were not Christian the communities were not necessarily Christian. Where people were Christian they might be of different denominations. There were also those in l'Arche who would not lay claim to any particular belief, though most assistants who stayed for any length of time, because of the very quality of relationship the life entailed, acknowledged the call to some form of prayer. Attempts at tidy definition tended therefore to crumble. At the heart of every community, however, be it in Belfast or Haiti, the aim to constitute a family in which people with mental disabilities could find security and peace in which to grow remained the same, as did the spirit – that of a special sensitivity to both the needs and the prophetic role of the poor.

L'Arche was lived on many levels, on a level so inexpressible that even to attempt to put the experience into words was, as one assistant put it, in some way to set fire to it; but on a level also which was very tangible and physical. Those levels were intimately linked. There was a stillness about the chapels and the oratory at Trosly, which was yet not separated from the reality of brokenness that is so much a part of our world. Mass there bore daily witness to a profound relationship between the broken bread upon the altar and the broken but life-giving presence of the people with disabilities who might shuffle their feet, comb their hair or even cry out their anguish, but whom no one could judge to be irreverent.

L'Arche, as distinct from many other communities, was founded not on the word but in a very particular way on the body. People with mental disabilities tended to be people of few words but people for whom the body with its pains, its pleasures and its capacity for expression and relationship featured prominently. 'God reveals himself to people first of all by the word which is very close to the spirit, filled with light and touches our intelligence and our hearts,' claimed Jean Vanier:

> And then there is the revelation of God through the body which seems to be the opposite of creativity, the power, the beauty, and the wisdom of the word: the littleness of the body, the fragility of the body, the ugliness, the dirt, the smell as it dies. With our people here there are little words and a lot of body.

Yet because of the mysterious relationship between the Word and the flesh, those whose bodies were broken, minds were disabled and hearts were open had the gift of revelation, and the capacity to lead others into the communion that is the life of God:

> In the beginning, before all things communion was: communion between God and the 'Logos' – the 'Word'[2] ...The Word became flesh and dwelt among us (John 1:14) ... God, the eternal God, Creator of the heavens and the earth became like us, a vulnerable, mortal human being ... He became part of history revealing to us a way to God and to universal peace ... He came to lead us all into this communion, which is the very life of God.[3]

The mysterious re-enactment of this reality was, moreover, sometimes best understood in the experience of 'living with'. To recognise the presence of Jesus in the poor and to talk about it was one thing; actually to be confronted by the poor person salivating, irritating, sometimes violent, uninhibited, intuitive, disconcertingly discerning and craving real attention was quite another. As one l'Arche assistant put it, 'You have to find out what it is to share a bathroom with these people.' Before a humanly speaking deformed face could be seen as extraordinarily beautiful, before the Word could be discerned in the flesh, there were often many barriers to be surmounted; there was a great deal of 'living with' to be done. The rich man of St Matthew's Gospel (22:1–14), present in all of us, found every possible excuse not to go to the wedding feast. Committing oneself to the poor person crying out for love meant in some way dying to oneself: to one's comforts, wealth, leisure, reputation, success, and possibly even one's family and friends. It meant becoming poor oneself, not externally but internally. It meant feeling oneself poor in the presence of the poor and so being 'reduced' to prayer. In the understanding of Jean Vanier God had a way of calling people to go forward into the double world of the poverty outside and the poverty within:

> For me the macrocosm and the microcosm are intimately connected, so that the whole vision of Jesus is the gradual discovery that the poor are not people whom we have to change from our pedestal and make them like us but people from whom we can drink. That means that the outside poverty and the inside poverty is the same reality to drink from. The presence of God is in our own littleness and poverty, in our need for love and recognition.

The parable of Lazarus and the rich man, between whom there was a great gulf fixed (Luke 16:20–31) applied to both the outer and the inner world. 'There is the gulf between the rich and the poor and there is the gulf of our own consciousness, and everything in life is the passage through that divide.'

My own first invitation to visit l'Arche came in 1988. It was accepted with what I would subsequently discover was a far from uncommon sense of being mysteriously drawn and yet afraid. I had little previous experience of people with mental disabilities and was acutely aware of my own overdeveloped if unwarranted sensibilities when it came to such superficial considerations as table manners and hygiene. I was given a gentle introduction. At table in the various houses to which I was invited I was tactfully placed next to people who were not too likely to deposit food in my lap. They were frequently gifted with the ability to allay my apprehension with the most beguiling of smiles. They accepted my silences and, because of their own speech difficulties, listened with exceptional patience and understanding to my halting French.

I had gone to Trosly-Breuil to gather material for a biography of the founder of the l'Arche communities. At Jean Vanier's suggestion, and almost without realising what was happening, I found myself next visiting not only l'Arche in England but also the communities of Daybreak in Canada, Erie in the United States, Tegucigalpa and Choluteca in Honduras, and some time later Asha Niketan, Kolkata. I journeyed from the snow of Toronto to the dusty heat of a Honduran *barrio* in an attempt to see how the initial vision of Trosly-Breuil expressed itself in different cultures, and in the course of those travels, the voice of the poor gained, as Jean Vanier had doubtless known it would, a special resonance.

I saw something of what it meant to welcome the poor in the relative material affluence of Canada and the United States, where government funding could not only provide but actually require a certain standard of living but where the struggle for a sense of community and simplicity of life was possibly all the harder for it. I saw a little of the many faces of poverty, of what it meant to be poor in Honduras, for example, where disabled children could be an intolerable burden on mothers with large families and no husbands to help care for them, but where the spirit of materially impoverished people spontaneously recognised the tiny symbols of hope that the l'Arche communities were. I took part in a Sariswati *puja* at Asha Niketan and witnessed the ongoing search for living models of inter-faith spirituality in l'Arche as the Hindu brahmin explained the meaning of a ceremony in celebration of and thanksgiving for the goddess of learning and inspiration. I lived moments gentle and not so gentle but often stripped of the barriers which the attempts to cover vulnerability more usually erect, and I learned something of the maturity and understanding of people with disabilities. Beyond the cultural differences it became possible to discern what it was that Randy with his television set, his readily available shower water at a prescribed temperature, his lunch box and his exercise bike had in common with Felipe, who had been left to fend for himself on the dirt tracks of the *barrio*, whose only means of getting about was an improvised wooden cart which someone else must pull for him, and whose poverty had brought him close to death. I discovered, not for the first time, what it was to be touched by the poor and to be sustained by them. It was not that the assistants were not welcoming. Far from it – they were extraordinary in their gifts, their acceptance of their own and others' disabilities and their generosity of heart, but in each community I learned to trust that it would be the 'disabled' people who would most astutely sense my weariness, feelings of strangeness or inadequacy, my own poverty and, in an intuitive, subtle way, effect some healing. For two days in Choluteca I found myself 'disabled' by my very limited knowledge of Spanish and of the Honduran way of carrying out the simplest daily tasks. I struggled ineptly to make tortillas and cook them over a wood fire and stammered inappropriate responses to well intentioned questions, only to find myself tacitly supported by Vilma, a Honduran girl, herself only barely able to speak. She could not know that I, like her, was virtually blind in my left eye – my handicap was less visible than hers – but she took me by the hand in moments of confusion and showed me where to go and what to do.

Overwhelmed with gratitude for the very people I had feared, for Johnny whose twisted smile was so infectious, for Lita whose uncontrollable dribbling I no longer noticed, for Dave who, with his pipe between his lips, would solemnly entertain me with stories of his early life that were so flagrantly but absorbingly untrue, for Peggy who concealed her disappointment so graciously when I and not, as she had expected, Princess Diana, arrived for dinner, and for the multitude of others I met along the way, Jean Vanier's vision of the poor as people from whom we might drink was rendered flesh. I had been borne along by the spirit of celebration which invariably greeted my presence as a guest, by the messages of welcome, the crayoned pictures on my bed, the flowers pressed into my hand on arrival, the prayers for my journey. Only in Miami airport as I re-entered a more sophisticated and individualistic world after my visit to l'Arche in Central America, did the profound suffering of those rejected for the strangeness of their bodies and disregarded for having something missing from their minds really strike me. The tears flowed quietly but embarrassingly persistently for some hours, and with them came a fuller appreciation of the gifts and strengths beyond the suffering, and an inkling of the extent to which the story of the person with disabilities at the heart of l'Arche was potentially the story of Everyman.

In 1989, when first we worked together on a book on l'Arche, Jean Vanier was at pains to disclaim the title of founder. Growth in community meant the progression from 'my work' to 'our work' to 'God's work'. More specifically, the foundation of l'Arche was as attributable to the inspiration of Père Thomas Philippe – the Dominican priest who had been the younger man's spiritual father – and to the disabled people who despite, or rather because of their physical and psychic wounds, were the source of the community's life. L'Arche, Jean Vanier insisted then, had begun as a response to the cry of the poor, had brought with it increased understanding of poverty, a sense of personal poverty on the part of those who set out to 'help' the poor, and ultimately the recognition that the cry was not only the expression of the need of the world but also of its hope. There had been the poverty, which Jean Vanier was quick to point out: his own. There had been the poverty of Père Thomas, who had known acute rejection and anguish; of the assistants; of the community; of those who did not know how to respond to the disabled person's call for love and relationship; and through all this poverty, there had been extraordinary grace and growth.

In 2004 Jean Vanier stood by that insistence. Some 15 years had elapsed since first I sat down in a pool of water on a bench outside the chapel at Trosly-Breuil, simply because Jean, oblivious to the dampness, had motioned me to do so. This time he had recently had a birthday, and the assistants and people with disabilities from the *foyer* to which he belonged, together with a few honoured guests required to wear festive hats, gathered for a belated celebration, a dinner of his favourite dish: roast lamb with mint sauce. At the age of 76 he was aware, with a certain sadness, that some of the simplicity and spontaneity had gone from his relationships with the younger assistants, that for some he had become the 'venerable founder', but he had lost none of his sense of humour and the childlike 'nonsense' quality that had long enabled him to take gleeful delight in water fights over the washing up, feigning exclusive possession of a box of chocolates or manoeuvring his 6ft 4in angular frame to the front of queues. After guitar strumming and general tomfoolery, a text from St Luke's Gospel (14:13) was read quietly to the assembled company: 'When you have a party invite the poor, the cripples, the lame and the blind' – 'and even an English author in a comical hat!' some generous soul appended.

Over 40 years of 'inviting the poor' and of 'living together' with people with mental disabilities, those afflicted with a very particular form of poverty, had reinforced rather than altered the conviction that God had chosen the weak, the 'crazy' and the despised to confound the strong, the clever and the respected. L'Arche had become more internationally famous, as had the man who was so reluctant to be revered and remained so wary of the seduction of being powerful even in order to do good. Insouciant about his appearance – he spent most of his life in a blue anorak and admitted to once having turned up to give a talk wearing one brown shoe and one black – he was as concerned as ever about his inner struggle 'between the desire to live simple relationships of communion with others and the need for power, to control others'. As he grew older he professed to being more aware of his own fears and blockages, of his difficulty in relationships and of the need for the love of God to transform his 'heart of stone into a heart of flesh, a vulnerable heart open to others.'

He was still slim and charismatic, a man of apparent strength and authority of body and mind. Hearing aids had recently resolved the problem of deafness and he was quick to emphasise the compensations of old age. He could now unreservedly enjoy being helped out of his chair or taking people's arms when he walked. Words still came quietly but with great fluency, delivered in a compelling voice and often emphasised with gestures of both hands. He remained by his own admission 'contained', not sharing his innermost thoughts and feelings easily. He struggled to do so in an atmosphere of trust but still spoke most readily of spiritual truths touching one upon another in a network of relationships which became ever more subtle with deepening understanding, and of others. Ask him to talk about l'Arche or about St John and he was fine, but take him to a dinner party and he would find that he had nothing to say.

Not long previously a bishop had told him, 'You in l'Arche are responsible for a Copernican revolution: until now we used to say that we should do good to the poor but you are saying that the poor are doing good to you!' In his seventies Jean Vanier seemed to be more aware of the wider implications of that 'Copernican revolution': that l'Arche had a message about liberation and morality, conscience and law that was relevant to the Church and to society at large. He was more aware that people with disabilities, both in and outside l'Arche, were not only the mystery of the hidden, vulnerable God, the littleness of God waiting, but simultaneously a revelation of the glory of God. More than ever he was conscious of the role of the suffering poor person, with whom Jesus had specifically identified himself at the heart of the Gospels, being also at the heart of the Church, most obviously and potently represented in the suffering servant figure of Pope John Paul II; and of the potential of this presence for the transformation, unity and healing of broken humanity. Gradually the network of relationships emerged with greater profundity and clarity: at the heart of l'Arche was the 'person with disabilities' who was not only the person obviously 'disabled'. Moreover, at the heart of l'Arche, as at the heart of the Gospel, as at the heart of the Church, that broken body which for all its dreadful frailty nonetheless maintained the two essential realities – the Word of God and the real presence in the Eucharist – was the mystery of poverty and pain that was yet life-giving.

Jean Vanier had just completed a book on St John's Gospel, the fruit of many years of reflection, study, prayer and living in community. Having written it, he claimed he had a feeling that there was nothing else to be done, although almost with the next breath he was modifying, as he frequently did, his own assertion. The book spoke of what was in his heart:

These insights that I share in this book come from the life of
Jesus in me, what Jesus teaches me in prayer and study.
They also flow from my life with people who are weak and
who have taught me to welcome Jesus
From the place of poverty in me.
This interpretation of the Gospel of John cannot be separated
from who I am, with all that is broken in me
And from the ways Jesus has guided my life.[4]

It was not difficult to discern in it the manner in which his
understanding of St John's Gospel had been fed by his experience
of l'Arche and his own life's journey, and how St John's Gospel
had simultaneously influenced his vision of l'Arche and life:

> Jesus calls his disciples to follow him as he goes towards the
> most rejected of people. He is revealing that he comes to heal
> the paralysis of our hearts and to lead us into life (John 5) …
> Jesus reveals that our final destiny is love and that we are called
> to a wonderful sacred wedding feast. But to live this celebra-
> tion the waters of our humanity have to be transformed into
> the new wine of divine love (John 2:1–12).

The subtle relationship between the revelation of the gospels,
particularly that of St John, l'Arche and his personal story was
one which Jean Vanier was readily prepared to acknowledge. In
the same book he had written: 'People reach greater maturity as
they find the freedom to be themselves and to claim, accept and
love their own personal story, with all its brokenness and its
beauty.' At the conscious level at least, he had reached such a
stage: 'What I would say of my own life is that it has been an
immense change from enthusiasm to self-knowledge.' He was
aware with the passage of the years of a growth in his understanding of truth, of a growth in his relationship with Jesus and readier
now perhaps to speak of the mystical element: 'the call of Jesus
for his followers to become one with him and to live with him
as a beloved friend'.

From this vantage point he could look back upon his own life
and charism and on the founding story of l'Arche with greater
clarity and possibly even understanding: 'What I am very conscious of is that there is a mission, a miracle, which is somewhere

in the retreats that I give, in the book on St John, in l'Arche. I am conscious of the mystery and conscious that I am an instrument.' Today, it seemed to him, so many people were not conscious of those experiences of God that they actually had. If there was a justification for writing about his role in the story of l'Arche it was in order that people might see that in his errors, weakness and brokenness, Jesus had used him to be part of the 'folly' of the plan of God, that they might discover that they too were called to intimacy with Jesus, to undertake a work of love, to be filled with God and so become a fountain of life for others; that they too might read the miracle of their own lives.

❧

TWO

'THE LIFE IS IN THE ROOTS'

WORKING IN THE GARDENS at l'Arche, Trosly-Breuil was a young man known to be something of a delinquent, who had been unable to find employment elsewhere. He was helping to plant out lamb's lettuce when suddenly, holding up one of the delicate seedlings in rough hands, he announced, 'It's extraordinary. All the life is in the roots.' This was a story which Jean Vanier liked to relate because the insight came from a boy who had no roots. He, by contrast, was aware of having roots which he could value and which had contributed in some way to his sense of mission. Part of his consciousness of a 'guiding hand at work' and 'the love of Jesus coming through' went back to his grandmother, Thérèse de Salaberry Archer and to Almire Pichon, the spiritual director she shared with St Thérèse of Lisieux.

Born in south-east Normandy in 1843, Almire Pichon was a gentle-hearted and profoundly spiritual Jesuit priest, staunchly opposed to the harsh Jansenist spirit still prevalent in Catholicism in France and elsewhere in the second half of the nineteenth century. His great emphasis was on self-surrender to God's love and devotion to that love through the Sacred Heart. In Canada, where in 1884 he was sent as a missionary, Père Pichon's affective approach to spirituality and his message of trust in mercy and forgiveness as expressed in the Sacred Heart earned him criticism and rejection in ecclesiastical circles. In 1886 he was obliged to leave North America and return to France for reasons which he never divulged. People flocked to the retreats he gave in various European countries but his enforced departure from America continued to be a source of suffering to him. For the remainder of his life he regarded himself as in some sense an exile.

Jean Vanier's maternal grandmother, who had been orphaned at an early age and who had first met the priest when she was just sixteen, was one of the few in Canada who kept in touch with him and continued to value his fatherly affection and guidance. Her husband, Charles Archer, was a successful lawyer who in 1911, at the age of forty-two, was named to the Superior Court of Quebec. Thérèse Archer was not without social ambition and enjoyed aristocratic connections but she was physically frail and beneath her enjoyment of the formal social round lay a yearning for a life of prayer and simplicity. Almire Pichon warned her against the frivolity that could lure her into a world of superficiality, encouraging her in the practice of good works but urging her not to back away from communion out of a forced sense of unworthiness. She should have confidence in God and be kind to her soul. She was in her grandson's words, 'a very holy little lady' and Père Pichon's spiritual direction of her and the friendship that developed between them had a profound effect that would be felt two generations later in her family, albeit in a way which Jean Vanier would find difficult to define. There was, he recognised with hindsight, a 'strange analogy' between Père Pichon and Père Thomas Philippe, his own spiritual father. Both had experienced rejection and exile.

Père Pichon had been very touched by Thérèse Archer's faithfulness to him and perhaps that had had some connection with the strong fidelity of which Jean was capable. Jean had kept the 110 letters written by Almire Pichon to the woman who had trusted him in adversity because 'There was something very special between them and I think perhaps that is all part of the story.' Jean Vanier was not sure whether he had been aware of it in the early days of l'Arche but he knew that with growing maturity had come an increased sense of something unfolding, of Providence, of something having been written in the Book of Life.

In 1898 an only daughter, Pauline, was born to Charles and Thérèse Archer. At the age of six she made her first confession to Père Pichon and in her correspondence with the priest, Thérèse Archer kept him in touch with her daughter's progress. Père

Pichon, for his part, seemed more and more convinced that God had special designs on the girl's future and that she was possibly destined for a religious vocation. In October 1919 the Archers visited France after an absence of five years and Thérèse Archer took her daughter to meet him. Pauline was by then twenty-one years old and six feet tall. Vivacious but also of a nervous disposition like her mother, she had an intense desire for greater depth in prayer.

She had already applied to enter a convent but been advised to wait for a while. In Montreal, over tea at the Ritz-Carlton hotel, she had recently met Georges Philias Vanier, a reserved young lawyer and distinguished and courageous soldier who had lost a leg in the First World War trenches in France. The meeting had raised doubts in her mind about her future. Characteristically Almire Pichon assured her of his prayers and urged her to have confidence in God's guidance and love. Père Pichon died in the following month. Two years later Pauline Archer married Georges Vanier in Montreal. Georges subsequently became aide-de-camp to Lord Byng, the then Governor General of Canada, and their married life began in Ottawa.

The first of their five children, Thérèse, was born in February 1923. Georges (nicknamed 'Byngsie' after his godfather Lord Byng) followed in November 1925 and Bernard in March 1927. In February 1928, in one of a succession of diplomatic moves that would take the Vanier family backwards and forwards across the Atlantic, Georges, Pauline, three children, a nanny and a nursery maid sailed to Europe where Georges was to serve as military adviser to the Canadian delegation at the League of Nations in Geneva. Pauline was by then expecting another child and it was a difficult pregnancy. In the summer of 1927 the family had narrowly escaped death by fire in their holiday cottage in Pointe-au-Pic on the shores of the St Lawrence River, and Pauline was still suffering from the trauma of the experience. The sea crossing was rough and shortly after the family's arrival in Switzerland, she nearly miscarried. She was obliged to spend the remainder of her pregnancy in bed. Jean or 'Jock' as his Scottish nanny would christen him and, as he would thereafter be known by his family and many personal friends, was born on 10 September 1928. The years following his birth were difficult ones for his mother.

Exhausted by her rapid succession of pregnancies, overwhelmed by the requirements of her social position and always inclined to be highly strung, she suffered a period of acute depression and anxiety.

The children were well cared for by their nannies. Asked years later whether he had been close to his mother Jean Vanier immediately referred to her state following his birth: 'I think as far as I can understand that for the first three years after I was born she was in clinical depression so in fact I was much closer to my nanny, Isabelle Thompson.' As Jean grew up his relationship with his mother would develop into one in which Pauline Vanier had the kind of overpowering need for proximity which 'scared' him. His nature had, by his own admission, not only the positive characteristics of containment but also those that could make life difficult for some seeking relationship with him. He was more spontaneously close to his father although it was only with hindsight that he realised quite how close.

The Vaniers spent much of the 1930s in London where Georges, then a Lieutenant-Colonel, was Secretary at the office of the Canadian High Commissioner, Vincent Massey. During that time Jock was sent to St John's, the preparatory school for Beaumont College in Old Windsor. Georges Vanier lost most of his investments in the stock market crash, a fact which paradoxically helped restore his wife to mental and emotional equilibrium but which meant that the family was obliged to move from a large house, complete with five servants, near Regent's Park to a more modest building in Oxford Square. The Convent of the Holy Child Jesus, where Thérèse went to school, allowed her to stay on for reduced fees, as did the Jesuits at St John's in the case of the boys. Their relatively poorer circumstances brought them into contact with 'reality' in a manner which Madame Vanier would later regard as salutary. None of the children would aspire to a life of material luxury.

As for their parents, they managed still to perform well as a glamorous couple in high society whilst sharing a deepening Christian faith. Georges Vanier's religion had initially been based very much on the rigorous rules that pervaded Quebec Catholicism. He frequently refrained from receiving Communion out of what some might consider an unfounded sense of unworthiness, failing to understand how his wife could dance the night away and drink champagne, then receive Communion at Mass next morning. Under the influence of Père Pichon's teaching, learned at her mother's knee, Pauline Vanier was more inclined towards an approach to God based on trust in his love. On Good Friday 1938 Georges was to undergo something of a spiritual conversion. Persuaded by his wife to go to Mass with her, he heard Father R. H. J. Steuart, a Scottish Jesuit, speak on the seven last words of Jesus. Thereafter he started to attend Mass and receive Communion more frequently. Together he and Pauline would spend half an hour each day in silent prayer. He also began reading books on Christian spirituality, his particular favourite being the autobiography of St Thérèse of Lisieux.

In the meantime the other of what Père Pichon had referred to as his 'two Thérèses' had moved to London, in order to be near her daughter's family. Charles Archer had died in 1934. The wife who had always been regarded as frail was in fact to outlive him by more than 30 years. Known to her grandchildren as 'Ganna', she was a loving and profoundly spiritual influence upon their lives. Like so many others, the Vanier family suffered dislocation during the war years. In 1939 Georges was appointed Canadian Minister in Paris. Abandoning the initial decision to educate his children in England, he tried to gather his family about him, if not in Paris, at least in France. At a time when families who could afford to do so were fleeing Paris and the threat of bomb attack for the safer villages to the south of the capital, Madame Vanier and her children found themselves living in a very large château in Baillou, la Sarthe, with a number of other people in a similar position. Jean and his two brothers were dispatched to a French school in the nearby town. Life in the château was possibly, according to their sister Thérèse, their first unfortunate experience of community.

In May 1940, as the German troops advanced, Madame Vanier, the children and their grandmother began gradually retreating with other refugees. In Bordeaux they waited to see what the next step was to be but, by June, Georges Vanier had joined them and the decision was made that they should return to Britain. The women and children of the family, together with others related to

British and Commonwealth representatives, were taken by a Royal Navy destroyer and put on board a British merchant ship, the S.S. *Nariva*, diverted from transporting meat from the Argentine to pick up refugees in Bordeaux. The journey to Milford Haven in Wales took five days. It was a memorable experience, both because of the possible threat of submarine attack and because of the contact with human distress it brought. As they were about to set sail a tug containing more refugees came alongside the heavily overloaded vessel. The captain, who later committed suicide, was obliged to refuse to take them in the interests of the safety of those already on board. The ensuing scene carved itself on the memory of Thérèse Vanier and doubt-less also on that of her younger brother.

The crew was under considerable strain. Their passengers were fed on tinned salmon, bread which the ship's baker seemed to be baking twenty-four hours a day and tea made with one-third salt water. It was Jock who went round with a bell calling out '*premier service*' to signal meal times. His father, who left Bordeaux after the rest of his family with the British Ambassador and others, was packed into a sardine boat and from there on to a British naval destroyer which landed him comfortably in England within 24 hours. 'Women and children first' was a principle which his family viewed thereafter with a certain ambivalence.

From England the Vaniers returned to Canada where in July 1941 at the age of 43, Pauline gave birth to a fourth son, Michel. In Canada his older brothers were sent to school at their father's alma mater, Loyola College. Georges Vanier was posted as General in charge of M.D. 5, the Military District of Quebec. His age and the loss of his leg prevented him from more active service. His third son, however, seemed destined from an early age to follow his father into a military career. At the age of 13, while still being educated by the Canadian Jesuits, Jock took it upon himself to apply to the Royal Naval College at Dartmouth. Armed with all the necessary paperwork, he requested an interview with his father in his office and asked him to sign his permission to pro-ceed with the venture. In an exchange which constitutes one of the few incidents of his early life about which the adult Jean spoke readily as relevant to all that was to follow, the General asked him why he wanted to join the Navy. Jean Vanier could not remember what he answered. He did remember that his father's conclusion was simply, 'I trust you. If this is what you want to do, then you must do it.' The fact that, despite all the obvious dangers of one so young crossing the Atlantic in wartime to join the British Navy, his father was prepared to trust Jean's intuition was 'probably one of the two most important things that happened, because if he trusted me then I could trust myself, and if my intuitions were true then I could work with them'. It also made the adolescent Jean determined not to let his father down.

General Vanier's attitude was very much part of the 'mystery' that would later confirm Jean in his sense of mission: 'I often say that when he said, "I trust you" he gave me life, and it is certainly true that the Navy prepared me to be where I am today'. It also enabled him in time to place the same trust in others and see the importance of setting them free to pursue their intuitions and act upon those 'moments in our lives when we do not reason things out, we just know in our hearts that this or that is the right thing to do'. Madame Vanier was in less ready agreement with her young son's aspiration: '1942 was the time of the worst torpedoing. The bombing was still going on in England and I just cried.' Her husband overruled her, however, with a vision and insight she later recalled with satisfaction: 'You know, we mustn't clip that child's wings. We don't know what he may become in later life.'

What was it that attracted a young French Canadian to Dartmouth and a naval life during the Second World War? Apart from his father's military example, there was the pull of a life of travel for one who had already travelled extensively. There was the challenge of actually being accepted for Dartmouth, the training ground for officers for what was then, as Jean was quick to point out to his father, 'the best Navy in the world'. Wartime had heightened the excitement of this challenge. It had exposed him to all the questions associated with war, and made him appreciate and admire acts of heroism. The return to Canada in July 1940 had given him a further insight into naval life.

Thérèse Vanier had been horrified by what she had seen of wartorn Europe and shocked at the apparent lack of interest she encountered in Canada. She returned to England with the Mechanised Transport Corp at the age of 18 and before Jean. Her work for the Free French organisation would subsequently earn her the Croix de Guerre. Jean, although much younger and unlikely to have expressed himself in the same way, possibly shared something of her feelings and desire to be actively involved. The adult Jean was reluctant to attempt analysis, whilst acknowledging that were he to do so, it was conceivable that his motives had been in some measure influenced by a quest for his heroic father's approval and the desire to elude his mother's possessiveness. Certainly at the time he would not have been able to say. 'What attracts when one is thirteen? I've no idea. Why I actually made the passage from the childish attitude to heroism and warfare, and then more deeply between the dream and the actual walking, the going steadily towards it, I've no means of knowing.' He could not even remember how he knew that there was a school that took 13-year-old boys.

Looking back on his departure on a troop ship from Halifax, Nova Scotia to Liverpool to join the Royal Naval College at Dartmouth, it seemed an act of madness. His companions aboard the troop ship were men belonging to different Canadian regiments heading for the war. At one stage there were as many as 400 German U-boats in the Atlantic seeking to sink Allied ships which travelled in convoys of about 40, escorted by Royal Naval destroyers. In the notes Jock kept about his journey he referred to depth charges launched by these warships – 50 of them – one after another – against the German submarines. The danger that had so distressed Pauline Vanier was very real.

Communication between Canada and England at the time was almost impossible, but somehow Thérèse, who was staying with friends of friends of the Vaniers in London, received a message to expect him some time within the next fortnight or so. She and her friends worked out a roster so that somebody would be at the flat most of the time to receive him. Nevertheless on the night he actually arrived, having caught a train from Liverpool to London and then a taxi, everyone was out. They came home at nine in the evening to find 'this pathetic little form sound asleep on the doorstep with all his belongings scattered about him'.

Jock Vanier was late joining his term of 48 young cadets aged 13 years at Dartmouth. He missed the official train at Paddington and, when he did finally arrive, distinguished himself from the other newcomers wearing Service uniforms for the first time in their lives by the fact that he was much taller than the rest and dressed in grey flannels and a trilby hat; he had not yet had the opportunity to visit the uniform suppliers. Yet for all the difficulties of his journey, he never doubted his decision. Nor was he unduly homesick for his family; 'It was as if I was carried along by a spirit of life, adventure, advancement, the desire to succeed. It's true that I didn't succeed better than the others. I was a good average but I was caught up in this military ideal and the desire to do my bit to defeat the enemy.'

In many ways Dartmouth was just like many other public schools of the day, except that in addition to the usual academic subjects and sporting activities cadets were also instructed in seamanship and sailing. It took time before they progressed to navigation and the more complex aspects of the Service, and the introduction to gunnery came only after they had left the Naval College. Academically, Jock specialised in French and Spanish and was put in the Alphas, the top dozen of his term, but in later life his contemporaries remembered him not so much for any outstanding academic achievement as for his performance on the tennis courts, where his height contributed to a powerful serve, and on the rugby field as captain of the second fifteen. They also recalled the occasional presence of General and Madame Vanier on the touchline.

In 1942, on the Sunday before Jock and other cadets were due back at Dartmouth for their second term, two Messerschmitt light bombers attacked the front of the college building and more or less put it out of action for the remainder of the war. The bombing took place at 11 a.m. Had it occurred only a week later, the whole college would have been on parade, providing an even more vulnerable target. As it was, the remainder of Jean Vanier's Naval College time had to be spent first near Bristol and then at Eaton Hall, just outside Chester. The College occupied not only the main Victorian building of the Duke of Westminster's home but also a number of Nissen huts, and instead of the superb facilities of the River Dart, students had to improvise on the River Dee.

It was an existence not devoid of pressures for boys between the ages of 14 and 17. Until the third term cadets had to move at the double everywhere in public throughout the day. It was entirely single-sex, very service-orientated and potentially in some ways a lonely experience. 'Jock' was a Canadian with a strange accent who had entered an unfamiliar world and did not see his parents very often. In April 1943 his father was appointed minister to the Allied Governments in London. Together with his wife who, with difficulty, tore herself away from her three sons in Canada, he moved to England but very soon afterwards transferred to Algiers and then, in September 1944, with the liberation of Paris, to the French capital as ambassador to France. Georges and Pauline Vanier's commitment to the war effort meant that they remained close to the French Resistance even whilst in Algiers. Because of these and other duties the time they were able to give to their children was limited.

The Vaniers did, however, have a network of friends in Britain, and Jean 'had resources'. He also had a gift for finding the amusing aspects of life. He was not a seeker after high visibility but a 'very likeable sort of chap' possessed of an authority for which he did not have to strive and capable of finding the potential for humour, even in practising flag signals by writing on his partner's back in the damp cold of an English winter's morning. His own memories of Naval College focused on one daily event in particular. Each morning there was a formal parade at which the order was given: 'Roman Catholics fall out', whereupon the handful of Catholics present would have to take a step forward, turn right and double away smartly. 'We would then go behind a hedge,' he recalled with full appreciation of the ridiculousness of the situation, 'and say the "Hail Mary" because the others would all be saying the "Our Father" so it wouldn't have made any sense for us to say that too!'

Although for some years not one to attend Mass regularly, Jean's father had always been a man whose spiritual life was (as Jean Vanier would later write in *In Weakness, Strength*,[1] his account of his father's spiritual journey) 'the source of his success in public matters'. In the same book there is a description of the General by one who had known him well:

> He was in many ways a living example of him whom the Bible and the ancients called the 'just man', the man of duty: duty to his family, his country, to his God. His motto might well have

been: 'I seek but to serve'. But these qualities of justice and honesty do not themselves explain the warmth of goodness that radiated from him. Many who wrote about him at the moment of his death spoke of another, even more impressive characteristic. They used the term 'love'.

As parents General and Madame Vanier paid a great deal of attention to religious instruction, placing considerable importance on the Sacraments, First Communion and Confirmation, and requiring great respect for people of God, for priests and religious. There were too, all the intangibles that went with the fact that both parents were practising Christians. They tried to lead good lives in the sense of caring for each other and their children and the people with whom they came into contact. *In Weakness, Strength* highlights the small details of human relationships, which others might have considered nonsensical but which were important to Georges Vanier, even once he became Governor General of Canada. Such shortcomings as his failure to enquire after someone's mother-in-law would be a source of considerable concern to him, possibly more so than his absence from Mass, although clearly in his case the two were closely linked. In Jean's life there was furthermore the influence of 'Ganna's' spiritual intensity with her continuing devotion to the memory and teachings of Père Pichon. At school in Canada, and even before that, he had gone to Mass daily.

To come from such a background, having had little if any contact with other denominations, to an environment where the 5 per cent of Roman Catholics were required to 'fall out', cannot have been easy: but the faith which in some sense separated undoubtedly also sustained. Apart from praying every morning on parade, Anglicans were encouraged to kneel and pray in the dormitory at night and to attend Communion Service on Sundays. Catholics went to the Catholic church in the nearby town and received religious instruction every week or fortnight. Jock did not find it particularly interesting or profound, consisting as it did very largely of apologetics, but he was aware of religious faith in general being encouraged by the College and of an atmosphere of moral rectitude and a religious perspective governing life amongst officers in the Navy. Although not one to talk about his religious convictions to his naval friends, he was remembered by one of them, who would himself become an Anglican priest and General Secretary for l'Arche in the United Kingdom, as 'pretty plainly Catholic and firmly so'. At the same time he was clearly 'quite touched and interested by the Anglican Church and by the college chaplain'. Some time after he had left the Navy, Jean Vanier in fact wrote enquiring after the Reverend Geoffrey Tiarks, who had been an outstandingly good college chaplain and who later became Bishop of Maidstone.

The adult Jean Vanier's remembrance of his faith at the Naval College and the subsequent years in the Navy was that it was 'real', if not very deep. It was, he maintained, 'simple' in the sense that, caught up in the love of his work, he never experienced any great moral or sexual temptations. He was in any case awkward in the company of girls and bored at the dances he was more or less obliged to attend. 'I wanted to love Jesus and the Navy supported me in that respect but no more than that … I never had any doubts about my Christian faith during my eight years in the Navy.' In fact at no stage in his life had he experienced real doubts about his faith.

By the time Jock and his contemporaries had completed their prescribed 11 terms the Second World War was drawing to an end. It had nevertheless affected Jock profoundly. Shortly after the liberation of Paris in January 1945, whilst on leave there he had accompanied his mother to a railway station where the Canadian Red Cross was receiving survivors from Buchenwald, Dachau, Belsen and Auschwitz. He would never forget those men and women 'coming off the trains like skeletons, their faces tortured with fear, anguish and pain, still wearing their white-striped uniforms'. It seemed to him unbearable that human beings could torture others because of their hatred and need to crush: 'horrible, too that tens of thousands were killed in an instant when the atomic bombs exploded over Hiroshima in 1945'.[2]

In January 1946 he was sent to H.M.S. *Frobisher*, a training cruiser, which the working cadets, despite their limited knowledge, manned virtually from top to bottom. Jean, who had been made a cadet captain in his ninth term and who had spent the last months at naval college dressed in butterfly collars with a gold chevron on his arm, found himself scrubbing decks barefoot at 5 a.m. *Frobisher* put to sea, for the first time after suspension during the war, in January 1946. In the course of eight months and two cruises the ship toured all the West Indian islands, including Jamaica and Montego Bay, and the coasts of Sweden, Denmark and Norway. Its cadets helped in the engine rooms and generally assumed the role of the seamen who were in short supply. Having completed their training at sea, they then became midshipmen and were allocated in groups of three or four to different ships as required.

In some ways Jean Vanier's had been an exceptional term: three of its number would later become admirals; one, William Stavely, would become a First Sea Lord. They went into the fleet at a time when there was considerable tension between naval men who had seen and were in many cases tired of the action of war and those concerned with the return to all the spit and polish of peacetime. Many ships' companies were made up of hostilities-only ratings who did not take kindly to young 'straight-ringed snotties', and in many instances the fresh young midshipmen did not take kindly to the loss of responsibility and range of activity which the return of more experienced officers meant to them. This did not initially, however, unduly affect Jean Vanier. He and his fellow midshipman, Geoffrey Upfill-Brown, who had both been in the same house and become cadet captains together, were among others to be appointed to H.M.S. *Vanguard* which was to take King George VI and the Royal Family on a cruise to South Africa.

Part of their implied duties during the cruise was to provide companionship for the royal princesses Elizabeth and Margaret who were about the same age. There were teas with the princesses and deck games, and officers took it in turn to dine with the King and Queen. A midshipman's log for the cruise contains accounts not only of such exercises as oiling at sea or instruction in radar jamming but also of careful rehearsals and rigorous snow clearing for their Majesties' embarkation at Portsmouth, the celebrations aboard when the ship 'crossed the line' and of subsequent ports of call in Cape Town, East London, Port Elizabeth and Durban. It may be surmised that the gunroom was fairly carefully chosen although Geoffrey Upfill-Brown doubted that there was any special method of selection: 'In my case I'm sure it was because I was quite good at cricket and they wanted a good cricket team.' A naval report on Jean Vanier commented at the time that he showed good qualities as an officer but lacked respect for his seniors. His father's response was characteristic 'As long as he shows respect for those under him, he'll be all right.'

Ill at ease at cocktail parties and similar social gatherings and not one for joining in the term reunions, Jean Vanier would later speak of his time in the Navy only in relation to the ways in which it equipped him for l'Arche:

> I needed to have been in the Navy. It formed my body physi-
> cally. When I compare myself to adolescents I meet now, boys
> of 16 to 19 are really fragile. I had an adolescence which was
> completely geared without the slightest wavering to one thing,
> and that thing was not at all materialistic. I see so many young
> people wavering now, not knowing what to do with them-
> selves, dissipating their energies. In the Navy there was a
> utilisation of energies and forces in a very constructive way.

H.M.S. *Vanguard* arrived in Portsmouth from Cape Town in May 1947. Some time that year, probably in Plymouth, as a midshipman Jean Vanier was in charge of a landing craft used to transport sailors ashore. The wind was gusting terribly, the sea was very rough and, as he tried to haul himself from his ship into the boat via a rope ladder, his muscles failed him and he fell into the sea. He lost consciousness immediately. Fortunately he was wear-ing a large lifejacket but the wind bore him swiftly away. He came to as he was hauled out of the water by the chaplain and some sailors who had promptly set out in a smaller boat to retrieve him.

There was no follow-up to this experience at the time. He was simply given brandy and encouraged to return to his duties. Reflecting on it years later, he could not be specific about the effects of this near-death experience, other than to say that he had been struck by the way in which he might quite simply never have recovered consciousness: 'What happens in the unconscious? I would think something may have imprinted itself there.' Perhaps the incident contributed in some way to the closeness he experienced later with people near to death. At very least the improbability of this rescue because of the strength of the wind underlined his sense of being somehow 'protected': 'It was perhaps the only experience I have had of coming close to death. I believe it was a small miracle of Providence that I was saved.'

After eighteen months as a midshipman aboard not only the *Vanguard* but also the *Renown* and the *Anson*, Jean Vanier began six to nine months of studies in science and literature at Greenwich. It was there that, by his own account, his faith may have begun to grow. He started going regularly to Mass in the parish church 15 minutes' walk away, and began reading books on spirituality. There was too the possible impact of his elder brother Byngsie's vocation. When the atomic bomb put an end to the war in the Pacific and to Byngsie's career in the Canadian Army, he had gone on retreat to a Cistercian monastery at Oka, near Montreal, to reflect upon a possible vocation to the priesthood. By the end of his retreat he felt instead that he was being called to a life of asceticism and silent contemplation as a Cistercian monk. He actually entered the monastery at Oka, where he took the name Benedict, on 14 November 1946. The Vaniers did not overlook the fact that this was the eve of the twenty-seventh anniversary of Père Pichon's death.

Some time in 1948 or 1949 Jean accompanied General Vanier to Lourdes. It meant a great deal to the young man to spend two days alone with his father and help him prepare to go into the baths. This venerable gentleman of considerable public position, with a high amputation which made it very difficult to get about, had the simplicity and faith to do what everyone else did at Lourdes. There could be no question of a cure. It was more a statement that this was a place of prayer and spirituality to which he was committed. There was furthermore a simplicity about such an action on the part of one who in some ways could appear quite complex, silent and not very open. Jean was at that age far more active than reflective. Nevertheless his father's entry into the baths and the presence of so many sick and disabled people using wheelchairs in an environment which contrasted starkly with his naval world, touched him. Years later he recalled the certainty he had, whilst at the Grotto, that one day he would leave the Navy 'to follow Jesus'.

After Greenwich he was required to take other sub-lieutenant's courses in different parts of England: courses in gunnery, submarines, communications, combined operations, fleet air arms and others. During those sessions he did everything he could to attend Mass at the nearest church. It was not always easy because his fellow officers were not necessarily similarly disposed. They never criticised or ridiculed him, however. One morning he was outside, enjoying the beauty of nature in the early hours, when he felt his heart fill with love and light. It was a sensation of overwhelming peace, which he would later identify as 'a real experience of God'.

Shortly afterwards Jean Vanier transferred from the British to the Canadian Navy. Somewhere inside him he was still a Canadian. There had been a number of Canadian midshipmen aboard *Vanguard* and they had possibly awakened in him some sense of his national identity. The founder of l'Arche could scarcely remember and thought it was more of an administrative move than anything else. The fact remains that by the time he was twenty he was an officer on the *Magnificent*, Canada's only aircraft carrier, based in Halifax. By then he was reading his breviary daily and thanks to the presence of a Catholic chaplain on board, attending Mass daily too. In Halifax Jean Vanier asked one of the priests at a local Jesuit house, Father Hector Daly, to become his spiritual director. His inner journey was becoming more important to him, as was the attraction to life among the poor. In December 1949, with the help of the Salvation Army and the local Catholic parish, he and sailors from his ship organised aid in the form of food and clothing for disadvantaged families in Halifax.

In April 1950, after a voyage to Cuba on exercises with the US Navy, the 'Maggie' put into New York. At the time Jean Vanier was reading Thomas Merton's *The Seven Storey Mountain*. Discovering how much the author had been influenced by Friendship House, founded by Catherine Doherty in Harlem for the city's down-and-outs, he telephoned the community and spent all his free time in New York with the occupants. He was deeply and spontaneously drawn to their life amongst the poor black Americans. They had a large store from where they distributed food and clothing. They themselves lived very simply in two apartments. On Easter Day Jean Vanier took them a large leg of lamb and at one point invited them all to come and eat in the officers' dining

room on board the *Magnificent*. Fifteen men and women in varying states of very poor attire formed a curious gathering in such
formal surroundings but one very much in the spirit of the
gospels.

Jean Vanier was highly disciplined, with all the efficiency of a
young man surrounded by older men of greater experience who
could afford to be more relaxed. When the conscientious young
naval officer found himself reading the Divine Office during the
night watch, he knew that he was not in the right place. On his
return to Halifax he went to see Father Daly to tell him that he
wanted to leave the Navy to follow Jesus and possibly become a
priest. Father Daly referred Jean to a Jesuit retreat house in
Montreal where he followed a discernment retreat based on the
Ignatian method, after which it was clear that he should leave the
Navy. Returning to his ship, he wrote to the Naval Minister in
Ottawa, tendering his resignation and in July received the
response: 'permission granted'.

A letter written in 1951, one year after he had resigned his
commission, sheds a little further light:

> I think that I might have felt that the naval officer's life and the
> life of a Christian were in opposition – if I did think that I was
> wrong – granted it is much harder to live completely the
> message of Christ for people will persecute you, think you are
> mad ... it takes courage but it is not impossible – the tempta-
> tions are much greater.

The same letter provides an insight into Jean Vanier's understanding of the officer's role as one for which he had the greatest
regard, that of assuming responsibility for a great number of men
not only from 'a service point of view' but also 'morally and in
education' in a way which 'touches the very roots of life for it is
a bit eternal':

> The officer in some ways has the responsibility of their souls.
> It is quite easy relatively speaking to die for one's men in time
> of action or emergency but to die by 'pin pricks' throughout
> one's life is a lot harder – I mean by that – devoting all one's
> energy to their welfare. The officer must love his men with a
> real love.

The writer did not feel that he had made a mistake at the age of 13½. The eight years he had spent in uniform had been invaluable. Nor did he leave the Service because of the Service – its defects were far surpassed by all the good points. Rather he left because:

> I felt that my place in the world was somewhere else … During courses I began to realise that my life has to develop along other lines – if not I would be stifling all my natural and supernatural inclinations – 'Thy will be done on earth as it is in heaven' – we all have our place, our vocation – my vocation wasn't in the Navy.

Asked once by a television reporter how it was that he had known that he should leave the Navy and follow Jesus, the older Jean Vanier likened it to the kind of knowledge people have when they propose to the person they wish to marry, a conviction not determined by reason but springing from 'our heart of hearts' … 'There is such a thing as *intuition*. We feel or sense things. They are not planned. That is where the Spirit intervenes, inspiring us to do things that we had not planned'.[3] His departure came as no real surprise to those who had been close to him in the Service, although in 1950 the chief of naval staff wrote to General Vanier in Paris expressing regret that the Navy was to lose an outstanding officer with a promising future. With hindsight Jean Vanier himself did not feel that he would necessarily have fulfilled that promise, acknowledging that there was a fear in him unsuited to making quick decisions under threat of storm and danger: 'There's a part of me where there is fear and how much fear there is and how much courage is still a question.' His father responded to the chief of naval staff at the time:

> Jock's aspiration transcends the human level. Knowing him as I do, I feel sure that he is answering to the Master's call. As you have been kind enough to ask me for my comments, I can only say that this is a matter between God and him in which man if possible should not interfere.

Yet again General Vanier exhibited his extraordinary trust in his son's intuitions and this time Madame Vanier readily understood and supported his course of action. On leave with them in Paris,

Jean had previously expressed the desire to consult a priest about his future. Madame Vanier had therefore introduced him to a French Dominican priest, Père Thomas Philippe, who had started an international centre called 'Eau Vive' (Living Water) on the outskirts of Paris. Both she and her mother had been deeply impressed by Père Thomas, 'Ganna' discerning in him the holiness and devotion to the love of God through the Sacred Heart that had so touched her in Almire Pichon. Jean Vanier's meeting with Père Thomas had been to use his own words, 'very, very deep'. Thomas Philippe looked at him as if he knew all that was within him – good and bad – and loved and accepted him just as he was. To be known in such a way was a liberation for Jean. It was in fact 'the second great thing' in his life.

On his return to the Navy the young man had corresponded with three priests. One of them was Père Thomas Philippe, who responded with a warmth and insight that seemed to Jean to stem from an extraordinary prayer life. When finally he handed in his resignation, in the conviction that his vocation was to the priesthood but uncertain as yet where he was being called to serve, he embarked upon 'at least a year of study, peace and prayer' under the spiritual direction of Père Thomas, a holy priest at whose feet he would 'receive the gift of prayer'.

'In the Gospel of John,' Jean Vanier was to write in 2003,

> I have come to see that to pray is above all to dwell in Jesus and to let Jesus dwell in me. It is not first and foremost to *say prayers*, but to live in the *now* of the present moment, in communion with Jesus. Prayer is a place of rest and quiet. When we love someone, don't we delight in being with each other? Now and again we may say a word of affection, we will be attentive to each other, but it is essentially a place of silence. The great Spanish mystic John of the Cross once said, 'Silence is the way God speaks to us.' I learned the silence of prayer and the prayer of silence with my spiritual father, Père Thomas Philippe.'[4]

THREE

THE MYSTERIOUS SOURCE

The man who Jean Vanier would later claim had recognised him as a person with a destiny and a mission was born on 18 March 1905 some 15 kilometres from Lille. Thomas Philippe was the son of a notary and one of 12 children, an extraordinary number of whom were destined for the religious life. His mother's brother, Père Dehau, was a Dominican priest, a man of great holiness and intelligence who undoubtedly watched over the upbringing of his nephews and in time became Thomas Philippe's spiritual director.

Père Thomas was aware of his vocation from a very young age. At just five years old he felt a strong attraction to Jesus in the Eucharist. In a manner that would subsequently have a bearing on his belief that very young children and people with disabilities, whose moral consciousness and rational capacities were not highly developed, could nonetheless experience a call to relationship with Jesus, he was convinced that he was being called to the priesthood, a role which he saw as bringing him as close as possible to Jesus. This conviction was one that he at first kept from his family, choosing only to tell his parish priest in the confessional. Young as he was, he was already capable of strong attachment and a response to a call from God which he identified as powerful, secret and belonging within the Church. The response, Père Thomas would afterwards insist, was also one which must be made in freedom. At the time his own local priest did not take the child seriously. On three successive occasions, however, the boy told him of his conviction. Finally the priest remarked to his mother that he was 'more sure of her little son's vocation than of most of the seminarians' to whom he gave instruction at Lille.

During the First World War Thomas Philippe's father spent four years in the Army and the family went through hard times. Barefoot or in rough shoes, the numerous children learned what it was like to go short of many things. Afterwards Thomas Philippe went to study with the Jesuits in Lille. In the absence of public transport during that postwar period he rode the 15 kilometres by bicycle each morning and evening, but not without a struggle. He was only 13, and it took him an hour and a half each way. He was also already having problems with his ears (deafness was a family weakness), as a result of which he had difficulty in hearing during lessons and became a subject of mockery among his classmates.

In 1923, at the age of 18, he decided to enter the diocesan seminary of Issy-les-Moulineaux on the south-western edge of Paris, but shortly before doing so sensed that his vocation was more specifically to be a Dominican. Not daring, however, to change course so swiftly, he followed the advice of his Dominican uncle to join the seminary for which he had already applied. If he was destined to alter direction it would happen of its own accord. At the seminary Père Thomas felt his call to be a Dominican, with a more religious and apostolic life than that of a parish priest, ever more strongly. After only two months he left to join the Dominicans. On the separation of the Church and State in 1905, all the Dominican monasteries in France had been obliged to relocate elsewhere so he continued his studies at Kain, some 20 miles east of Lille, in Belgium. In July 1929 he was ordained at the unusually young age of 24. In his family two elder sisters had already joined the Benedictines. Another younger one would follow them. His younger brother, Marie-Dominique, would become a priest shortly after him. Another sister became a Dominican and two other brothers started their Dominican novitiate. Of these one died during the war; the other left the order. Only three of the children married.

In 1936 Père Thomas went on to the Dominican university in Rome but during the Second World War was enrolled into the Army, albeit only briefly. By 1942 he had become a professor at the Angelicum University in Rome and a 'Master of Theology'. That year, relatively young though he was, Père Thomas was sent by the Holy Office in Rome as an 'Apostolic Visitor' to the Dominican Priory and house of studies on the outskirts of Paris, the Saulchoir, with a view to 'rectifying' the Saulchoir and removing its leading theologian, Père Chenu, and his disciples. It was the time of considerable ferment among Roman Catholic institutions in Europe that preceded the Second Vatican Council. This was the era of such radical French thinkers as Lèon Bloy, the novelist, critic and polemicist who preached spiritual revival through suffering and poverty; of Ernest Psichari, the writer and soldier whose works combined militaristic sentiments with a semi-mystical religious devotion; and the Roman Catholic philosopher Jacques Maritain, highly regarded by many both for his interpretation of the thought of St Thomas Aquinas and for his own thinking, based not only on Thomism, but also on Aristotelianism, and drawing upon anthropology, sociology and psychology. His themes included the contention that science, philosophy, poetry and mysticism were among legitimate ways of knowing reality, that moral philosophy must take into account other branches of human knowledge, and that people holding different beliefs must cooperate in the formation and main-tenance of salutary political institutions. This was also, however, the time when the conservative Cardinal Ottoviani presided over the Holy Office and the tension between conservative thinkers and those in the Church seeking new ways to respond to the challenges of Communism, psychology and Freud was mounting. Relations between Rome and the Dominicans in the Province of Saulchoir during the 1940s and 1950s were particularly strained. In the 1950s Rome saw fit to condemn worker priests and oblige the Provincial of the Dominicans in Paris to resign; the Dominicans did not take kindly to these and other interventions.

The issue in contention as far as Père Chenu was concerned appears to have related to dogma. Père Chenu was trying to show the historical reasons for the proclamation of dogma almost to the point of exploring the psychological explanations for it. In Rome there was a fear that he was in some sense humanising the divine and that he was not sufficiently respectful of the transcen-dent aspect of dogma revealed to the Church by the Holy Spirit.

The Dominican priest originally appointed to be the Apostolic Visitor, nervous of the consequences, delegated the task, with the result that Thomas Philippe, who had barely been ordained 15 years, was sent to remove from his position a man many years his senior who was the highly respected hero of a strong contingent in France. Père Thomas, whose position was the orthodox one that dogma was a religious truth established by Divine Revelation and defined by the Church, nevertheless did what he was asked to do reluctantly and out of obedience. What compounded the difficulty of his predicament was the fact that, in an unusual breach of general policy, the Church authorities then required him to step into Père Chenu's shoes as Master of Studies at the Saulchoir.

Père Thomas did his term at the Saulchoir but found himself in the almost untenable position of being perceived by those about him as Rome's man, hence an arch-conservative and even a traitor. Not so much an arch-conservative as an obedient servant of the Church, Thomas Philippe was also very mystical. In 1947, having completed a difficult and painful period as Master of Studies at the Saulchoir, he decided that, in Jean Vanier's words,

> the way to help people discover mysticism and a relationship with God without being too humanistic was to create a place near the Saulchoir where they could discover a really good theology which for him was Thomistic, and really enter into communication with Jesus.

In response to the expressed needs of a number of his students, he founded a small community 20 minutes' walk from the Saulchoir in premises purchased by the 'Felix Dehau Foundation', Felix Dehau being Père Thomas' grandfather. More accurately, it consisted of three large houses built side by side, one of which became known as the Pavillon Maritain because Jacques Maritain came there for a number of years to give summer courses. The study of theology and philosophy at the Saulchoir necessarily implied a commitment to enter the Dominican novitiate, but Père Thomas had recognised that there were those who, though not intending to commit themselves to the priesthood, were still potentially interested in the study of theology and philosophy. A vocation might well reveal itself in the course of those studies. If it did not, Père Thomas was still able to perceive the value of the knowledge acquired for a layman in a world craving peace, and in which countries long dominated by colonialism were being given independence.

He had identified the need in that postwar period for what he described as an 'international work of the heart'. His 'school of wisdom', 'Eau Vive' would become a 'small international centre for students who wanted to get to know something of the spirituality of the Church, for lay people who wanted to know more and who would afterwards take that knowledge back to their respective countries and use it to help shape future development.' Père Thomas believed that to gain real knowledge of philosophy and theology, it was important to live in a Christian milieu, a prayerful community.

The centre began with ten students but their numbers very soon multiplied. It attracted all kinds of people. It was in fact the first place of study in France to take in a German student after the war, an act of reconciliation that was a very concrete expression of what the community was trying to live. An extract from the diary of a friend from Jean Vanier's naval days who visited Eau Vive in 1951 also noted the presence of 'Arabic philosophers, a Persian merchant, several Germans, a woman who went into a concentration camp for being a key worker in the "underground" during the war'. In all there were some 20 countries, including Syria, Lebanon, Egypt and Morocco, represented by the 80 or so students. In the month of August summer courses were held to which friends of Père Thomas, including not only Jacques Maritain but also Charles Journet, who later became Cardinal Journet, and Olivier Lacombe, a renowned specialist in Hindu mysticism and religious experience, came. All in all, Eau Vive was a highly diverse assembly with a strong intellectual element, but in its community life it tried to live as the early Christian communities lived, particularly from the point of view of unity based on the directive, 'that you may be one', a unity founded on love and charity. Eau Vive became known as a place of peace and grace. Most of the 'students' left after completing their studies. The permanent members were for the most part women who did the housekeeping and cooking. Accommodation was often provided in huts or stables and food was very simple. It was a lifestyle that enabled even the poorest to participate in and listen to the new thinking prevalent amongst the Dominicans at the time.

By his own admission, in the pursuit of this spiritual and intellectual life Père Thomas paid scant regard to the financial running of the community. There came a point, however, where Eau Vive had run into such financial difficulties that he was obliged to try and raise funds. As Canadian ambassadress in Paris, Pauline Vanier was known for her generosity of spirit and active involvement in Red Cross work for refugees and others. Père Thomas appealed to her to help him organise a charity sale at which he would sell rolls of fabric manufactured by friends of the Philippe family. Recalling their first encounter, Madame Vanier claimed in 1989 to have been very rude to this unknown and somewhat importunate priest: 'Firstly I'm not a good organiser, and secondly I was far too busy. I got up and made him understand that the conversation had ended; but he was a very persevering man.'

Two or three weeks later he came to her again, this time with the suggestion that if she was not prepared to organise a bazaar, she might at least be willing to contact any wives of ambassadors who would be interested in and prepared to support the work that was going on at Eau Vive. Despite herself, Madame Vanier found herself agreeing to do so. What was of greater significance to her, however, was the fact that in the course of conversation Père Thomas, who was still very much a stranger to her, informed her that he felt she was searching for direction in her spiritual life. This was indeed the case. She had been looking for a Carmelite convent where she could go and pray. Père Thomas' next unprompted suggestion was that she might like to come to some talks on spirituality that he was giving in a Carmelite convent near Paris. His intuition shocked her, but it was the beginning of a profound friendship – Thomas Philippe in fact became her spiritual director – and the basis for her suggestion to her son when he too was 'searching', that he should talk to Père Thomas.

There is much about Père Thomas and his relationship with Jean Vanier that defies words. 'The meeting with Père Thomas was deeply moving,' Jean Vanier recalled years later,

> I suppose somewhere because of my freshness I needed a master, a teacher, a spiritual father. I think I knew that I knew

nothing. There was a sort of experience of Jesus and I felt bonded to him. How can one explain that? We are touching on the inexplicable. But in the Gospel of John, two disciples leave John the Baptist to follow Jesus and the first words of Jesus are 'What are you looking for?' (John 1:38) and they say 'Rabbi, teacher, where do you live?' 'Come and see', says Jesus. And they dwelt with him for a day. And before that *dwelling* they referred to him as 'Master' and afterwards they called him 'Messiah'. I lived at my level a similar experience with Père Thomas.

The use of the Greek word *menein,* to 'stay', to 'abide', to 'dwell' was, according to Jean Vanier, special in the gospel of John:

> If John uses this word to signify 'staying in a particular place', he uses it even more to signify a friendship where we 'dwell' in another person. A 'mutual in-dwelling' is a permanent, deep friendship. It is an intimate, dynamic relationship between two people dwelling in one another.

It is a definition of relevance to Jean Vanier's relationship to a priest who by his very presence seemed to communicate a presence of God that filled him with inner peace and silence and drew new life from him.

Père Thomas, for his part, recognised when Jean Vanier left the Navy that the young man was seeking primarily 'to know God better'. His response to Jean's request to come to Eau Vive was typed by a former art student in Paris, Jacqueline d'Halluin. She had been invited initially by the first German student at Eau Vive to spend a day there, had fallen in love with the trees that surrounded the community houses, had later returned for a week knowing that she was in some way taking a definitive step, and remained for seven years. Meeting Père Thomas, she had agreed to help him and thinking it impolite to say 'No' to a priest, had not admitted when he asked her to do some typing that she had never used a typewriter. In those days she believed not so much in the will of God as in inspiration and intuition. Not for the last time, for she would later follow Père Thomas and Jean Vanier to l'Arche, the priest's intuition with regard to the young naval officer surprised her:

It took me three days to type that letter because I had never typed anything in my life before. People were impressed by my industry because they could hear the typewriter going constantly, but in fact I was typing the same thing over and over again with one finger and filling up the waste-paper basket. I said to myself, 'This young man is crazy. He has everything going for him at sea.' But, at the same time, what Père Thomas said to Jean Vanier in his letter about the Holy Spirit made me enter into something different. I didn't keep a copy of that letter but not surprisingly I know it off by heart.

Jean Vanier had been seeking. Père Thomas Philippe's response, like that of Jesus to the two disciples in the Gospels who wanted to know where he lived, was an invitation to 'come and see'. Accordingly Jean spent the month of August 1950 on holiday with his family and arrived at Eau Vive at the beginning of September.

Having come from the Navy, fresh, naïve and open, knowing something about guns, torpedoes and aircraft carriers but relatively little about theology and philosophy, he plunged himself into the life at Eau Vive. He lived poorly but went to the Saulchoir to study theology, philosophy and Latin with ordination in mind. Listening to Père Thomas, seeing how he prayed, there was no doubt in his mind that this was a man of God whose disciple or spiritual son he wanted to be. Jean joined the queue of people outside Père Thomas Philippe's door seeking his spiritual direction and by the time he actually saw the priest it was often late at night. At 22, having no knowledge of the kind of conflicts that had preceded Père Thomas' founding of Eau Vive, he was completely uninfluenced by all the contemporary undercurrents of thought and values. He was simply a very disciplined young man of good will, whose virgin intellect was ready to soak up the kind of knowledge of theology and spirituality that Père Thomas could impart. During those meetings with Père Thomas the priest's words seemed to penetrate his heart and open it up. Listening to him, simply being with him, he felt transformed, and the older man became for him 'a presence of God'. Fifty years later Jean Vanier would be able to remember the detail of the talks Père Thomas gave on 'silence' as if it were yesterday. As a result of these encounters, with the priest's active encouragement, Jean Vanier spent much time in prayer.

In November 1950 Jean Vanier accompanied Père Thomas to Rome by train for the proclamation of the dogma of the Assumption of the Blessed Virgin Mary. It was a very important occasion for the priest because the belief that Mary, having completed her earthly life, was in body and soul assumed into heavenly glory, was at the very heart of his mystical life and theology. Significantly also, Jean would subsequently refer to his 'second conversion' and resignation from the Navy as occurring 'in the year of the proclamation of the dogma of the Assumption'. 'That is why', he added, 'I feel so much a child of the Assumption.'

It was not Jean Vanier's intention to remain at Eau Vive indefinitely. Nor did Père Thomas try to persuade him to do so. All the Dominican wanted of his spiritual son was that he be faithful to the Holy Spirit. In February 1951 Jean Vanier spent ten days at the Carthusian monastery of La Valsainte in Switzerland. He lived in the Carthusians' 'little house', participating totally in their austere life of solitude and attending their night offices. At the end of those ten days it was clear, however, that such a life was not for him.

Thanks to General Vanier his son had the use of a car whenever he wanted it. Consequently Jean Vanier was able to drive Père Thomas about. In September 1951 they drove together to La Salette, a place of Marian apparition in the canton of Corps, where they spent five or six days, then to Saint Maximin, in the heart of Provence, where Père Thomas gave a retreat to students and their instructors belonging to the Dominican Province of Toulouse, then to a retreat for the Dominican Sisters of La Tourelle. In later life Jean Vanier would advocate for others in community what he described as 'filiation', as opposed to the structured acquisition of knowledge based on clear principles which 'formation' implies, as the only means by which certain knowledge at a spiritual level can be transmitted. In 1976 he would write in *Community and Growth*:

> Today many ministers and priests are formed in universities and seminaries, by professional teachers. In India, if you want

to become a guru, you live with a guru until he confirms you and sends you out to be a guru who forms disciples in his turn. These days we tend to believe that everything can be learned from books. We forget that there is another way to learn: by living with a master.

In Père Thomas he identified such a master. In his small room in a hut, the wide windows of which gave out on to trees and grass and birdsong, Jean seems also to have found peace and an excited enthusiasm for the spiritual writings of St Francis de Sales and the primacy of love as revealed in the New Testament. In a letter to a friend he wrote at that time:

> Alas, Christians everywhere – and Catholics are no exception – have lost faith in the truths of the New Testament. We have lost the sense of prayer, forgotten that 'without me you can do nothing', forgotten that all is *love*: *Deus caritas est*, that God is love – he is the way, the truth and the life – that the meaning of the cross is love – Christ died out of an excess of love. 'God so loved the world.' Read in St John at the Last Supper how many times the word 'love' is used.

In April 1952 Père Thomas Philippe was called to Rome by his superiors. Without knowing the reason for this sudden summons, Jean Vanier drove day and night to get him there while his spiritual mentor prayed continuously in the passenger seat beside him. Jean Vanier had thought that the priest's absence from Eau Vive would be a short one. In fact he would never return to the 'school' he had founded. Père Thomas had been denounced and accused of unorthodoxy and spiritual direction that was too mystical.

Even after the elderly priest's death, Jean Vanier would remain reluctant to speak of what he considered to be essentially private to Père Thomas, 'the secret of his relations with God, Jesus and Mary'. In 1937, however, while he was teaching philosophy and theology at the Angelicum in Rome, Père Thomas Philippe had spent many hours (sometimes as many as five or six in succession) in the small 'Mater Amabilis' ('Mother deserving of love') chapel of a church just off the Piazza di Spagna. In the course of those periods of prayer he had undergone a mystical experience of profound union with the Virgin Mary. All that he underwent at that time during the long periods of prayer in the presence of Mary he recorded in notes to, and under the supervision of Père Dehau, his uncle and spiritual director. What he sought throughout to know was her will and that of his God for him. On his return to France, Père Thomas continued to experience what he regarded as graces inspired by God, which rendered him nonetheless open to misunderstanding and criticism. Called to account by Rome, Père Thomas was so convinced of the divine inspiration of what he had lived through that he believed he must defend it theologically. The theology he expounded related to the role of the body in the incarnation and the transmission of grace through the body.

Required to leave Eau Vive, Père Thomas asked Jean Vanier provisionally to assume responsibility for it. By his own account, Jean was naïve and ill-prepared for such a role. He had never been at the centre of the community and had much to learn, but he was aided, trusted and supported by those around him. There came a time, however, when the Father Provincial of the Dominicans, who had assumed that the successor to the Dominican Père Thomas would be another priest of the order, wrote to the Association of Friends of Eau Vive to inform them that a Père Desobry OP had been appointed as director. Notwithstanding this, the Association formally instated Jean Vanier.

Shortly before leaving for Rome, Père Thomas had met a psychiatrist who was working at UNESCO at the time. Born in Mexico City, John Thompson was originally a US citizen but became a Canadian after the Second World War and served with both the Canadian Air Force and the British Army as a scientific intelligence officer. A consultant psychiatrist at the Nuremburg trials, he had worked with Jung and had considerable influence on the thinking of Père Thomas, particularly in relation to the mother–child relationship and the infant's need for love being greater than the need for food. Dr Thompson had rather assumed that in Père Thomas' absence he would take over the running of Eau Vive. He was, after all, a much older and more mature man than the ex-naval officer. He remained, however, supportive of the community, bringing in his friends and connections to take courses, and in 1954 left UNESCO and began to live full time in the grounds.

The Dominicans' reaction was less constructive. They proceeded to prohibit students at Eau Vive from studying at the Saulchoir. It was a move which cut away Eau Vive's very reason for existence. The group of 70–80 people rapidly dwindled to 15–20 and those who remained were obliged to continue their studies at the Institut Catholique in Paris. Jean Vanier did two years of philosophy, travelling to Paris virtually every day by train, and under his leadership Eau Vive survived. It continued to take in groups and run summer courses until, in 1955, with the appointment of a new Dominican Provincial, an agreement was signed between the Dominicans, the Eau Vive Association and the Bishop of the Versailles diocese. Eau Vive was recognised once more, an Assumptionist priest, Père Cayré, was appointed as chaplain and the students were able to resume their studies at the Saulchoir.

Jean Vanier had also been greatly encouraged by Père Marie-Dominique Philippe, Père Thomas' brother, and others, to seek ordination as a priest. It was decided that he should apply to Monsignor Roy, Archbishop of Quebec, to be a member of his diocese. The intention was that Monsignor Roy would ordain him and send him back to Eau Vive as director and chaplain to the Canadian students in Paris. It was an arrangement that seemed acceptable to all. Jean would spend a period of time at a seminary in Quebec prior to being ordained a deacon.

Tensions had arisen at Eau Vive, however, between the chaplain and the director. Père Cayré was a man whose sympathy for and understanding of the principles of Eau Vive was limited. With hindsight Jean Vanier also admitted that he had not been sufficiently diplomatic in dealing with those areas in which temporal and spiritual responsibility overlapped. Nor had he been sufficiently respectful of the priest's role. When Père Cayré informed him that he had written to Rome to the effect that Jean's spirituality was false, the young man realised that the chaplain was trying to have him removed.

On 8 June 1956 Jean was asked by the Holy Office to leave Eau Vive. The following day the Provincial of the Dominicans in Paris, whilst assuring Jean Vanier that there was no stain on his character, nevertheless informed him of two conditions imposed upon him. The first forbade him from being involved with any other 'EauxVives' and the second informed him that if he wished to become a priest he would have to spend not just a brief spell but several years at a seminary. In his old age Jean Vanier could look back on the episode with humour. He had been given a paper to sign to the effect that he accepted these conditions. He signed without looking at the contents. Only afterwards did the authorities realise that they had given him the paper stating that he did not agree, and send him another. At the time, however, the apparent injustice must have been painful. He was given no explanation and no opportunity to speak, nor was he given any financial compensation. He was simply put out without anywhere to go.

Jean's parents were deeply distressed by their son's departure from Eau Vive but Jean himself was able to accept the move peacefully. When Père Cayré was surprised at the apparent lack of resentment with which Jean agreed to go, remarking that he had thought the young man was very attached to Eau Vive, the response was unhesitating, 'Of course, but I am even more attached to Jesus.' As with his departure from Canada in 1942 and his leaving the Navy, he went ostensibly without regrets although probably with more pain than he acknowledged ... 'looking to the future, seeking to be close to Jesus'.

It was with the desire to know what it was that Jesus wanted of him that, on leaving Eau Vive, he went to the Trappist Abbey of Bellefontaine. All his plans for ordination seemed to be shattered. Should he abandon his life in France, the spirit of Eau Vive and his links with Père Thomas and Père Marie-Dominique, who had also been very supportive of him since 1952? In the course of a year spent in the guest house at Bellefontaine, rising early in the morning to pray, then studying in his room, following the liturgical readings, doing some manual work in the garden, walking and reflecting, it became clear to him that he should not go back to Canada and pursue the priesthood in the diocese of Quebec, but wait to speak to Père Thomas who was, after all, his spiritual father.

Père Thomas, however, was for the most part out of his reach. Having been numbered amongst others condemned by the Church authorities at that time, the priest spent a while first in a psychiatric hospital in France, and then with the Trappists in Frattochie, 30 kilometres from Rome, and in Santa Sabina. Jean was able to meet him from time to time in Rome but only in secret. At first the Dominican was not permitted to celebrate Mass, hear confessions or have any other form of ministry. This period of isolation and exile was one of extraordinary anguish for him but he continued to centre his life upon Jesus and Mary, living exclusively with them, spending entire days and a good part of his nights in prayer. It was also during this period that he really developed his mystical theology. Writing helped him. He wrote at length, for example, on the Eucharist and on Mary as a model for the contemplative life, and Jean Vanier was able to type some of the texts for him.

At the heart of Père Thomas' theology was the hidden life of Mary, the insight that she had become holy and grown in holiness by virtue of the presence of and contact with Jesus, the Word made flesh. The mystery of the Annunciation, the body of Mary, the life of Jesus in her, the birth of Jesus, Mary nourishing Jesus, the love between Mary and Jesus, all led to a mystical understanding of the place of the body, which in the light of Mary, became the privileged instrument of grace. Jean Vanier was aware that some of the texts were open to misinterpretation by those who might fail to afford the Holy Spirit its proper place in Père Thomas' mystical experiences, and was reticent in talking about Père Thomas' thinking on love in its different forms, and grace in relation to the body. Yet they remained very important to him.

Père Thomas' theology gave him strong and solid principles to the extent that he did not really seek any elsewhere. They also gave him a freedom to think for himself so that in later life, when commenting on the gospels or theology he did not feel obliged, as others might, to quote other sources or authorities, but rather had a strong sense of the synthesis of his own knowledge and experience. 'If people find that I am very free in my intellectual life,' he was to write many years later, 'even in my interpretation of the Gospel of St John and in my development of an anthropology which is bound to human and spiritual reality, it is because I was moulded by the thinking and methods of Père Thomas.'

It was under the influence of Père Thomas and his brother,

Père Marie-Dominique that Jean Vanier had begun a doctoral thesis on the ethics of Aristotle whilst studying in Paris. Years later he explained his interest in the Greek philosopher in terms of an attraction to his realistic vision of the world:

> The intuition of Plato stems from his inner experience whereas Aristotle is something about outer experience. Somewhere in Christianity is the harmonisation of the two, but from a philosophical point of view just to love reality and to touch, to look at things, to listen to people is very Aristotelian.

He would not, however, have been able to offer that kind of reason at the time he made his choice. It was one which seemed then to arise quite spontaneously from conversations with the two Thomist Fathers, Marie-Dominique and Thomas Philippe and others. Two questions underlay his leaving the Navy: What did he want to do with his life? And what would make him a fully accomplished man? He was seeking the meaning of life in Jesus' message of peace and in his vision of humanity. He also sought answers from philosophers and from wise men and women who were convinced of the beauty and value of human beings. That search led him to the works of Aristotle. As to why he specifically chose Aristotelian ethics, at the Institut Catholique in Paris he had had a very good teacher: 'A fearful man like an eagle but clear in his thinking. He certainly helped.' Jean Vanier continued to work on his theology and his thesis at the Trappist monastery of Notre Dame de Bellefontaine.

His parents continued to be anxious about his health and state of mind, but his letters of that period invariably addressed to 'Dearest Mummy and Daddy' and slipping sometimes even in mid-sentence between French and English, were full of reassurances that he was at peace and able to see to what extent his time at Eau Vive had been shaped by the 'desire for success'. He had now, he insisted, been given an opportunity to draw closer to the will of Jesus and Mary. At Eau Vive a whole new world had been opened up to him, at the centre of which were Jesus and Mary. In this he identified one grace. 'And the second is to have made me make the sacrifice of Eau Vive and of all immediate active life in order to live for Jesus alone.' He wrote of how fruitful his theological studies had been from an intellectual point of view:

One begins to realise that the mystery is much deeper than one might ever have believed ... like small children we must advance in this knowledge of the truth ... bearing in mind all the time that this theological knowledge is nothing compared with knowledge through Love in which I attain God without any reasoning, without any intermediary.

By September 1957 he felt called to a life that was even more solitary and went to live briefly in a very small farm in Crulai, in Orne. It had no running water, only a well with drinking water and a small stove on which to cook. This was the only source of heat for the whole house. There too he was happy, although the older Jean Vanier acknowledged a certain fear of nights spent in such isolation, admitting that he would go to bed early in order to avoid the darkness. Every morning he would cycle 5–10 kilometres to one of the local villages for Mass. He was deeply moved by the fidelity of the priests who said Mass quietly in icy churches with only one or two elderly women present.

As early as 1953, however, Dr Thompson, who had been very touched by Fátima in Portugal, had suggested buying a piece of land there. Land at Fátima was cheap at the time and with Jean Vanier's parents' financial backing it had been possible to purchase a plot with the vague possibility of creating another Eau Vive in mind. When, after leaving Eau Vive, Jean was looking for intimations as to which way to turn, the possibility of living in a place of prayerfulness and pilgrimage seemed like a small sign. For a while his letters to his parents were full of detailed plans for the building of a modest cottage in which to live. Designs and measurements reflecting the naval officer's attention to practical precision were interspersed with theological reflections on St Augustine, St Thomas, the primacy of charity and words of spiritual consolation to his mother in particular. Permission to build in Fátima was initially declined for practical reasons but Jean Vanier was able to move into an existing cottage there belonging to some American Dominican nuns:

> Our Blessed Lady has been good to me. If I have difficulties concerning the construction of a little house, I have none concerning my life here. The American nuns have lent me their little gardener's house – which has all the conveniences –

kitchen, running water etc – I am able there to continue the
life I have been leading for two years.

The very modest house in Fátima was subsequently built and he
was able to settle in it. Repeated reassurances to his concerned
parents revealed the maturity with which he had been able to
approach his own and Père Thomas' apparent mistreatment:

> A small point we forget too, is that God cannot stick us together
> unless we are somewhat in pieces, and those he wants for
> greater strength in the Church have to be in pieces, in order
> that clearly, tangibly, immediately and actually it is He that
> sticks them together. Never be alarmed or dismayed when you
> see religious suffering or on trial, and never examine the causes
> or motives or intentions on the immediate plane. Every detail
> has passed through the beloved Hands of God for His eternal
> purposes and eternal glory.

The Vaniers had rejoiced in the prospect of their son's ordination. Madame Vanier had even purchased a chalice and cassock in
anticipation. Seeking to alleviate the isolation and prohibitions to
which Père Thomas was subjected and also to have the restric-
tions imposed upon his son lifted, when in 1959, Cardinal
Roncalli was elected Pope, General Vanier wrote to him on their
behalf. As Canadian ambassador to France he had known Angelo
Roncalli well while he was the Papal Nuncio in Paris. Monsignor
Roncalli had even visited Eau Vive and in an exchange with Père
Thomas had given his whole-hearted approval to the
Dominican's recipe for a life in which Muslims, members of the
Orthodox Church, Catholics and Protestants could pray har-
moniously together. Thomas Philippe had advocated praying
together but the avoidance of contradictory discussion. If people
wished to talk they could do so privately with him. It was, the
future Pope had agreed, 'a good method'.

Having become Pope John XXIII, Roncalli granted General
and Madame Vanier and Jean a private audience and a visit to the
papal apartments, showing his guests the shutters he had changed
in his bedroom in order to be able to see the crowds in St Peter's
Square. As the small lift took General and Madame Vanier to the
ground floor, the Pope took advantage of a moment alone with

their son to advise him to separate himself from Père Thomas Philippe. Like General and Madame Vanier, Jean remained nonetheless unwavering in his belief in the priest's good faith: 'I was so interiorly convinced that Père Thomas was a man of God that it was clear to me that my future was not in an ecclesiastical career.'

In September 1959 Georges Vanier's distinguished career as a soldier-diplomat culminated with his appointment as Canada's first French Canadian and Roman Catholic Governor General. The new tenants of the vice-regal mansion, Rideau Hall in Ottawa, were hailed by the Canadian nation as a gracious couple committed to national unity and the continuation of the social work that had always formed part of their life together. Their son meanwhile continued his life of prayer and study. Despite a severe bout of hepatitis in July 1959 from which it took him some time to recover fully, he completed his work on the ethics of Aristotle. In June 1962 he defended his doctoral thesis on 'Happiness as Principle and End of Aristotelian Ethics'. It was a gruelling three-hour experience at the end of which a jury of five members unanimously pronounced him a Doctor of Philosophy 'cum maxima laude'. Canon Lallement, who had helped Jean Vanier as a metaphysician, philosopher and Thomist, wrote afterwards to Georges Vanier in glowing terms of how even the new dean of the Catholic Institute, who was least close to Jean in his interpretation of Aristotle, had recognised the great value of his work. The author of the thesis, however, still had no very distinct idea what his next step was to be.

❦

When in 1989 I first met Père Thomas Philippe in his room at the Farm – the collection of converted farm buildings at Trosly-Breuil where by then he was available six days a week to welcome people, guide them and often suggest to them truths which they would carry with them for the remainder of their lives – he was able to trace quite clearly a path which led almost inexorably to the creation of l'Arche. In his eighties, despite the constant demands made upon his theological and spiritual resources, he was still somehow a priest with time. He spoke in a distinctive high-pitched voice, his sentences punctuated with the often repeated question, '*Vous voyez?*' ('Do you see?'), his body craning forward for further confirmation that he had been understood, and in compensation for the deafness that had grown more acute with his advancing years. He was manifestly a man of suffering, indeed it seemed to me one whose suffering was at the very source of l'Arche, but he chose to say nothing of his years of painful exile and rejection during which, even after he had been permitted once more to say Mass, he had been deprived of all ministry. Nor did he refer to the extreme disabilities of his old age other than with a certain rueful humour.

He spoke of Dr Thompson, not as the friend who had been to Rome in 1953 and 1954 and been a support to him throughout the some ten years of his 'exile', but as one who had above all else, opened up for him the dimension of the heart. Dr Thompson had been not only an eminent and discerning psychiatrist, a disciple first of Freud and then of Jung, but also a man capable of integrating the human heart into the philosophical vision of Père Thomas Philippe. Père Thomas had been particularly moved by the knowledge that Thompson had adopted a German Nazi boy he found lying in the street and by the fact that so respected a man had been touched in a very particular way by the papacy. Dr Thompson, originally a Protestant, had become a Roman Catholic because Jesus had appointed to the head of his Church a servant of the servants of God, not a doctor or a prestigious man but Peter, a simple fisherman. Based on his experiences at international UNESCO meetings, Dr Thompson had also drawn Père Thomas' attention to the fact that group decisions could be prudent and reasonable, but they could not be compassionate. Only the human heart, he maintained, could be that.

Dr Thompson was a sensitive advocate of St Augustine's emphasis on the richness of the human heart and simultaneously an extraordinary thinker well equipped to help Père Thomas discover a new dimension in psychology. The Dominican priest had been familiar with the work of Freud but less so with that of Jung. Through Thompson he discovered the 'communion' of mother and baby, the idea that it is only through the child's experience of its mother's love that it realises it is loveable, and the anguish arising from the rupture of that communion. Such an understanding of the importance and implications of the mother–child relationship, now widely recognised, came as something of a revelation at that time. It formed the basis of much of Père Thomas' subsequent thinking and that of Jean Vanier. Years later Jean Vanier commented:

> I find that we've been clouded by Freud in the understanding of the mother–child relationship. I find he's lost some sort of simplicity in the bonding between mother and child. The child is not an egotistical creature but very fragile. There is this incredible relationship between the mother and child in which the child is filled with love and peace, communion.

What he and Père Thomas together were to discover in l'Arche was the particular wound of the person with disabilities stemming from the experience of 'broken communion'.

It was Dr Thompson who had used his influence to have Père Thomas, whilst still under condemnation by the Church authorities, moved from Rome to a monastery in Citeaux. It was Dr Thompson also who had introduced him to Dr Préaut. Dr Préaut was a man highly respected in Oise, with many years of experience with people with mental disabilities. In 1960 – together with a Monsieur Prat – he had begun in the village of Trosly-Breuil a home and workshop for mentally disabled young men known as the Val Fleuri. Monsieur Prat was himself the father of a boy with mental disabilities. Reluctant to put his son into a mental institution and concerned for his future, he had been persuaded by Dr Préaut to use the legacy intended for his child to open a home to help not only his own boy but others too. A condition had been built into the agreement that his son would have a place there for life.

Between 1952 and 1963 Père Thomas had at intervals spent time with Dr Préaut at a school for delinquents the doctor had founded about 10 kilometres from Trosly-Breuil. The two men had come to know each other well and in 1962, in his capacity as chairman of the Board of Directors, Dr Préaut invited Père Thomas to come as chaplain to the old village château and stables that were now the Val Fleuri and its protected workshops. The ageing priest was by this time living with his elderly mother. He had long been attracted to the poor, sensing in them the special action of the Holy Spirit, but his vision of the poor had focused first on manual workers or dockers with their 'simple working life'. His years at Eau Vive had brought him into contact with another Dominican priest who worked amongst the dockers and who had impressed upon Père Thomas his own discovery that 'though they were in many respects coarse and rough, they often had extraordinary hearts'. Progressively Père Thomas had discovered what it meant to be a delinquent or marginal and, in a very personal way, what it meant to be rejected. Dr Préaut's intimation that there was special work to be done among people with mental disabilities, that they were people who were poor and weak in the extreme, and that they needed teaching not through force but through trust, touched a chord of recognition.

He accepted the invitation, arriving in Trosly-Breuil shortly before Christmas 1963 as one of the poorest of the poor. He was poor in the material sense, having many years previously chosen a way of poverty. He was also poor in the sense that for some ten years he had been an outcast deprived of the ministry to which he had been called at so early an age. Moreover, even in the place where he had finally been invited to stay he found there were those who did not want him. Among the educators at the Val Fleuri were a number of former seminarians who had been turned down for the priesthood or who had opted to leave the seminary before ordination. Strong feelings of anti-clericalism prevailed, and Père Thomas was quick to sense that they would prefer him not to live with them in the building which was later to become the place of welcome for l'Arche in Trosly-Breuil.

A priest did not impose his presence, nor that of the Sacraments. Instead, he sought a place to live in the village where those who wanted the Eucharist could have ready access to it. He found two rooms off the village square, the Place des Fêtes, one of which was to become a chapel. In the corner which would later become a sacristy, he had a bed, a desk and the few possessions he needed to live. There was no electricity. When it was cold Dr Préaut's son would bring him wood from the forest to burn, and when it rained the water poured in through the leaking ceilings of his dilapidated rooms.

This poverty made him all the more readily accepted by the local villagers, many of whom were themselves elderly and poor, and he felt at once drawn both to them and, in a very particular way, to the people with disabilities in his pastoral care at the Val Fleuri. They had been born poor, and the aim was not so much to help them out of their poverty – as in the case of delinquents – but to help them accept their poverty and enable them to see in it the grace granted by God, to show them that their handicap was not necessarily a curse but could be a mark of God's special love for them.

Dr Préaut had begun a programme of research to identify the principal characteristics of the mentally disabled people with whom Père Thomas found himself involved. His investigations revealed that

> mentally disabled people in psychiatric institutions were considered to be gregarious in the sense that they flocked together and appeared to need to be led. They were regarded as having an intelligence far inferior to the rest of humanity and more on a par with that of animals. But it was society and its overbearing attitude of superiority that made disabled people 'gregarious'. By nature they were the most spontaneous beings, who actually found living crowded together very difficult, who when approached roughly withdrew into themselves, but who when approached with love, responded with extraordinary warmth and generosity.

Their intellectual knowledge was limited. It was frequently hardly worth teaching them to read. Yet one of the first revelations to surprise the psychiatric profession was that they could make beautiful mosaics. With encouragement they could display quite extraordinary artistic gifts. Though their intellectual qualities were limited, they were rich in qualities of the heart, and those qualities of the heart called directly to people. They had a profound need for relationship, and in relationships of trust, love and freedom their particular gifts would flourish.

Père Thomas related the journey of discovery he had made with Dr Préaut to what Thompson had already shown him with regard to human consciousness and its operation not only at the level of reason and the mind, but at the level of the heart. Thompson had cited the example of the human baby, born in a state of such dependence on its mother that, without assistance, it is incapable even of turning itself over to avoid suffocation, as an example of how a child is obliged to put its trust in its mother and is thus made to be a religious being. If man were a purely rational being, Thompson had argued, this would constitute premature birth. Philosopher and skilled theologian that he was, Père Thomas aligned himself with the visionary French Jesuit, palaeontologist, biologist and philosopher, Pierre Teilhard de Chardin, whose writings he knew well: 'With all the discoveries that clever men have made about life, our world and the universe, Teilhard de Chardin was not able to find any single philosophy capable of assuming them all in a synthesis, other than the teachings of Jesus.' Those teachings emphasised the importance of, indeed found their most potent expression in, the 'little' people of this world.

Père Thomas, for all his scholastic language and intellectual abilities, was a man in whom the heart consciousness was already well developed. His own experience as a small boy had shown him that the 'smallest' and the 'poorest' could be called into a profound and direct relationship with Jesus, a relationship intended uniquely for that person which he called 'mystical' in the sense of being hidden to all others. For him evangelisation meant enabling people to enter into this direct relationship. By his own account, however, his ministry among mentally disabled people brought home to him more powerfully than ever the need to 'rediscover all my theology under the sign of the heart'. It reinforced the conviction that the Church, which he consistently referred to as 'the Church of Jesus', had been established first and foremost for the 'little' people and the poor, in whom the Holy Spirit acted from preference, and from whom others must be prepared to learn if they were to enter into its life. 'What enabled me most to understand disabled people', he subsequently claimed, 'was my deafness. My suffering brought me nearer to them. They would shout quite brazenly, "He's deaf. He can't hear us." But with such affection!'

Anxious to refurbish, not so much the room where he was living but the small chapel that was to house the Blessed Sacrament, Père Thomas set about doing it himself. He borrowed tools and enlisted the help of some good friends, among them Jean Vanier. He invited Jean to prepare the dilapidated chapel to receive and welcome Jesus in the Eucharist, in much the same way as he sought to enable Jean to welcome Jesus from the place of poverty within him.

Jean Vanier helped his spiritual father set himself up in his simple lodgings, and Père Thomas – feeling that there was a vocation there for the ex-naval officer who in his mid-thirties was still uncertain of what he was going to do in life – suggested in his gentle way that there was something special to be done among disabled people. Jean Vanier, for his part, found himself self-conscious and a little apprehensive amongst Père Thomas' new friends, men who were weak and powerless in a way that he had never previously encountered. He felt, nevertheless, that Père Thomas had 'discovered something', and was deeply impressed by what the priest had learnt of the spiritual openness of disabled people and of their place in the heart of God. In December 1963 he was present at a theatrical production put on in the large hall of the Val Fleuri. In those days there were men in the home who were violent and noisy. His first encounters with them left him both touched and fearful. He enjoyed the production but, by his own admission, did not feel fully at ease.

In the following January Jean Vanier took up a post at St Michael's College at the University of Toronto to teach ethics. His thesis on 'Happiness as Principle and End of Aristotelian Ethics' had come into the hands of Larry Lynch, dean of the philosophy faculty there, who had written to invite him to give a course on ethics from January to May 1964. He had been due to lecture on justice but, deciding that that was not a subject of great interest to his students, changed his theme to friendship, love, sexuality and atheism, which attracted a sizeable following.

It came as an extraordinary revelation to him to discover that he had the 'power of teaching'. It had never previously occurred to him that he had the capacity to teach. He had studied but, compared with others in his position, had read less than most. He had, however, listened intently to Père Thomas. From the manner in which, without having taken notes, he found he could give the priest's words back as if recorded on a tape, he recognised that he had been 'formed very deeply', and once again felt this was as an experience of God. At St Michael's College, without his fully understanding why, the fruits of all that had gone before began to come out with great force. He was asked to give talks to the whole college and the hall would be packed to bursting point. It was an experience that had great relevance to his agreement a few years later to take a retreat in Toronto and to the many other retreats that developed out of it. 'It is one of the advantages of getting older', he confided much later when the mystery of his life had become more readable to him, 'that you can see how everything had meaning. You think everything is your choice but it's not. Gradually there is the discovery of being chosen, of being shaped in order to be an instrument.' Asked whether a process of 'osmosis' would be an accurate description of his relationship with the priest who did much of the shaping, he replied:

> Probably but it's an osmosis, some form of communication, born in the spirit. I gave up an ecclesiastical career and my only intention was to be with him even if that brought difficulties so there was an element of choice, a renunciation that was somewhere at the basis of that osmosis.

At the time, despite being offered a permanent position at St Michael's College, he knew only that he did not see teaching as a permanent option, that Jesus wanted him to be close to Père Thomas and that he was still in a state of waiting to discern where the Holy Spirit would lead him.

Some months later, on his next visit to France and Père Thomas, there was the same gentle hint, the same question: was there something special to be done among people with disabilities? Encouraged by Père Thomas and by Dr Préaut, he went to see the person in charge of people with disabilities in the Oise area, who confirmed what by this time was shaping itself into the resolve 'to do something'. In the late spring of 1964 he began visiting different centres for people with mental disabilities. He was overwhelmed by what he found, especially in the asylum of St Jean les Deux Jumeaux south of Paris, where some 80 mentally disabled men lived together in two dormitories in chaotic and violent conditions. Forbidding concrete walls surrounded buildings constructed of sombre cement blocks. The occupants had no work. They ate together in a vast refectory and otherwise spent their days going round in circles. From 2 p.m. to 4 p.m. there was an obligatory siesta and then a walk. One man, Dany, had spent his life in a cellar and spat at anyone who approached him. 'There was something terrifying about it but at the same time something difficult to touch, something profoundly of God. I have found the same thing in prisons and places for leprosy sufferers,' Jean Vanier reflected with hindsight. 'In places of horror there is a kind of presence of God. Peace and chaos – one is frightened yet captivated.'

The horrifying, chaotic, repellent conditions in which many people with disabilities were then obliged to exist would not in years to come be a reality to many of the assistants who followed Jean Vanier into l'Arche. At that time, however, Jean Vanier felt acutely the dreadful disparity between the gospel message of compassion, mercy and justice, and the plight of people with disabilities. All that he had read and all that Père Thomas had communicated to him about the primacy of love was in shock-ing contrast to what he was now encountering, and he was moved by the inner pain of it to do something, however imprecisely formulated that 'something' might be. Combined with the clear inner certainty that he was to remain in close proximity to Père Thomas, his spiritual father, a man of God, a friend of Jesus and of Mary, gradually the conviction that 'Jesus wanted something to be done' was becoming more concrete. For one, moreover, who was always inclined to live the present moment with a certain naïvety and trust, if Jesus wanted it, there were no real questions to be asked.

It was a conviction not so readily shared by everyone. Madame Vanier reacted strongly against what her son was proposing to do. It was Tony Walsh of Benedict Labre House in Montreal who helped her and her husband to accept the decision. An Irishman by origin, he had gone out to Canada to teach Indian children in the North-West Territories and to help them rediscover their roots and their identity at a time when the Indian culture in Canada had been strongly repressed. He had then gone on to found a house in a very poor part of Montreal, which provided accommodation for a number of 'gentlemen of the road' and was a centre to which people would come for a meal and a chat. Both General and Madame Vanier used to help there. Pauline Vanier, who had a special regard for Tony Walsh because he had recog-nised that, 'for all my apparent wealth, I too was poor', waited at tables and served meals, especially at Christmas, and kept the men amused with her talents as a raconteur and clown. Benedict, Jean and Thérèse Vanier all knew Tony Walsh.

Thérèse Vanier acknowledged that he influenced her in the direction of l'Arche and that he probably influenced her brother in a similar way: 'For someone of his generation he was extremely radical as far as the Church was concerned and yet extremely anchored, very sure of his place in the Church, very challenging of its attitudes, but acting out his challenge in what he was doing.' He was a layman who had voluntarily adopted a life of smallness, simplicity and poverty, one who in a quiet, unobtrusive way reflected the love of God to his fellow man, and who conveyed a message to the Church and to the world about the place and the power of the poor, not merely by words but through his very life.

The adolescent Jean Vanier had loved the spirit and power that came with naval life. People there had not been his prime concern and even when he chose to leave the Navy it was not primarily people or relationships that interested him. Looking back, he could see that it was more a question of devoting himself to an ideal of peace and Christian life and to the study of philosophy and theology. Certainly he wanted to follow Jesus but at this stage it was more out of idealism. 'Jock', Tony Walsh told Madame Vanier at the time, 'has to go to the end of his ideal, that of poverty'. He would do so in the conviction that, as Jean himself had once written to her, 'The ways of Jesus are very different from the ways of men. He alone sees the heart – the deep aspirations and the profound intentions – we only see the "unimportant".'

❧

FOUR

A SCHOOL OF THE HEART

JEAN VANIER HAD HEARD what he would subsequently call 'the primal cry of people with disabilities', a cry which expressed in their very flesh a yearning for friendship combined with a sense of being unworthy and the doubt that anyone could ever want them. In some ways horrified and afraid, but also deeply moved by the new world of suffering he was entering, he embarked upon a plan of action. He was after all 36 years old, full of energy and a man schooled in efficacy and efficiency, with both a naval training and the experience of running Eau Vive behind him. Before he had even found a house in which to live, he informed Père Thomas that he would open a small *foyer* on 4–5 August, two saints' days representing for him fidelity to the Holy Spirit: that of Saint Dominic (because Père Thomas was a Dominican) and that of Notre Dame de la Merci. Thereafter, with the help of Louis Pretty, a Canadian architect who had come to France to visit Taizé and see something of the newly developing Christian communities, the plan evolved very rapidly.

Père Thomas gave free rein to Jean Vanier's impulses. At one point the priest suggested he look for a house in Vieux Moulin, a village some 5 kilometres from Trosly, but Jean Vanier refused. He wanted to be close enough to his spiritual father to attend his Mass every morning. A small house in Trosly-Breuil, only a few minutes' walk away from both the Val Fleuri and the tiny chapel behind which Père Thomas was living, seemed a suitable property. The owner had had no intention of selling but obligingly agreed to do so. A legal structure had to be created to carry responsibility for what was to come into being. Dr Préaut suggested that it should become part of an already established charitable organisation, SIPSA (*Societé pour l'instruction des enfants sourds, muets ou arriérés*) and that this society should undertake any necessary administration. Jean Vanier agreed subject to two conditions: that he be chairman and that he appoint half the members of the board. It was also agreed with the appropriate government health authority that the house should be considered a 'placement familiale' linked to the Val Fleuri.

This was a time when many people with disabilities were frequently still hidden away by their parents. Jean Vanier once encountered a teenager on a farm chained up in a garage. Officially, however, the general climate of the day was conducive to the new venture. The policy of French legislation was to facilitate and encourage the creation of homes for mentally disabled people. In other respects too 'everything was given' in a way that made it swiftly apparent to Jean that he was embarking on something definitive.

Madame Martin, the directress of St Jean les Deux Jumeaux, the asylum Jean Vanier had visited near Paris, was an extraordinary woman. By packing 80 people into a former convent where she was only supposed to care for 40, she had created a very closed and disturbed institution. At the time Jean felt himself too ignorant to be unduly critical but later he described it as repellent in the absence of any real attempt to achieve the well-being of its inmates. Yet Madame Martin was also possessed of a certain generosity of spirit. She gave the young man advice which, despite the fact that she herself was a woman in a house full of men, included the directive never to have women assistants to live with disabled men. She also supported him in his venture. Eventually it was she who suggested which three men he should invite to live with him from amongst the many he had identified as crying out for love and relationship. It was decided that Jean Vanier would move into the small *foyer* on 4 August and on 5 August she would bring these three, Raphael, Philippe and Dany to join him in time for lunch. The initial invitation was for a month's holiday, and if all went well they would be asked at the end of the month whether they would like to remain permanently.

For some years Jean had been living on a shoestring, subsidised by cheques from his father and parcels of clothing and food from his mother. With very limited funds, he and Louis Pretty hired a small truck and bought some second-hand furniture from Abbé Pierre's Emmaus Community. Other necessities were lent or given. By the time the day of welcome arrived the furnishings in the little house included a small statue of the Virgin Mary, which would remain in what was to become known as the 'Foyer de l'Arche', and a dining table. Madame Martin brought with her a celebratory meal for the newcomers and the welcoming party, which included Père Thomas, Dr and Madame Préaut and others whose help Jean Vanier had recognised he would need. Afterwards, however, the guests all left and he found himself alone with his three new companions.

'I was completely lost', he recalled, 'especially with Dany. He couldn't hear and he couldn't speak. It was crazy taking him. I should never have been asked to remove him from his highly closed institution to a free situation.' In a state of total insecurity, Dany began to hallucinate. He ran out into the quiet streets of Trosly-Breuil and made menacing gestures at the uncomprehending passers-by. The night of 5–6 August was a memorable one for Jean. Failing to find the electricity meter, although there was one in the house as he was to discover a few days later, he and his companions spent the first night in darkness and turmoil with Dany constantly on the move and Jean Vanier unable to get any rest in his bed up in the loft. The walls of the little house were sound but the interior left much to be desired. There was no lavatory, only a bucket.

Next morning the practical side of him recognised that it was impossible for Dany to stay. From the telephone in the village café he called Madame Martin and with great sadness asked her to come and collect him. From that very first founding night Jean Vanier experienced the need to make choices, and suffering; his own suffering and sense of failure and the suffering of the men who had come to live with him.

Both Raphael Simi and Philippe Seux were to some degree physically as well as mentally disabled. Raphael had had meningitis when he was very young. His vocabulary was restricted to about twenty words and his understanding was very limited. His balance was shaky, and he could easily fall over. He communicated by grunts and had the real appearance of a disabled person. In Philippe's case the physical disability was more obvious in that he could not walk without a crutch. Encephalitis had left one of his legs and one of his arms paralysed. He talked a lot but frequently about the same things and lived to a large extent in his own dream world. Both had been placed in the asylum in Seine-et-Marne on the death of their parents. Yet Philippe, not realising that his mother was dead, constantly asked after her. Madame Martin had told Jean Vanier of the woman's death but no one in the family had thought to inform Philippe. In response to Philippe's persistent questions Jean set about finding a member of his family to tell him the truth. An uncle came to Trosly-Breuil and Jean asked him to take Philippe to his mother's grave and help him to accept the reality of her death.

> He threw himself on his mother's grave and howled and howled in a way that you could hear for miles around, and I think those howls were not only because his mother, the only person he had ever loved, was dead but also because no one had treated him as her son.

Being plunged into this world of suffering was to bring about a gentle revolution. Like Père Thomas, Jean Vanier was poor when he arrived at Trosly-Breuil. To wait until his mid-thirties to find his true vocation had been an impoverishing experience and, as one friend put it, 'he had lost a lot of baggage' along the way. The life he led with Raphael and Philippe in their little home with one tap and one wood-burning stove was simple in the extreme. They went shopping together, prepared meals, cleaned the house, and did the washing. Raphael and Philippe helped as best they could with the different chores in the house and garden. In the morning they went to Mass and in the evening they said part of the rosary together. The house looked straight out on to the road, without a wall or garden to separate them from passers-by. Raphael and Philippe manifestly inspired fear in some of the villagers and an unhealthy pity in others. The more his friendship with the two men grew, the more Jean Vanier found himself hurt by such attitudes and even by people applauding him for what he was doing.

He was conscious of a bond of commitment, a 'covenant' between himself and Raphael and Philippe which in some mysterious way flowed from the covenant that existed between God and the suffering poor of the world (Exodus 3:7–8). He wanted to create a family around them, a place where they could grow in all the dimensions of their being. They began to get to know each other, to learn how to live together, to care for one another, to have fun and to pray together. It was a life which Jean Vanier would look back on as being open to the action of the Holy Spirit and in some sense 'prophetic'. Because of its poverty, he shared Père Thomas' experience of the generosity of the poor, particularly in the guise of the local village women who brought apples and soup and whatever else they could offer – parcels of food even arrived through the post – but also in the form of the disabled men and all that they had to show him, for in their shared life he was to learn the value of really listening to them:

> The idea of living together was there from day one, the idea of living happily together, of celebrating and laughing a lot, came very quickly and spontaneously. When the idea of the poor educating us came, I don't know exactly. The words of St Vincent de Paul, 'The poor are our masters', were always there, but when they became a reality is uncertain.

The change of attitude from 'wanting to do things for' to 'listening to' was one which took some time but it was a revolution no doubt made possible by his own openness and readiness to be shaped by experience and events. Despite the barrier of preconceived ideas and psychological defence mechanisms that he was obliged to recognise existed even within himself, he began to realise that he had everything to discover about people with disabilities, whom at that stage he referred to as 'boys'. During those first months he learned a great deal, not least that Raphael and Philippe did not want to live with a retired naval officer who ordered them about and thought himself superior. Nor did they want to live with an ex-professor of philosophy who thought he knew all the right theories. He had left the naval world where weakness was something to be shunned at all costs and joined a different world at Eau Vive, the world of thought where once again weakness, ignorance and incompetence were things to be shunned. Life with Raphael and Philippe moved him into a world of poverty, weakness and fragility in a way which supplemented his ideas and theories about human beings with the discovery of what it meant to be really human.

Neither his family background nor his time in the Navy had really encouraged him to grow emotionally and develop his capacity for relationships. In Raphael and Philippe's hearts, however, he discovered not only immense pain but also beauty and gentleness, a capacity for communion and tenderness. Dimly he began to sense how living with them could transform him, not by developing his intelligence or talent for leadership but by awakening the qualities of his heart, the child within him. The man who had on occasions had to make an appointment to see his own father was moving towards the understanding that 'to love someone means being prepared to waste time with them'.

Jean Vanier was happy to command, teach and obey. He was less well schooled in the art of listening and friendship based on parity. He had taken it for granted, for example, that he and his companions would lead a 'gospel' life. Of course there would be grace before meals and even a decade of the rosary. Everyone would have to go to Mass at 7.30 a.m. which meant getting Philippe and Raphael up very early. One morning Philippe asked him why he should. Only then did Jean Vanier realise that in order to remain there and not return to the institution, Philippe would have agreed virtually to anything, even to going to Mass when he did not want to. Yet the Holy Spirit could only express itself in freedom. The realisation dawned that the more fragile a person's liberty was, the more it must be respected and protected. This was the pedagogy, not of force but of freedom, which Dr Préaut and Père Thomas had recognised disabled people specifically needed. It was a principle absolutely fundamental to the communities that would follow.

Jean Vanier professed not to be a man of much vision. There had been no clearly defined desire to found a community. He claimed to be conscious of only two things at the beginning of l'Arche, two things which he would not have been able to put into words at the time: one was that he was doing something irreversible; the other was a somewhat ambivalent feeling about possible growth – 'If nobody came we would remain the size of a car so that we could still travel together, but there was also a desire to start building little barrack huts right from the beginning.' Somewhere in his heart or head there was a model of community which consciously or unconsciously he was following.

Not only was there the influence of Catherine Doherty's Friendship House and Tony Walsh's Benedict Labre House as communities based very much on pain, mercy and welcome, in which lay people lived a life of simplicity and poverty with the very poor, but in 1954, in Montreal, Jean Vanier had come to know the Little Sisters of Jesus and their fraternity based on the spirituality of Charles de Foucauld. L'Arche would come to feel very close to the Little Sisters and Brothers over the years, discovering a common basis in the spirituality of Nazareth, the recognition of Jesus present in the poor, the simplicity of their daily life and the quest for unity. Eau Vive had undoubtedly also left its mark, although there for Jean Vanier it had been more a question of discovering the ways of the Spirit in the sense of trying to be faithful to what Jesus wanted. Dorothy Day's paper, the *Catholic Worker*, had made a profound impression on him. He had also visited the Foyer de Charité begun by Cardinal Leger in Montreal. There people with physical and mental disabilities were welcomed in a spirit of prayer. Elements of all these would find their way into l'Arche.

On 22 August 1964 Henri Wembergue, a cousin of Père Thomas and brother of Sister Marie-Madeleine, a Carmelite who would hold l'Arche specially in her prayers, came to help. In September Dr Préaut asked Jean to welcome another disabled man, Jacques Duduit. At the beginning of November, a Sister Marie Benoit who was living in the village with two other Sisters asked to come and work on a regular basis in the house. Meals improved dramatically. Then, in December a social worker asked them to welcome Jean-Pierre Crépieux. The little family was gradually growing.

Jacqueline d'Halluin, who had remained close throughout his long years of waiting, was by this time dividing her time between Paris, where she was looking after three invalids, and the small house in Trosly-Breuil. Its garden was so overgrown in those days that it seemed to her very much part of the surrounding forest.

Drawn once again to the trees and the new life which she sensed somehow to be being born there, it was she who was called upon to write a prayer which members of the tiny community could say as they gathered together round the flickering light of a candle.

The l'Arche prayer was based on suggestions made by Jean Vanier even before the arrival of Raphael and Philippe. It was addressed to Mary, in whose life was contained the mystery of the relationship between the Word and the body:

> Mary who lived off and was nourished by the prophetic Word as a young girl, filled with grace until the incarnation when it's no longer the Word but that silent body, first of all inside her and then in her arms.

The prayer was also centred upon three invocations of Saint Vincent de Paul:

> Lord, bless us through the hands of your poor,
> Lord, smile at us through the faces of your poor,
> Lord, receive us one day into the happy company of your poor.

It would be modified over the years to enable non-Christians and Christians of different denominations to join together in worship all over the world. Sung to the accompaniment of guitars, murmured softly against the roar of traffic beyond thin wooden walls, uttered falteringly by those able only to say the first line over and over again, in Spanish, English, French and a multitude of other languages ... in its essential it would not change, for it reflected the special relationship of reciprocity at the very heart of l'Arche, which altered only in its deepening:

> O Mary,
> we ask you to bless our house,
> keep it in your immaculate heart,
> make l'Arche a true home,
> a refuge for the poor, the little ones,
> so that here they may find the source of all life,
> a refuge for those who are deeply tried,
> so that they may find your infinite consolation.

O Mary,
give us hearts that are attentive,
humble and gentle,
so that we may welcome with tenderness and compassion
all the poor you send us.
Give us hearts full of compassion
so that we can love, serve,
dissolve all discord
and see in our suffering and broken brothers the humble
    presence
of Jesus.

Lord,
bless us with the hands of your poor.
Lord,
smile at us through the eyes of your poor.
Lord,
receive us one day
into the blessed company of your poor.
Amen.

When it came to deciding what the small community should be called, Jacqueline d'Halluin was asked to make up a list of biblical names. When Jean Vanier read it he chose 'l'Arche', the French word for both 'ark' and 'arch', without a moment's hesitation. In fact it was so self-evident that with hindsight he would say that it was more a question of sensing that 'it had been chosen'. A letter he wrote to his parents on 2 June 1964 said that the project he was starting would be called 'l'Arche' after Noah's Ark

> because it is the name of the work that takes in all the little animals to save them … and which floats (but don't tell the Holy Office) on living waters! It is also the Ark of the covenant: Mary, Mater Misericordiae, who holds out her arms to embrace all the suffering of the world.

At the time the choice had been instinctive: 'I'm one of those people, I think, that discovers reasons afterwards but I think we're in a domain which is symbolic, not rational. It goes very, very deep'. In 1989, he delved into the depths to produce a series of reasons which failed still to satisfy him completely:

The passages in Genesis which tell the story of Noah are rich and meaningful. The Ark is the first covenant between God and humanity even before the birth of the Jewish people. So it's the whole vision of a boat where we welcome people who are in pain. It's the place where we are saved. It's the place of the covenant, and that's very important to us. Also Mary, who carried the saviour in her womb, has been referred to by the Fathers of the Church as the 'Ark of the Covenant'. Then there is the whole idea of the arch as a bridge, the bridge between two worlds. Then the ark of the covenant as the inner sanctuary, and then, something which is possibly deeper, the idea that we're looking at humanity somewhere before today's Christianity and we welcome people because they are people and not because they are baptised.

He was also a naval man, and to one who when speaking English frequently broke into French, not always in an attempt to find the *mot juste* but sometimes simply for the sake of euphony, there was also the attraction of the sound of the word 'l'Arche': 'It's not a hard "k"; it's something soft, gentle and holding.'

Somewhere in the early vision, of which both Jean Vanier and Père Thomas were a part, was the idea of welcoming anyone who wished to come, be they the very elderly, drug addicts or simply 'gentlemen of the road'. At Christmas 1964 Jean Vanier went to collect his sister Thérèse who was arriving at Compiègne station from England. On the way there he noticed a man walking along the road and, seeing him again on the return journey, invited him for Christmas lunch. Showered and refreshed, Gabriel presided over the Christmas festivities, smoked cigarettes and regaled the assembled company with stories. He had previously tried his vocation as a Dominican but had remained for only a few months. He was now a traveller and after a couple of days was back on the road with an open invitation to return. This he did the following month but, as soon as he decided to install himself on a more permanent basis, it became quickly apparent that he was not really suited to living in community. He was very jealous of Raphael and Philippe. The two archangels in particular did not get on and, when finally Jean Vanier walked into the dining room one day to find plates flying through the air, it was decided that for the sake of Raphael and Philippe, Gabriel must leave. For Jean Vanier the vision was gradually focusing: l'Arche, as far as he was concerned, could not take in all who were in need but must be for those suffering from a specific form of poverty, people with mental disabilities.

Brother Andrew, co-founder with Mother Teresa of the Missionary Brothers of Charity and one with whom l'Arche felt a close affinity, recalled the question of the nature and focus of community arising during his very first meeting with Jean Vanier in Calcutta in the early 1970s. As Superior of the Brothers, Brother Andrew had just had to ask two much loved men with very good qualities to leave the congregation. One had become too political in his approach to the problem of poverty; the other had a taste for drinking and was influencing others in that direction:

> When Jean arrived I had just gone through this painful business and I told him about it. Everyone knows Jean's great love for the human person, and I was surprised by the promptness of the response. He said that he believed that one of the prime roles of the superior or leader of any group was to discern who had the spirit of the group and who had not. And if there was a destructive influence he had to send away the person from whom it came. No matter how loving and kind one wanted to be, the greater good of others was a vital consideration.

The special call to people with mental disabilities was powerfully endorsed when, at the end of 1964, a crisis occurred at the Val Fleuri as a result of which all the staff handed in their notice. Three months later, in the following March when their resignations became effective, Jean Vanier was asked to take over as its director. Relations between l'Arche and the much larger residence, which housed 32 disabled men, had been a little strained. The director there, a Monsieur Wattier, had been a good man but not one who was very creative or rich in ideas. Conscious of Jean Vanier's friendship with both Dr Préaut and Père Thomas, he appears to have seen the French Canadian's presence in the village as a threat. He had allowed Raphael and Philippe and subsequently Jacques and Jean-Pierre to go to the Val Fleuri for showers but otherwise there was little contact between the two houses. In those days the residents of the Val Fleuri were kept firmly under lock and key except during a daily walk which was taken in a line with one member of staff in front and another bringing up the rear. The atmosphere inside the building was disrupted by noise and violence. It was not without a certain apprehension that Jean Vanier responded to Dr Préaut's request to pick up the pieces following the departure of all but two of the staff. There was a reluctance too to take a step that would radically alter the prophetic little family in the Foyer de l'Arche. As one of the earliest assistants put it: 'The community there was poor in every way except in its prayer which was magnificent, but it got poorer because we could not even have the kind of community we wanted.'

It was Jean Vanier's conviction that what people with disabilities really needed was a *foyer*, a home, a hearth, a family, because at that time in particular they were frequently not understood by their parents and brothers and sisters, and even if their blood relatives did understand them they were inclined to be too paternalistic, treating them like children and failing to take into account what Dr Thompson and others had found them to be capable of. These alternative *foyers* needed above all to be 'homes', but 'homes' which would provide something deeper than the family home. Père Thomas saw Mary as the mother of this alternative family unit and Jean, who had 'a great gift for organisation' as the father. Jean Vanier himself described his feelings in relation to the early days of l'Arche as those of one who had 'come home'. At the Farm in 1989 Père Thomas recalled how Jean Vanier loved his little *foyer* and the family life he led there, where he did the cooking himself and was dependent on the villagers for help, and how the assumption of the directorship of the Val Fleuri and consequent uniting of his small family with a much larger State-supported structure was not a transition easily made: 'Jean did it only because he felt it was the will of God.' Jean Vanier for his part remembered:

> I had told Père Thomas that I wasn't capable of running it, but he thought it would be right. In many respects it was madness. I had just no idea how to look after 32 people with a lot of violence and screaming.

As at previous significant junctures in his life, however, he took the circumstances as they arose without excessive questioning or introspection.

> I suppose there has always been something in me. There is naïvety, but there's also risk and trust in self which is both good and bad. You just keep going. I think those are strengths that carry weaknesses also. You make mistakes, but I think also, as you look at the story, there is the presence of Jesus, of one who is using me with all my defects, fragilities and qualities, and bringing something to birth.

'Here in l'Arche all is well', he wrote to his parents in February 1965, 'I am to take over the running of the Val Fleuri on 22 March – there are 30 boys. I am putting all my trust in Jesus.'

On Sunday 22 March 1965 he took charge of the Val Fleuri. The outgoing director had no great desire to show him how the place functioned. He pointed out some of the books and handed him a heavy bundle of keys to cupboards, offices and files. The younger man set up his office without even knowing the names of the people who lived in the building. Within an hour someone had stolen his bunch of keys. With only two of the original staff members remaining to help him, the house, workshops and garden were swiftly reduced to chaos. There was no nurse so Jean Vanier had to learn how to give injections. One man was a diabetic and needed injecting every morning so the new director found himself practising on an orange.

The need soon attracted help. Volunteers appeared from the village and elsewhere to assist with the book-keeping, gardening and cooking. It was a time when the social services were trying to organise themselves a little better and they sent a representative to help straighten out the finance and administration. At a congress in Paris for professionals working with people with disabilities Jean Vanier stood up and spoke about community life with disabled people in a way that he subsequently recognised must have seemed very naïve to those with infinitely more experience than he had. Nevertheless, a lady psychiatrist present, a Dr Richet who at the time was practising at Clermont psychiatric hospital 40 kilometres from Trosly, approached him afterwards and they became friends. She would help Jean Vanier and other assistants to a deeper understanding of the suffering and psychological needs of the men in the Val Fleuri and to increased knowledge of how to help them.

Furthermore, for all his protestations of ineptitude and lack of experience of anything but naval skills and Aristotle, the Navy had undoubtedly taught someone endowed with a natural authority something about management and discipline. It had given a boy who in his sister's recollection was something of a dare-devil non-conformist, constantly up to mischief and dis-inclined to toe the family line if he could avoid it, a certain respect for discipline. It had developed the capacity to cast aside important issues and go for even more important ones, combined with extreme self-control in areas which he recognised as crucial, such as prayer and work. His dedication to both of these stood him in good stead in the chaos of the early days of the Val Fleuri. Not at any stage did he feel the challenge was not for him.

> There were obviously times when it was hard, when I was angry, but I just kept going. I suppose there is also an element of – I was going to say proving oneself, but that's not entirely true. There's a sort of tenacity. Grace is there but there is also a human element. I had to go through many breakages after-wards but the Val Fleuri was an interesting time.

For all its 'prophetic' nature there had been a certain amount of formality and professionalism involved in the original setting up of the *foyer*. Three disabled men could not have simply been removed from an institution without it. The taking over of the Val Fleuri, however, moved Jean Vanier and l'Arche into the world of greater regulation and administration. It brought with it a 'prix de journée', a daily government subsidy for those living in the Foyer de l'Arche and hence greater external control. It also opened up the dimensions of the workshops. Work had to be found of a kind which would allow mentally disabled people to develop their particular gifts and give them access to the dignity of a salary, no matter how small. There was an unmistakable happiness that sprang from a disabled person's discovery that he or she could make something beautiful or useful. Opportunities to nurture that happiness had to be created.

Gradually it was recognised that on the road to greater autonomy a person might need to have two places of operation –

the home and the workplace – and that there was something to be said for these two places and the relationships that went with them being largely separate. In that way if things were going badly in one, it need not necessarily affect the other. In time this would prove a strong case for those capable of doing so going out to workplaces outside the community. At the same time, close co-operation between home and workshop could provide a more unified and effective approach to a disabled person's overall growth and development. With the passage of the years the assistants in the workshops in Trosly-Breuil would be quite distinct from those living in the houses, although the two groups liaised regularly. In the workshops the ratio of assistants to people with disabilities could be as high as one to three. In the right conditions people with disabilities there, and in l'Arche communities elsewhere, showed themselves to be very gifted in the making of mosaics and pottery, woodwork, weaving, gardening and a wealth of other creative skills. In the 1960s, however, such avenues were still being explored and there were possibly one or two assistants for 32 people. 'Of course I just opened up the gates. I wasn't going to have 32 people controlled by two.'

Jean Vanier's days were full. In March 1965 his thesis was published. As soon as he had a spare copy he sent one to his parents and his father professed to be so interested that he read a page of it daily. The Vanier parents were still faithfully supporting their son both materially and spiritually in all that he was doing. Jean remained affectionately appreciative, assuring them that he was united to them in the Heart of Jesus, but the workload in l'Arche meant that his letters were neither as long nor as frequent as they might have wished. At midday Jean Vanier would eat his meals at the Val Fleuri in a single vast dining room that was later divided into three still sizeable rooms. In the evenings he would return to the Foyer de l'Arche to relax over dinner. His office and his bedroom were at the Val Fleuri. He slept poorly during those initial years, for there were invariably disturbances in the night. Nevertheless, in the tumultuous atmosphere of the Val Fleuri, where there was much shouting and where at times men would go into uncontrollable fits and have to be restrained by force, Jean Vanier was still able to perceive the mysterious presence of God. In all the suffering and the madness there was yet something profoundly of God.

It was the religious element, Père Thomas emphasised, which alone could unify the increasingly diverse aspects of home life (be it in the Foyer de l'Arche or the Val Fleuri), activity in the workshops and external involvement in the form of a growing number of people who came to help. In the village of Trosly-Breuil Père Thomas made himself available in his room behind the chapel in the Place des Fêtes, where the Blessed Sacrament was reserved, to those who sought his counsel or simply his presence. Sometimes he would celebrate Mass in the nearby church at Pierrefonds. Often he visited the sick and the elderly. The figure in the white habit pedalling his bicycle or kneeling in silent prayer in the little chapel soon became widely known and accepted by the local people as 'le Père blanc'.

He had long felt a calling to be present in a special way to the dying. Early in his priesthood he had discovered how important it was for the dying to have a priest at their side, and Dr Thompson, who had influenced him so markedly, had maintained – as Freud also had done – that what troubled people most was fear of death. When he arrived in Trosly-Breuil 90-year-old Madame Bertrand, one of the village ladies who used to take soup to the Foyer de l'Arche every Friday, confided in Père Thomas that she had been praying that there would be a priest with her at her death. She welcomed him precisely as one who would accompany her in her last hours and, as it transpired, she did die with Père Thomas saying the rosary beside her. Thus, very quickly, Père Thomas found an eschatological role.

Within the first year of l'Arche a young person with disabilities died in humanly-speaking tragic circumstances. One Sunday night he suffocated during a fit. His parents could have taken him quietly away to be buried without much being said. For Père Thomas, however, it was a highly significant event which raised very early on in the history of l'Arche the question of how death should be approached. Dr Thompson had maintained that the fear of death, while it remained half conscious and unexplained, acted like an abscess beneath the surface of human consciousness. The suffocation of that young man provided a unique opportunity to let people with disabilities, most of whom had never seen a dead person before, face death. The manner in which they

gathered to pray round the body and afterwards came to talk to
Père Thomas about what death was and what happened afterwards, marked that day as a special one in his apostolic life. It
underlined his belief that disabled people, far from being like
animals, were in fact extraordinary for the understanding and
maturity their response displayed.

In October 1988 I stayed for a week in La Petite Source, then
one of the newer houses in Trosly-Breuil. The youngest and most
recent member of the household that made me so very welcome
for that week was Pascal, whose ability to speak was limited but
whose capacity to communicate by means of grunts and smiles
and touch was more than eloquent. Each time we met he would
press his hands together with a look of entreaty and say the word
'Papa', which I came to understand was a request that I pray for
his father. Pascal's mother was already dead; his father, a policeman, to whom the boy was particularly close, was now gravely ill
in hospital. At lunch one day Pascal gave us all to understand via
Joseph, one of the assistants, that he had something to say after the
meal. Over coffee in the living room Joseph announced on
Pascal's behalf that his father had 'gone to be with Jesus'. Little
was said in response. There were hugs for Pascal and tears and
prayers that were touching in their lack of inhibition. There was
no denying Pascal his grief. He would disappear at intervals and
I would hear him sobbing in the night; but there was also no mis-
taking the way in which during the days that followed he was
tacitly carried in his suffering by other members of the *foyer.*
Small acts of special consideration, a touch, a look, expressed far
better than any words the fact that those about him knew his
anguish better than most others, and he was not alone.

Père Thomas spoke readily of how among people with disabilities he had discovered a language of the heart 'which is not
written but which passes from person to person'. 'For the Holy
Spirit to operate through a sermon', he claimed as we sat side by
side on his worn settee, 'there needs to be personal contact.' He
recalled asking himself in the early days of l'Arche, whether he
should not teach the disabled people the rudiments of reasoned
theology relating to the God who had created them; but in the
years leading up to 1968 he had been struck by the fact that it
was often the assisted who helped assistants going through

difficult times with regard to religious belief and the Sacraments to rediscover their religious faith. There was of course great diversity among disabled people: not all of them had a highly developed spiritual sensitivity. Nor did all of them live in intimate communion with God. Each had his or her own particular struggles and temptations. But in all his years of pastoral care Père Thomas claimed never to have come across a mentally disabled person who was an atheist.

> They were all believers. I won't say practising, but they were believers and they were best helped by introducing them to the Gospels and the Sacraments as Jesus presented them – Jesus who is paradoxically head of the Church by virtue of his heart, not because he was capable of giving talks that could unify Aristotelianism and Platonism, not because his teachings were more beautiful than that of the Old Testament prophets. Jesus surpassed the prophets in his littleness.

Père Thomas had found that disabled people, who related much more readily to persons than to structures or abstractions, quickly discovered the name of Jesus very powerfully. It was also his experience that they discovered Jesus much more readily through the cross than the manger:

> The first name which disabled people respond to is not Christ or Lord, not the social functions of Jesus, but Jesus the person, through the heart of Jesus. I discovered that rather than teaching them about the creator God, through Jesus it was possible to help them discover the Father, the Holy Spirit, Mary. It was very simple to prepare them even for First Communion through the cross of Jesus.

If mentally disabled people were touched in a special way by the cross of Jesus, they also had a way of pointing others to the inner meaning of the crucifixion and the actuality of death leading to life. Years later Bishop Stephen Verney, one of a succession appointed to 'accompany' l'Arche in the United Kingdom, recalled an incident that occurred one evening at a gathering of disabled people and assistants in Lambeth. In the course of the evening a disabled woman of about 45 had given voice to that 'primal cry' that the world had abandoned her.

She had been rejected by her family and this was the deep, deep trauma inside her which nothing could ever cure. I tried to comfort her by assuring her that she had a new family in l'Arche, but she made it quite clear that that was nonsense really. She had been rejected. Next morning one of the assistants said to me, 'That woman's cry last night pierced into my heart, broke through my defences and showed me the deep cry within myself which I had never realised was there. I knew last night that cry within myself and this morning for the first time I know that I can be loved.' What went on there is such a mystery, but it seems to me that the disabled woman's cry somehow unlocked the door in the assistant to her own inner need and longing, and at that point she could meet God and discover she was loved. So one begins to see how Jesus actually saves us on the cross. One sees that because he cries out, 'My God, my God why hast though forsaken me', which is exactly the same cry as that woman's, he can actually touch the inner cry in my heart, your heart, everybody's heart. If we can stop pretending and all stand there together in compassion, which means after all 'suffering together', then we begin to know that we can be loved. I see the mystery of the death of Christ happening in l'Arche.

The germ of that vision – which saw in the weak, the broken and the rejected, the Jesus who was also rejected by his own, tortured and condemned to death, and which perceived also the saving power of those suffering people – was already present in the early days of l'Arche. Père Thomas had seen the gift of disabled people and allowed himself to be touched and shaped by them. He had discovered too, that disabled people were particularly sensible to the presence of Jesus in the Sacraments. They came to the confessional not because of a sense of wrongdoing but because they felt sad. They might not have a very developed sense of sin but they knew the inner turbulence and pain that was counter to the peace of communion, the peace to which Jesus referred when he said 'my peace I give unto you'. In the vision of Père Thomas therefore, they had a better understanding of the true nature of the Sacrament of Reconciliation: the gift of peace by means of which Jesus restored them to the way of faith. When it came to the Eucharist also, because their primary interest was in the heart, they were less deceived by the exterior beauty of the ceremony and more discerning of the attitude of the celebrant.

> I remember once a very lovely midnight Mass. One of the assistants serving had made it a most beautiful ceremony and I recall being a little caught up in the beauty of the occasion myself. Afterwards in the sacristy, I commented on how lovely the service had been to one of our disabled men and he told me that he hadn't been able to receive the Sacrament. He had sensed that there was too much concern for the ceremony.

From the very earliest days of l'Arche Père Thomas had understood that when disabled people serving at Mass placed their sometimes clumsy and often grubby fingers on laundered napkins, he could not be excessively concerned with the outer trappings of ceremony. He had also understood that something in their approach enabled them to discover the Eucharistic presence in a special way. 'With their hearts they went directly to the presence of Jesus, and they needed a priest who was not so much a showman as a man who celebrated the Eucharist with faith and love.'

Père Thomas was not specially present in the *foyer* at the beginning of l'Arche. He had undoubtedly felt the need once more to witness something being born. He had always needed to confront his spiritual life with something concrete. To be a Dominican or a teacher had never in itself been enough. That was why Eau Vive had been born very spontaneously, as if out of a seed that had somehow been sown in advance. L'Arche grew in much the same way. This time, however, Père Thomas assumed a less obviously central role. He did not involve himself in the daily tasks of the little household. Perhaps once a week he would eat with them and sometimes the small family there would take him food, but he wanted to retain a certain freedom in order to live his priesthood fully, to pray for l'Arche and also for the people in the village and surrounding area.

His unassuming, prayerful presence was nonetheless essential. In fact one of the extraordinary aspects of l'Arche derived from the fact that it was founded not on one but on two complementary but different vocations. Its history would be very largely determined by the tension between the two. The ageing priest, whose vision of the Church gave primacy to love and the poor, made it very clear from the beginning that the priest in l'Arche could not be a leader or director. That was to be Jean Vanier's role. In l'Arche the priest was not to be a father as in the Foyers de Charité but more like a brother. He was to be the shepherd and servant of the poor and their advocate in time of need. His role on the community council for example, was to defend the interests of the poor person when problems arose. As a servant of the poor, he was also himself among the humblest, entrusted by God with the service of the Sacraments so vital to the life of the heart, especially in the very poor. Père Thomas was always convinced that it was not for him to lead or make decisions but rather to ask the questions, 'Where are we going? What are our primary values?' In this way he might be considered to provide a kind of yardstick of the values of the heart against which the movement and direction of the community could be measured.

Inevitably such questions gave rise to tension between the questioner and the one who had actually to take charge, a man who was by nature inclined 'to go ahead because I just feel it's right' and who had been trained to be 'efficient'. There were differences of emphasis. Both men had been drawn to the poor, both shared the recognition that the poor were teachers of the heart, that they themselves could learn from the poor rather than the reverse and that the poor needed relationships of love and freedom in order to shine. Both had recognised from the beginning of l'Arche a fact which constituted a significant difference between it and many other places that took in suffering people: that 'if you go with the poor it's for life', that if you entered into a deep relationship with someone you could not simply end it after a few months or years.

For Père Thomas, however, drawn as he was to the accompaniment of the dying, the emphasis was upon being with the poor person to the end of his life in order to accompany him to his entry into heaven, to assist him towards the final step of passing to the Father. For Père Thomas the whole community was growing towards what was really an Ascension. For Jean Vanier, the pragmatist with an Aristotelian approach to happiness it was important to accompany the poor man to the end of his life but also to spend that life with him and see that he was happy. When Père Thomas emphasised celebration it was in connection with the Eucharist; for Jean Vanier celebration was also an important part of birthdays, festivals and the joy of living. The two dimensions – the pull towards heaven and the simultaneous recognition that life in this world must be lived with happiness, arguably part of the tension experienced in the Church as a whole – were to be clearly present in the history of l'Arche, straining one against the other.

Père Thomas Philippe also maintained that a welcome should be extended to any poor person. The first manifesto of l'Arche, written by him, reflected a wider vision of a community encompassing families, old people, the dying and marginal people of all kinds. The door should be open wide to all who were poor. Père Thomas felt there was a unity that existed between the poor regardless of the particular form that poverty took. Jean Vanier on the other hand, on the basis of his experience of having to make choices in relation to Dany, Gabriel and others, had identified the need to be selective; if l'Arche wanted to help people with mental disabilities it could not for their sake take in marginal people and drug addicts also.

In time these tensions would be experienced in the different l'Arche communities throughout the world. Indeed, these tensions – the tensions of the modern world – seemed to be an integral and difficult part of the l'Arche vocation. They brought suffering to the various communities as they undoubtedly brought pain to the two men whose relationship reflected them. In 1989 Jean Vanier spoke of how Père Thomas had the eschatological dimension, the vision, and he was 'just walking with it'. He referred to the priest as a rock, then qualified his comment with the words, 'and sometimes a wounded rock'. As to his own role; 'I think there had to be a number of knocks on the head. Now I have a much greater consciousness that it is God's project. But it wasn't always like that.'

Père Thomas had given Jean Vanier everything that he most valued. In many ways he had been born from the elderly priest and for years their relationship had been one of total submission on his part. As Thomas Philippe's spiritual son he had written him notes explaining what was going on within him, and followed the priest's direction implicitly. With hindsight Père Thomas was quick to insist that because of his age and deafness it would have been a grave handicap for l'Arche if he had assumed the prophetic role that was to become Jean's. Despite his recognition of Jean as head of the *foyer*, however, and his conviction that Jean had 'an extraordinary sense of the Word', the priest had probably hoped and imagined when l'Arche began that he would determine its orientation and Jean would follow. There came a time, however, when Jean Vanier had to evolve from being the spiritual child to adulthood and the maturity of someone who could make judgements for himself. There was, even at the most basic level, a generation gap between the two. His years of exclusion had moreover left Père Thomas in a fragile state. With increasing confidence Jean Vanier began to respond differently to the needs of a different age from Père Thomas, whose theological formation and the greater part of his ministry had taken place in the years prior to the Second Vatican Council.

'Communion despite difference' was how the complex relationship between the two men was sometimes described. It was an attractive idea but the suffering involved was very real. There were times when communication would have virtually broken down between them had it not been for Jacqueline d'Halluin, in particular, bearing messages and building bridges. It was painful for Jean Vanier and possibly even more so for Père Thomas because he was, according to Jean, the more sensitive of the two and because, while the priest had the spiritual authority, the younger man had the practical power.

In his seventies Jean Vanier was able to admit that, although he had never experienced depression 'in the real sense', he could understand people feeling that they were no good: 'There are strange powers that come up from within saying you're of no value, that you can do no good'. He was capable of being quite easily hurt or wounded. The pain of alienation from and even rejection by his mentor must have cut very deep. After all, Jean Vanier was aware that Père Thomas had experienced much the same tensions with Père Déhau, his own spiritual father, a man who was also hidden and who had in his old age known the disability of blindness. Humanly speaking Jean might have hoped for greater acceptance of his differences and his 'coming of age' from one to whom he had sought to be faithful at considerable personal cost. Throughout their differences, the belief that Thomas Philippe was a man of God to whom he was deeply and enduringly united had remained unshaken.

> I knew that what is deepest within me came from him so I could not deny him without denying myself. So it was not just a question of being faithful to each other. It would have been suicide. That was why it was so painful.

Beyond the protestations to his parents, for example, that there were 'not too many problems in l'Arche. Jesus is there', beyond his tendency to portray difficulties in terms of an ever-positive Christian message, lay a raw reality of suffering and rejection, from which Jean Vanier himself was not exempt. Nevertheless the miracle in it all was still discernable: their unity had been much deeper than any tension. And even the tension, he believed, was fundamentally wanted by God. Their complementary differences were a great safeguard for both, guaranteed the humility and poverty of both and made possible extraordinary growth.

FIVE

SHARING THE WORD

AT EAU VIVE THE AIM HAD BEEN to unify the world through an intellectual élite. In l'Arche Père Thomas and Jean Vanier began to realise more fully that there was 'an élite of the heart' which was of even greater relevance to the world. Even in the early years the world began to converge upon Trosly-Breuil in a very significant way. It came in the form of the growing number of disabled people needing places and in the form of young assistants who arrived from as far afield as Canada and the United States. They came and gave their services in exchange for their room, board and a small stipend because it was believed that the absence of a regular salary would help assistants pursuing an ideal of community to deepen and clarify their motivation. They also seemed to arrive in just sufficient numbers to keep pace with the community's expansion. By the autumn of 1966, Jean Vanier was writing in his regular circular letter, which the increasing number of people showing an interest in l'Arche and its activities had made necessary, of how he received requests several times a week for places he could not provide.

He was still returning to Canada at intervals to lecture. His courses on artistic inspiration, on friendship and affectivity, and on the cry of the poor attracted large audiences. From Toronto he wrote of how at a talk given to 1,800 students he had felt the current of generosity among them. 'We must create situations in which these young people can dedicate themselves and serve,' he wrote. 'L'Arche must seek to fulfil this function also and so become a sign of hope for many others throughout the world.'

Disclaiming any definite ideas about the formation or growth of the community, he would subsequently say that he knew only that he must go ahead. 'There's something naturally speaking, or supernaturally perhaps, that means I am able to form community, so it just happened.'

The combination of the needs and the increasingly recognised gifts of people with disabilities and the untapped and unfocused energies of the generous-spirited young people he was encountering came about with extraordinary dynamism. The early letters reflect breathtaking activity: the production of 10,000 paper bags a week in the workshops; the organisation of leisure activities that included a more creative element than watching television – photographic clubs, country dancing, cycling, fishing, stamp collecting, painting, singing; celebrations; excursions that included a flight for the disabled men in Canadian Air Force Dakotas from Montmedy; renovations such as the installation of central heating in properties already owned, and the acquisition of new ones. Fortunately, the growing number of requests from parents, the social services and psychiatric institutions, especially the nearby Clermont psychiatric hospital, coincided with considerable financial encouragement on the part of the mental health authorities. It became possible to meet arising needs in a way which might not otherwise have been feasible. Some of the men at the Val Fleuri very obviously needed to leave the noise and bustle of so large a building for a smaller and more intimate environment. In 1966 Steve and Ann Newroth, who later founded the Daybreak community near Toronto, welcomed three men from the Val Fleuri to another house in the village which became known as Les Rameaux ('Palm Sunday').

L'Arche began to buy up as many available houses as possible in Trosly-Breuil and its environs and to give them the names by which the community would know them. By November 1965 they had acquired the use of Les Hirondelles ('Swallows'). In 1968 they opened L'Ermitage ('Hermitage'), and in 1969 Valhinos, which had once been the old presbytery in the adjacent village of Cuise-la-Motte. The 'little valley', as the name means in Portuguese, provided a home for ten disabled women.

Women had been part of the community at l'Arche from the earliest days. They had been numbered quite spontaneously among the assistants who arrived, often for a week, and found themselves staying for very much longer. The possibility of welcoming disabled women had occasioned some concern about mixing the sexes. Nevertheless, in the conviction that their arrival was something that was meant to be, Jean Vanier did what he called his 'naval officer stuff' and disregarded such anxieties; 'I just knew that it had to come and that if I listened to the community here it wouldn't, so I bought a house. And as I was president of the Board of Directors I just created a new community there.' Afterwards he was obliged to pick up the pieces, but by then the important step had been taken.

Towards the end of the 1960s l'Arche began to take in day workers, people with disabilities who lived with their families and came to the community to work during the day. Often they were less disabled and often they were more problematic, requiring a lot of 'accompaniment' because in a sense they were living between two worlds. Between 1970 and 1977 a further twelve houses were opened in Trosly, its neighbouring villages of Breuil and Pierrefonds and the nearby town of Compiègne. These included La Grande Source, previously Trosly-Breuil's café-hotel. Hitherto guests had been given accommodation in the various *foyers* but when the visitors themselves were people in need, such an arrangement sometimes proved unsatisfactory. La Grande Source became first a *foyer* and then a place where visitors could stay. So the remarkable growth went on: in 1968 l'Arche had welcomed 73 disabled people; by 1970, 112; by 1972, 126. By 1995 because of the number of houses and people in the Trosly-Breuil region the need would be felt to give greater independence not only to Compiègne but also to Pierrefonds and Cuise-la-Motte as separate communities.

🌺

From Rideau Hall in Ottawa and the heavy draped splendour of the Hotel Royal Monceau in Paris where 'Ganna' had been living since just after the Second World War, Jean Vanier's parents and grandmother followed the early stages of this explosive development with concern but satisfaction. The spirit of l'Arche could not be entirely divorced from the spirit in which the Vanier parents had sought to live. It also reflected much of the spirit of Thérèse de Salaberry Archer, formed as she was in the way of the heart by Almire Pichon. This was not Jean Vanier's only family legacy however. Hand in hand with the spirit of the Beatitudes went a certain social confidence that came with belonging to a prominent family. The son of the Governor General of Canada made a point of introducing himself to the local *Préfet*[1] of Oise who was so moved by what he was told about l'Arche that he awarded him the medal of Oise at a public ceremony. 'That's the strength of coming from a family of diplomats. You know what to do.' Jean Vanier had conversed with royalty and church dignitaries and the generally influential at a relatively young age. His letters to his parents during the early years of l'Arche contain the occasional remark such as 'Do you know Princess Grace of Monaco?' On the whole however, he insisted, there had been no need to pull too many strings: 'Strangely enough there was very quick recognition.'

Since her husband's appointment as Governor General, Pauline Archer had been made Chancellor of the University of Ottawa and Canadian Woman of the Year for 1965. When General Vanier wrote to inform her mother at the Hotel Royal Monceau, it was with characteristically self-deprecating humour:

> What's happening to me in all this? For many she is no longer the wife of the Governor General, but I have become the husband of the Chancellor and the Woman of the Year. Sometimes also, since there has been so much publicity about Jock's work, I have another title, that of the father of Jean Vanier of l'Arche of Trosly. Don't you think it's time for me to depart before I become the son-in-law of Madame Thérèse de S. Archer, the queen who sits upon a throne at the *Royal* Monceau!

General Georges Vanier in fact died quietly and at peace on 5 March 1967 in Ottawa, scarcely an hour after he had received Communion. By what he saw as the grace of God, Jean Vanier was with him at the time. Although he had not been in the habit of returning home very frequently, he had been able to spend some time with his parents at Rideau Hall. 'I remember I'd go into his room every morning before breakfast or just after breakfast because he would stay in bed until about 9 a.m. when he was

Governor General, and he would certainly share quite a lot.' Both his parents, he recognised, had been 'instruments of his vocation'.

There were memories of his father that he valued greatly, such as the occasion when he had said to his son, 'You know I love you', 'in a way that few fathers would', or the times when he had come to visit Jean on holiday and they had knelt and prayed together for an hour. The full extent of his father's spiritual life had nevertheless remained unknown to him.

The day after the General's death, his son was going through his papers and found a number of brief notes which were very simple but clear intimations of a special intimacy with Jesus. An estimated 30,000 people filed past the coffin as it lay in state in the Senate Chamber. In the light of this display of affection, virtually unprecedented in Canada, it seemed right to Jean Vanier that the many who so manifestly loved his father should be given a glimpse of the source that had helped him to be what he was. *In Weakness, Strength*, one of Jean Vanier's first books, was an insight into the spiritual pilgrimage which had been so essential a part of General Vanier's life as a lawyer, soldier, diplomat, ambassador and, for seven years, Canada's Governor General. It was written with no pretensions to biography or completeness, and was the kind of book that Jean Vanier himself might find acceptable in similar circumstances: written in order only that those who knew and loved him might see just a little more of the light and loves that had guided such a man. It pinpointed the motivating sources of the General's life as confidence in God, an everpresent sense of the Holy Spirit and a contemplative prayer life. There was, Jean Vanier was quick to point out, very little in the book apart from quotations from letters Georges Vanier had written to some Carmelite Sisters and his notes. His family had no wish to betray the discretion the General himself had exercised but rather to show very simply that 'there was this exterior dad and then there was his interior'. The book was so simple in fact that at least one Catholic publisher rejected it and it was eventually published with great appreciation by Griffin House, a non-Catholic publisher.

In the mid-1980s a preliminary investigation was begun to guage the opinion of people who had known Georges Vanier about the possibility of introducing a cause for his beatification at some future date. This was encouraged by Marcel Gervais, the Archbishop of Ottawa, in part because of Pope John Paul II's desire to recognise married life but also because there was a general appreciation that the Vaniers, and particularly Georges, were remarkable in having combined a very deep spiritual life and the exercise of that spirituality with diplomatic representation and all that that entailed. The preparation of the necessary documents was subsequently placed in the hands of a theologian, Monsignor Quesnel, who pursued it with recourse to the national archives in Ottawa and the help of Jacques Monet, a Jesuit and historian, and Thérèse Vanier. This recognition of married life and the manner in which the General and his wife, regardless of their other, public commitments in Government House or elsewhere, had always taken the opportunity to attend Mass and spend half an hour in prayer, was something which both Jean and Thérèse could commend.

General Vanier had helped l'Arche financially from its earliest days but he had never visited Trosly-Breuil. His son remained uncertain whether he had understood what people in l'Arche were endeavouring to live. In other respects their interests had been somewhat different. After the General's death Jean found the published copy of his thesis on Aristotelian ethics, from which his father had claimed to read a page each day, with most of the pages still uncut – 'It wasn't really his kind of thing.' Of one thing he was sure, however: that his father had loved Père Thomas, sensing that there was a mystery of pain in the priest who meant so much to his son, that he had trusted him, and that that trust had been invaluable.

In the absence of his father, Jean Vanier assumed greater responsibility for his elderly grandmother. He had always been fond of and in a way close to her, although he was the first to question what closeness really meant in the Vanier family. He had visited her regularly in her suite of rooms at the Hotel Royal Monceau while he was in Paris and reported back to his parents. Even while l'Arche was expanding rapidly and consuming much of his time and energy, he looked after her finances and found her a nurse to provide her with the increased care she needed. For many years she had gone to Mass daily but otherwise rarely left her rooms, though managed nonetheless to maintain numerous friendships and keep up a correspondence that suggested a lively intellect and frequently provided spiritual counsel. The hotel staff looked after her with kindness but when finally she succumbed to senility and was found, one day in 1968, wandering in her dressing gown, not knowing where she was, they could no longer accept responsibility for her. The house across the street from the original l'Arche came up for sale. It was a white, low-lying building at the end of a gravel walkway, half concealed by the chestnut trees that would give it its name, Les Marroniers. In the recollection of Pauline Vanier:

> Grandma had simply told Jean that she wanted to come and live near him and Père Thomas. Oh my – she was 88 then and her mind was failing. They had a terrible time finding this house, and when they did it was in a dreadful condition. They started restoring it, and in the meantime grandma was living in a hotel in Paris. The bathroom there was pink and black, so the bathroom here had to be pink and black. Knowing she wouldn't be used to the kind of furniture people had here, particularly in 1968, they acquired two velvet-covered chairs for her, but she died without ever seeing the house.

On 28 February 1969, four days before her ninety-fifth birthday, Thérèse de Salaberry Archer died in her familiar hotel room. Not long afterwards Pauline Vanier visited Trosly-Breuil. She had previously visited the Foyer de l'Arche while her husband was still Governor General and found her son living 'in a terrible state'. In the course of her second visit she informed him that he was to have Les Marroniers for l'Arche. During that same visit, however, an assistant suggested to her, with what at the time she considered extreme impertinence, that she should come and live in the accommodation prepared for her mother. The suggestion infuriated her but the seed was sown. In October 1971, uncertain what she should do with what remained of her life, she spent a week's retreat at a Carmelite convent in Montreal where she had special permission to enter the enclosure. On the very last day the gospel was the story of the rich young man required to sell everything he had in order to follow Jesus.

'I didn't want to come here. I was afraid', Madame Vanier later acknowledged. Nevertheless she left her splendid house in

Montreal in the charge of one man-servant and gave herself a six-month trial period in the house set in the garden studded with chestnut trees at Trosly-Breuil. At the end of those six months she sold everything and moved permanently into Les Marroniers complete with its pink and black bathroom and its two velvet chairs. It was not an altogether easy transition for her. The depression of her earlier years returned as her body deteriorated. Despite her protestations that she was just a 'fat bourgeois amongst the poor' and despite the fact that even in the context of l'Arche she remained very much the 'grande dame', she nevertheless discovered a much valued role as a grandmotherly adviser to young assistants who arrived full of idealism and then found the challenge more taxing than anticipated. Her son, whose relationship with her was shaped as much by duty as affection, did not fail to recognise the significance of her presence. 'The gift of youth to community is the gift of wonderment', he wrote in *Community and Growth*, 'that of the elderly is the peaceful wisdom of age ... Grandmothers sense certain things. And there are things which can be confided only to them. They are important to a community.'

The community expanded in a fashion which Jean Vanier would subsequently consider wildly haphazard, borne along in no small measure by his enthusiasm. Writing in 2003 of the journey of life,[2] he referred to the progression from the lack of self-esteem to self-acceptance in a way that begged the question of whether he had ever lacked self-esteem.

> Probably not because when you're enthusiastic, it carries you. But there is a very thin and fragile line between the conscious and the unconscious. Above the line is the capacity to do, to want to do, peace, and apparent courage. Then under the line there are a lot of elements, in my case, related to fear.

Once in the road in Trosly he was accosted by a large, muscular man from the village. He was hurling abuse at l'Arche, at people with disabilities and at Jean, all of whom he seemed to hate. The man hit Jean on the ear but not quite hard enough to knock him to the ground. Jean found himself standing firm and heard himself saying, 'You can hit me again if you want.' Flabbergasted, the man took him by the hand and invited him into his house. Jean

Vanier had been able not to show his fear but his heart had been beating furiously and underneath it all he had been terrified. 'I can be very quickly frightened or feel anguish or guilt.' Of what precisely he was frightened or guilty he could not say. He knew only that above the line there was a consciousness of being looked after but below it were all the signs of being afraid.

In the early days of l'Arche he simply acted with all the apparent courage and enthusiasm of his convictions, as the need and opportunity arose. A house would fall vacant and he would buy it and fill it, without really ascertaining in advance whether it would suit the particular needs of the people who were to live in it. There were times when the arrival of assistants did not keep pace with the number of people with disabilities, and there were days when one single assistant had charge of 20 disabled men in the workshops. Nevertheless, as early as 1965 Jean Vanier wrote:

> The first months of l'Arche have been lived in poverty and simplicity. Now that the first foundations have been laid, we must give it structure, organise, grow. We must make a solid work that will last.

He also wrote of how he realised that while l'Arche had been profoundly inspired by the gospels, and while it was to be a community lived in the spirit of the Beatitudes, there was also a need to make full use of medical and psychiatric techniques in close co-operation with the relevant health authorities. Père Thomas, despite the insights he had received from Dr Thompson and Dr Préaut, was less inclined to acknowledge the requirement for professional care and more reluctant to accept the controls that inevitably went with government funding, seeing them as a potential threat to the spirit of gospel poverty. Jean Vanier, however, recognised the importance of professional competence and encouraged it within the community, accepting with relative ease government stipulations with regard to structure and care, boards of directors and living conditions.

The story is told of how one government inspector had satisfactorily completed his tour of inspection of the very primitive 'Foyer de l'Arche', much to the relief of Jean and his fellow residents who had been specifically briefed not to draw attention to the outside lavatory, leaving as it did quite a lot to be desired. The inspector was about to leave when Jean-Pierre, with habitual amiable helpfulness intervened, 'You're welcome to see our toilet.' Another story tells of how a representative from the Department of Health was invited to lunch at a time when l'Arche was seeking the Department's financial support. After the meal this very important person found himself enlisted to help with the washing up. Washing up in l'Arche would long remain a time of particular fellowship, of relaxed and simple conversation and jostling horseplay in which everybody was invited to take part. In those days the tea towels were not always very clean or dry. People used to like the hot soapy water and race to do the washing, and it was not unheard of for Jean Vanier to leap over a table to get to the washing-up bowl first. The official from the Department of Health afterwards admitted to being deeply touched at being asked to help with this simple domestic task. He had felt welcomed as a man and not merely in his official capacity, and over the kitchen sink an enduring friendship with Jean Vanier and l'Arche was born.

Nearly 40 years on, some of the early assistants at Trosly-Breuil who had remained in l'Arche would look back with a certain nostalgia to the days when numbers were relatively small, when contact with Jean Vanier was much closer and when, although the need for greater order was recognised, their lack of competence in many fields allowed the poor to reveal themselves in a special way.

From the very first Jean Vanier had seen the importance of journeys and celebrations in lives that might otherwise be monotonous and devoid of hope, to keep up spirits and open hearts and minds to other realities. For centuries Jews, Muslims, Hindus and Christians alike had valued a sense of pilgrimage. The experience of journeying together to a holy place, a place of prayer, was important for everyone but possibly even more so for the poor person and for the person with disabilities. Leaving some of the familiar routines, meeting new people, facing fresh challenges and needing one another along the way healed divisions, cemented old bonds and created new ones. It became a potent symbol of what people in l'Arche were trying to live. The community would set off in processions of private cars to Rome, Lourdes, Fátima or some other distant destination. Often the cars

would break down en route. There would be other minor setbacks, but ones which were often turned upside down and made
wondrously acceptable and even happy by people like Dédé who
would look at a shattered windscreen and see not the brokenness,
the inconvenience and the work involved in its replacement but
only the beauty, the way it shone like crystal in the sunlight.
There would be moments of relaxation, joy, renewed hope, and
for some the beginnings of a new and more peaceful life, a life
more open to the world, society and other people.

Michel took part in one of these early pilgrimages to Rome as
part of a short stay to see whether he would remain in l'Arche.
At the hospital where he had been living he had been told simply
that he was to stay for a trial period and not to expect anything
very different from his hospital life. Suddenly he found himself in
a car in St Peter's Square and chattered with great excitement
about his wishes, fears and feelings. The l'Arche assistants had no
official file for him so only later discovered that in hospital
Michel had not uttered a word for many years. Their lack of
knowledge had made it possible for him to react to them quite
differently from the way he had responded to professionals. As
one of the early assistants recalled:

> There was a lot of madness. We were incompetent in many
> ways. We were young and threw ourselves into this new idea of
> 'living together' without any regard for how late we went to
> bed, conserving our energies or having a private life of any
> kind, but in a way that madness, that incompetence was justi-
> fied by the fact that we were possibly the first to say to people
> with disabilities, 'You are loved just as you are.'

Though not given an unqualified welcome by all members of
the community and not always up to the professional standards of
others, greater competence would come. Dr Leone Richet was
the first to help the community grasp the particular therapy of
l'Arche. For several years she came to Trosly-Breuil for a few
hours a week. When she left the area she found another psychiatrist, Dr Erol Franko, who helped and supported the community
and also played a vital role in Jean Vanier's own intellectual
development and the therapeutic aspect of l'Arche. In 1982
Patrick Mathias took up the relay. None of the psychiatrists and

psychologists at Trosly-Breuil, and few working with communities elsewhere, were people who would call themselves Christian. Asked what it was that had attracted them to l'Arche in the first place, they cited such practical considerations as salary or convenience of location. All, however, were men and women with a profound respect for people.

L'Arche had come into being at a time when professionals in the field of mental disability had generally received a scientific education based on the philosophical thinking of the nineteenth century: evolution, natural selection, relativism, determinism, positivism and Marxist or Freudian interpretations of idealism which subsequently worked themselves into popular thinking. From such a vantage point it could be considered logical to see a person with disabilities as an unfortunate happening, a disastrous mistake of nature. Fortunately the hearts of many had not fully accepted what their heads had been fostering. L'Arche was greatly encouraged to encounter many clear-minded professionals who regarded their clients as people like themselves, who recognised the pain caused by the fact that they were made to feel extraneous to human society in a multitude of ways, and who worked with generosity, compassion and integrity for more human conditions for disabled people. Some professionals, for their part, found in l'Arche a new vision of how their skills could be exercised. With the realisation that the psychiatrist alone had neither the time nor the capacity to bring about healing came the recognition that an environment such as l'Arche could provide 'family therapy'. As the tendency in some Western countries to dehumanise 'patients' into a series of symptoms that could be stored in a computer increased, so an environment that was sensitive to the needs and engaged the active participation of people with disabilities gained in importance. At the same time, professional carers presented l'Arche with a challenge to be more competent and confronted it with insights drawn from a different perspective and different reference points.

With the help of Dr Franko, who 'worked magic' at a time when the men in the Val Fleuri really needed a magician, Jean Vanier began to integrate both professional and spiritual insights into life in l'Arche. He sat in on the meetings when the psychiatrists and assistants from the *foyers* and workshops came together to talk about a particular person and their problems and received what he called a 'great formation in the link between the chemical and the psychological and how to approach people and listen to them'. He came to see unusual or abnormal behaviour – such as violence, or delirium, or the refusal to eat or speak – not primarily as a symptom of mental illness to be categorised and medically cured but as a language to be listened to. Such behaviour showed that the person concerned was living in a world other than the 'normative'. People who were well integrated into society, who lived according to established norms, were often afraid of those who acted strangely. In their fear they tried by every conceivable means, even violence, to change 'abnormal' people and make them act in an acceptable way. At the same time those who felt excluded and labelled 'mentally ill' tended to build their own isolated world. Their behaviour became more and more odd, and people about them became increasingly frightened. It was a vicious circle which often ended in a complete break and hospitalisation. Yet strange behaviour was first and foremost a way of saying: 'I'm suffering, come and help me. I feel alone and unable to find my way in the chaos.' Sadly the response was frequently defensive rejection, and the person whose cry for help was the loudest was often the one most categorically rejected. The person who most needed to be understood and supported was often the one who found him or herself most misunderstood and alone.

L'Arche in general was learning to listen, to listen to the wisdom to be gleaned from outside the community even when the demands made exposed its own mediocrity, to listen also to what people with disabilities were saying and so discover there a value and a light. Some years later on a pilgrimage to Assisi and Rome a group of l'Arche people had an audience with Pope John Paul II. As Père Thomas often pointed out, for mentally disabled people who do not relate well to structures but rather to persons, the Roman Catholic Church has the advantage of having at its head an actual father, one person whom they can love, the Pope. On this occasion the Pope went along a line, greeting people who were waiting to meet him. Men bowed their heads, women curtseyed in respectful silence until eventually he came within sight of Alice, a woman with disabilities, who called out as soon as she saw him, 'John Paul, John Paul, we love you.' He sought her out and took her in his arms. 'She had said', reflected one of the assistants, 'what everybody wanted to say but did not feel they had the right to.'

The presence of people with disabilities meant that anything could happen anywhere: a server at Mass could pour water for the celebrant, then wander off and water a flower; a disabled person arriving at Tel Aviv airport at a time of great tension could walk up to an armed guard, push the man's gun to one side and hold out his hand to be shaken. 'The basic gift of a person with mental disabilities', it was acknowledged,

> is that of having kept the heart of a child. Much of the person with disabilities' personality is still that of the child we can no longer be. Even at the age of 40 or 50 a disabled person can be quite without restraint, react as a child would and so cast a different perspective on theology, philosophy and our world.

At one High Mass to mark the conclusion of a pilgrimage a cardinal sat high on a throne looking down on the congregation, surrounded by an entourage of bishops. During Communion the cardinal rose to administer the Sacrament and as he did so one of the disabled men slipped up into the chancel, sat himself in the cardinal's seat and gazed about him, as if he really wanted to know what sitting on that exalted seat did to the person occupying it. There was much agitation amongst the bishops. Some evidently thought they should do something; others apparently felt they should ignore the situation completely. In the end nobody did anything. When the cardinal had finished distributing the host he took a stool, placed it next to the throne, sat down and chatted to the person with disabilities. It was, in the recollection of the accompanying assistants, quite a sight:

> The cardinal sitting on the stool and the disabled person look-ing down at him from the throne, the cardinal's humility was very beautiful, and the disabled person had given him the opportunity to show that for all his importance, he too still had the heart of a child.

Visitors who came to Trosly-Breuil did not fail to be marked, as Jean Vanier and Père Thomas had been, by people who were so poor and so rejected yet were the carriers of so much life and love. Their thirst for friendship and communion, devoid as it was of the masks to which people with power and intellect are given, invariably provoked a strong reaction. There were those who hardened themselves and rejected; more often people opened themselves to simple relationship built upon trust and those small acts of kindness which precluded the need for too many words. There were difficult moments in the life of various houses, times of crisis and violence, but for the most part people were happy together. L'Arche was experiencing the paradox that the people whom the world considered useless and only fit to be put away in institutions – those who were regarded as a heavy burden and a financial problem – were actually sources of light and life. It was also recognising in that paradox, the paradox of the Beatitudes, of Jesus, of the message of the Good News that gave cause for celebration. There was a good deal of laughter in the community over simple things. Mealtimes were occasions for jollity and celebration; people's birthdays were celebrated; their arrivals and their presence were celebrated. There was a growing appreciation of celebration as something different from a party at which friends met and drank and laughed, but where often the laughter was hollow and the drinks were necessary to warm hearts and spirits.

'To celebrate',[3] wrote Jean Vanier whose own heart had undoubtedly been touched and opened,

> is to give thanks for the gift God has given us in having brought us together from a place of loneliness into a sense of belonging. I know that you have accepted me and I you. I know your gifts, and I also know your darkness. Yet I accept you as you are, not expecting more and not weeping because you are not exactly what I wanted you to be. So to celebrate is to give thanks for all you are and all we are together.

On this divided earth celebration was never perfect. There was always a note of suffering: perhaps some members of the community were not there, some had withdrawn or were in pain, some might have broken away. Whilst celebrating the unity that had been given it was still important to be open to the suffering of the world. Indeed, celebration did not happen if the weak and the

frail, if children or old people were not present. In the same way
that the quality of the prayer after the evening meal was remarkable precisely because of the special potency of hearts turned in
extreme simplicity and sincerity towards God, so at the heart of
every celebration were the eyes and laughter of those who were
most fragile and most vulnerable.

This witness of people with mental disabilities in daily life was
one which readily engaged the interest and commitment of
young people in the late 1960s. In the Church this was the time
of renewal that followed the Second Vatican Council. In the
world at large a climate of economic prosperity and security
prevailed in which Third World countries were gaining their
independence. There was a great desire for liberation which gave
rise to problems with authority in the Church and institutions in
general. Associated with it, however, was the impulse to create
and commit oneself to something fresh and new. There was a
feeling that most religious orders had lost sight of the original
intention of their founders. There was also a desire to get away
from the need to compromise with society, wealth and power.

Young people coming to l'Arche were highly educated and
formed in their ideals and attitudes, and needed in some way to
emerge from that and find their own space and creativity. The
idea of living with the person with disabilities as one of the poor
presented them with a fresh and purer basis for a harmonious life
together. Assistants of that generation spoke readily of the
poignant difference between the community life in l'Arche and
the life they experienced in the 'outside world'. They committed
themselves in a way which produced great dynamism but which
was not devoid of problems. It compounded the tension which
always existed to a greater or lesser extent in l'Arche between the
need for professionalism and the desire to remain open to divine
providence and the Holy Spirit, between what some would
consider necessary detachment and commitment to the point
sometimes of self-destruction. It also aggravated the problems
which by the late 1960s were beginning to arise with the local
people of Trosly-Breuil.

At the very beginning the villagers, though possibly taken
aback by the people with mental disabilities who suddenly
appeared on their streets, accepted their presence with good

grace. The arrival of assistants from all over the world, however, many of whom were not very well dressed and who behaved in a way which seemed strange to elderly neighbourhood residents, inevitably gave rise to apprehension. The local people saw Canadians and English people squatting on the pavement chatting with their bikes on the ground beside them and they wondered how Monsieur Vanier could possibly have assistants like that to look after people with disabilities. Monsieur Vanier, for his part, afterwards acknowledged with regret that in his enthusiasm to help disabled people he had been undiplomatic and insensitive to the villagers. The tension mounted as he, a foreigner, bought up more and more of the local houses. Most of the people in the neighbourhood had lived there for several generations. Their land and houses represented their history and cultural patrimony. There came a point when these seemed under threat from one who appeared to have unlimited financial resources, who, though he spoke French, did not speak their language, and who did not go about things in their way.

When Jean Vanier wished to act he did so through the local *Préfet*. In some ways socially sophisticated though he was, he was not aware that in a French village there were a mayor and councillors and that the councillors were there in the very next street. Neither he nor Jacqueline d'Halluin nor Père Thomas had really lived village life before. They noticed a little too late that they had failed to communicate what they were trying to live to the people on their doorstep. Finally, in 1972, l'Arche recognised the need to stop and reassure. The community undertook to set a limit to the number of people with disabilities it would bring into the village. There would be no more than 66 living in Trosly-Breuil. The figure was agreed with the local mayor and was afterwards respected. It was also agreed that no more houses would be bought there without the consent of the council.

The arrangement proved in fact to be in the interests of l'Arche also, for although the growth in Trosly-Breuil had produced a 'motherhouse' equipped to welcome and introduce a large number of assistants to life in l'Arche, who would in their turn go out to found or become part of communities elsewhere in France or the world, it had also presented the very real, if not immediately recognised, danger of creating merely another kind of institution or ghetto in which people with disabilities were set apart and ostracised. The smallness and the attitude of the village had obliged Jean Vanier and l'Arche to discover that one of their aims was 'insertion'. If one of the prime objectives was to help the person with disabilities to lead as full a life as possible, it was important that his or her life was integrated with that of the neighbours and the village. L'Arche, however, had failed to make the villagers understand this, and it took a while for the wound to heal.

This was not the only incidence of opposition from neighbours experienced by l'Arche. There were other instances of the 'Not in my backyard' syndrome, perhaps the most significant of which occurred in 1984 when plans were being made for a new community in Kansas in the USA. A neighbourhood was chosen and the project explained to many local people, but when it was formally presented to the municipal council it was rejected. Neighbours protested that they did not want to live next door to people with mental disabilities. Three times the founding director went through the same experience, and only in 1988 was the opposition surmounted.

Yet the growth was apparently unstoppable and Jean Vanier's 'extraordinary sense of the Word' was another contributory factor. In 1968 he was invited by a group of Catholic priests in Toronto to lead a retreat for the Toronto diocese in Marylake. As a layman, he was somewhat taken aback by the invitation and his first reaction was to decline. After an interval of prayer and reflection, however, it seemed very clear that if he was to take the retreat it should not be just for priests but for all the people of God. He suggested that the participants should be made up of one-third priests, one-third religious and one-third lay people. The retreat would last for eight days and a considerable part of it would be spent in silence. Jean Vanier had never given a retreat before, so it was with a feeling of confusion that he entered the room marked 'Retreat Master'. Nevertheless, 'incredible grace was given, something so strong'. With hindsight he attributed his ability to give things very simply in a way that touched people partly to the fact that he had never really been in the world of church conflict. At the time, he made a discovery related to his experience as a teacher of 'something inside myself which flowed out with conviction and force and obviously touched people'. He was aware of the mystery of the Word that can penetrate people's hearts rather than their heads and change them:

> It's funny how often I find people say, 'You never say anything that I don't know.' It's as if the Word penetrates right into the very depths and puts a word on what people already know, gives the revelation. You don't actually teach anybody anything. All you do is give them the consciousness that they know it.

Looking back on that retreat and the many that followed, he valued them as experiences of vital importance, both for l'Arche and for him, in that they enabled him to discover the power of the Word of God, the Word which is 'the good news announced to the poor and the promise of the presence, the forgiveness and the sustenance of Jesus, which awakens in us new energies of love, which purifies and liberates, which reveals to each his true identity as a child loved by the Father.' Announcing this Word, he often felt as if he was the first to hear it. Years later he referred to speaking from the solar plexus as opposed to the head, which meant that he could speak fluently and at length without feeling any fatigue. And it did him good, not least because it gave him the sense of 'being chosen to be an instrument'.

As a priest formed in the pre-Second Vatican Council Roman Catholic Church, Père Thomas did not approve of a layman taking retreats. Paradoxically, Jean Vanier felt that what was deepest within him, what was therefore at the source of his retreats and calling forth a response in others, came from Père Thomas. If what he said was very simple and in a sense not in any way new, but contained more than the intelligibility of what he actually said, it was in some profound way due to Père Thomas. Yet Père Thomas could not accept his assuming such a role. Again paradoxically, this non-acceptance by Père Thomas strengthened the younger man in his own sense of mission because the signs were there that he was nonetheless performing the will of God. People embraced Jean Vanier's experience as he expressed it and sensed it touched their own deepest needs. They were profoundly moved by the way in which he was endorsing the gospel message relating to the poor, the sick and disabled people with whom

Jesus had specifically identified himself, with his actual experience of life with disadvantaged people. To them the word born of silence and of personal experience seemed to have a special force. Some were particularly touched by what he had to say about the poor, some by his vision of community, but somewhere beyond it all was a glimpse of the lived actuality of the Word become flesh.

As a layman conducting that first Marylake retreat for some 60 people of whom approximately a third were priests, Jean Vanier felt the need for the presence of a priest and a friend. He therefore invited Father O'Connor, a priest whom he had known at Eau Vive and who continued to visit him at l'Arche Trosly-Breuil, to join him. Father O'Connor was very involved in the charismatic movement begun in the United States in the early 1960s. At the retreat he spoke a number of times about charismatic renewal in the States and every night he had a prayer meeting. Jean Vanier recalled him saying at the end of the gathering that he did not understand why, when at his other prayer meetings gifts had been given, they had not apparently been granted there. Had the gifts of tongues and prophecy to which the priest was referring taken over, which Jean acknowledged they could have done because he was 'open to anything' at the time, many things would have been different in l'Arche. As it was, what seemed to be most healing for people was the adoration of the Blessed Sacrament. Jean Vanier felt close to the charismatic movement in the Roman Catholic Church, both in the United States and France. There was something 'incredibly beautiful about it', but somehow he was always more drawn to the silent worship of Charles de Foucauld and the Little Sisters of Jesus from whom, in Montreal, he had learned the importance of periods of quiet adoration.

Gifts were given at the retreat in Marylake, though possibly not in the form that some had anticipated. There were many who perceived in the talks, the periods of silent adoration, the Eucharist and the times spent in groups of eight sharing, as distinct from discussing, their faith, the presence of the Holy Spirit. From the desire to continue what had begun there sprang the decision to arrange two further retreats for the following year: one which Jean Vanier would again give in Marylake and another for those who had already taken part in the first retreat, organised by one of those participants. So it was that the 'Faith and Sharing' movement was born to organise retreats based on the model of that first one. Jean Vanier would go wherever he was invited next. A group would be appointed to organise the retreat for the following year. Having given a retreat in Ottawa in French, he was afterwards asked to give one in French in Montreal. If there were people from Quebec at the Ottawa retreat, he decided, he would give a retreat a few months later in Quebec, and so it went on. In this way small groups of people wishing to meet, pray and share emerged quite spontaneously, as did priests, religious and lay people who were willing to give retreats. The sharing aspect was essential.

The initial insight of conducting a retreat for all the people of God was remarkably endorsed. Lay people, clergy and religious, married and single, young and old, all came. From the first also there was an attempt to bring together different social groups, particularly people who were in some way disadvantaged, be it through material poverty, disablement of mind or body or through some other condition which placed them on the margins of society. The occupants of old people's homes were invited together with mentally and physically disabled people and those living alone. In the groups which eventually met all over Canada, the United States and Britain there were one or two active organisers, but often they were predominantly 'little people'. As in the parable of the wedding feast, Jean Vanier pointed out, there were many in the world who had no time to come to such gatherings, but there was also a whole class of people – the elderly, disabled people and the lonely – who had too much time and were glad to come. Their presence proved invaluable.

Often new l'Arche communities sprang up in the wake of these retreats. The communities in Edmonton, Calgary, Mobile, Cleveland, Victoria, Winnipeg, St Malachie and Erie all had their roots in the retreat movement. Among the many who were deeply and lastingly touched by Jean Vanier's talks was a Canadian religious studying at the University of Toronto. Sue Mosteller had first heard him speak at the university and been moved by what he had said about the circle of poverty:

I remember him saying that the person who is poor or suffering does not take care of himself, looks as if he is suffering and is therefore not attractive. Consequently we are not attracted to him and he feels rejected. He is stuck in this circle that ostracises him, while we who are stronger, who have education, friends and wealth, and who can get out of our own pain are in another circle with people who like us. We stay in that circle and don't step out, so we don't have any ugliness. If we don't like people we walk away and so we keep our circle going while the circle of the poor spirals down.

On the strength of this insight and of Jean Vanier's emphasis on the message of Corinthians that the poor would confound the wisdom of the prudent, Sue Mosteller went to the retreat in 1968:

I was at a point in my religious life where I was searching because I wasn't finding. Jean called us to prayer. He called us to silence, and it was the first time in the whole of my religious life that I felt that the silence was not empty, that it was full of the presence of God, that God was acting in my emptiness. There was a need in me, and that word came and filled the vacuum for me. I wanted to be more faithful, more radical.

Three years later she found herself at Daybreak, the first l'Arche community to open in Canada.

Also at the Marylake retreat in 1968 was a Superior General of Our Lady's Missionaries, Sister Rosemarie Donovan. At the end of the eight-day gathering she felt moved to offer l'Arche a house and some seven acres of land in Richmond Hill, once the site of the order's novitiate on the outskirts of Toronto. The offer coincided in an extraordinary way with the return of Steve and Ann Newroth to Canada. The Newroths were Anglicans; Steve had in fact completed studies for the Anglican ministry. Since opening Les Rameaux in Trosly-Breuil, they had spent a year at the Ecumenical Institute of Bossey near Geneva. The couple's creativity combined with Jean Vanier's Toronto retreat and the offer of the property suggested that the Daybreak community in Richmond Hill was given in a very particular sense. A board of directors was promptly formed. In addition to the seven acres

given by the Our Lady's Missionaries the new l'Arche was able
to take up an option the Sisters had held on another 13 acres
owned by the Basilian Fathers. They also leased a further 150
acres directly from the Fathers for the princely sum of one dollar
a year. Against the background of a move in North America
towards the introduction of group homes instead of large institutions for people with mental disabilities, Steve and Ann Newroth
brought with them to Canada their experience of Trosly-Breuil
and the vision of building ten homes which would not be exactly
a village but in some ways self-contained, like the community at
Trosly – the limitations of that self-containment had not yet been
discovered. Also integral to their initial vision was a farm. Steve
Newroth was the son of a farmer and was attracted to farm work
as good, physical, meaningful work which could be therapeutic.

Daybreak opened its doors in October 1969. To the 'Big
House', originally the home of Our Lady's Missionaries, the
'New House' was swiftly added. From there most of the 'folks', as
the people with disabilities became known in l'Arche in North
America, went out to a local sheltered workshop, but some
remained to look after the cattle, sheep, horses and, at one stage,
a milking cow. In the early days it was also very much the pattern
that all the male assistants went out to work on the farm while
the women remained in the house to do the cooking. Inevitably
that initial vision would be subject to change. As it transpired, the
'Green House', built in 1974, was the last constructed on the
original land to provide living accommodation for the people
with disabilities. The philosophical trend in North America
towards 'normalisation' highlighted the value of living, not on a
farm which in those days was somewhat isolated from the city
centre, but in an 'ordinary' street from which people could walk
to the local store or doctor or bakery.

Steve Newroth, and through him Jean Vanier, had come to
know Wolf Wolfensberger, one of the exponents of 'normalisation' in the United States fighting most effectively for the rights
of people with disabilities. Jean Vanier and l'Arche identified a
beauty and a truth in his theory. People with disabilities, it
maintained, had the same rights as any one else, and should be
welcomed into society on an equal footing, They should be able
to go to the municipal swimming baths, cinema or church like

anyone else. They should even be able to go to school like other children. The worst thing for a disabled person was exclusion which brought about a wounded self-image and ultimately feelings of guilt. Everything should be done to help people with disabilities to have confidence in themselves, to rediscover their human dignity and develop their intellectual and manual capacity.

The dynamic in North America in this direction raised a number of salutary questions in l'Arche. Were the communities sometimes overprotective? Did they show enough belief in the ability of the people they welcomed to grow towards independence and the rediscovery of their dignity? Was there not perhaps a danger inherent in the gospel vision of the prophetic poor of being too quick to spiritualise the disabled person's need to grow, of being too ready to see his or her poverty as something 'divine' and therefore not helping him sufficiently towards greater liberty in human terms? Love should never inhibit the competence necessary to help someone to develop to his or her full potential.

In 1974 Daybreak opened its first house off the main property, in downtown Toronto, and the experience showed that many of the 'folks' could learn to take the subway and the buses and benefit from access to more vocational opportunities. One house for more independent people in the city had been part of the founding vision, but by 1989 there would be more people living off the original property than on it. The building boom around the city of Toronto filled the community's once rural setting with an ever increasing number of new houses in such a way that it was no longer 'normal' to maintain a farm there. In any case the community was obliged to recognise that many assistants and people with disabilities, coming as they did from a restless, hectic consumer society, were not naturally drawn to farming. The farm was gradually phased out.

Much earlier in its history the community had been obliged to acknowledge that l'Arche in North America would not be able to draw on quite the same spiritual resources as l'Arche in Trosly-Breuil. In France, as the Dutch priest and author Henri Nouwen who spent the last ten years of his life at Daybreak, later pointed out, there were at least pockets of spiritual intensity, which were not so readily found in North America. Daybreak had no Père Thomas, and Richmond Hill was not Trosly.

This is the Americas and we are in a very hedonistic country. There is an American religious life that is very young, a reality of religious pragmatism and good works, but where do you go when you really want to be nourished spiritually, when you want to be surrounded by the mystical knowledge of God?

Here as elsewhere in Canada and the United States – where in the delicate and constantly shifting balance in l'Arche between the two complementary elements of professionalism and spirituality, people would perhaps more readily align themselves with the former – the challenge was to find a life that was North American but deeply spiritual. In this challenge, retreats once again had a crucial role to play as a call to prayer and as a reminder not only to the North American communities but to l'Arche as a whole that it was founded first upon the gospels before being a professionally run home for people with disabilities. They were also a reminder that whilst l'Arche set out to encourage maximum autonomy and normalisation for those capable of it, the ultimate aim for people with disabilities – as for all human beings – was growth in love, in the welcoming of others and in service and holiness. At the same time this growth did not in any way preclude the communities from seeking every possible means of helping disabled people to achieve as much independence, knowledge and ability as they could or to be better integrated into society and the Church.

For Steve and Ann Newroth, the founding directors of Daybreak, there was an additional challenge which Trosly-Breuil, for all its universality of heart had not yet had to confront in quite the same way. Given the recognised need for a spiritual life, what form should that life take when they themselves were Anglicans, an increasing number of assistants were Roman Catholics and the people with disabilities came from a culture which included Anglicans, Catholics and members of the United Church? Theirs was the first experience of trying to express the vision of Trosly-Breuil in terms of a different culture. They had brought their own modifications to it, and the culture and the community rooted in it would bring others. By 1970 a newly-formed community in Bangalore, India was facing similar questions, questions which in time would be confronted by communities all over the world:

what were the elements of life in l'Arche on which it was inappropriate to compromise and in what ways was it right that the original intuition should remain open and receptive to creative change?

❧

SIX

BETWEEN TWO WORLDS

'IT IS SUCH A GREAT GRACE to be here,' wrote Jean Vanier from India in November 1970, 'I sense such a change taking place in me. I would like to become poorer, much less aggressive, more gentle and non-violent ... more welcoming ... pray for me that I may be faithful.'

Extraordinary circumstances had once again contrived to bring a small l'Arche community to birth, this time in the land of Mahatma Gandhi. Among the assistants who had come to l'Arche in Trosly-Breuil as early as May 1965 was an Indian girl, Mira, the Roman Catholic daughter of a Hindu mother and a Muslim father still living in Madras. When her father subsequently fell ill she found herself torn between the need to return to her homeland and what she felt was a calling to l'Arche. To use Jean Vanier's expression, 'This triggered something.'

Could l'Arche begin in India? In Montreal Jean mentioned the idea to Gabrielle Einsle, a German woman in charge of the Carrefour centre for foreign students. She too felt drawn in a particular way to the Indian subcontinent. At the same time he came into contact with a Major Ramachandra, a follower of Gandhi who wanted to create schools for disabled people in India. A fortuitous encounter with General Spears, head of the Canadian International Development Agency, Canada's government programme to support overseas development, provided the necessary finance. Finding himself with a surfeit of funds for that financial year, the General agreed that if Jean Vanier could provide a profile and compile a budget for his proposed project in India as quickly as possible, CIDA would provide a third of it. Jean had no idea how to set about it but managed nonetheless to work out a budget for $100,000, and within a few weeks had $33,000 dollars in the bank. The 'folly' of l'Arche in India was no longer a dream but a reality.

On 30 October 1969 Gabrielle and Mira set out on a three-month exploratory journey in India. Shortly afterwards Jean Vanier followed them to a country where he already sensed the role of l'Arche would not be to help people with disabilities from a vantage point of superiority but rather to become in some ways like the local people. It was his first journey to the East. He was prepared for it in that he had read and digested the spirituality and teachings of Mahatma Gandhi, but that did not diminish the impact of the Indian culture, of a people he perceived to be profoundly religious and not motivated by the individualistic materialism so often found in the West, of the continuing relevance of the teachings of the Mahatma and of the suffering poor. 'I suppose there are two things that left a very, very deep impression', he remarked 20 years later with a certain critical detachment in constantly modified phrases:

> One is the immense poverty, the poverty of humanity, the littleness of humanity and the relativisation of everything that I had done before that was so small in size compared with what was happening in India. The other is what I call the whole mystery of Mahatma Gandhi – a gift to humanity, a spirituality, a prophetic vision, the vision of the Harijans[1] and the vision of *ahimsa* or non-violence, and in both cases a depth of spirituality and union with God and a sense of the continual presence of God in his heart, in his flesh, in his being.

Gandhi's very deep sense of his own littleness and poverty had 'imprinted itself, given new certitudes, enlarged my tent.' Non-violence was 'being prepared to be vulnerable'.

During his first travels in India and on numerous subsequent visits he wrote back to friends, ever more widely distributed throughout the globe, in a way that suggested a new sense of his own poverty. He visited schools for mentally disabled children, homes for those with physical disabilities, psychiatric hospitals and leper asylums. In the psychiatric 'hospitals' of India were men and women confined naked in 'lion-cages' built more than a hundred years previously, with no toilet and no bed, only the bare floor and bars. Others were kept in enclosed wards and almost never went out except to receive electric-shock treatment. Their need was crying out for a response. It was madness, Jean Vanier acknowledged, to start a house for people with mental disabilities in India, knowing virtually nothing of the language, traditions and culture. For him, however, it was a question of being poor and trusting enough to allow a new kind of community to develop, a community for which there was no prototype other than the idea of living with people with disabilities, be they Muslim, Hindu or Christian, praying with them, eating with them and generally walking with them on the journey that was life.

✳

From Bangalore in 1970 he wrote of how he had been reflecting on what 'we in the West have done with the gospel'. He had also been re-reading what Gandhi had written on prayer, the love of God and humility:

> I would especially like to live it! I sense all that is happening within me. I feel impatient. How urgent it is for men of peace to rise up in our world. The spectrum of violence is so present. We must react quickly with the folly of works of peace that completely surpass our own capacities, without fear of the violence that can strike us and our world. We are called to oppose violence with non-violent action, based on trust in the Holy Spirit. Although I sense within me a divine impatience, I also know that I must become poorer and trust more fully our Father in Heaven in order to do things that are even more foolish. I have the feeling that we must move more quickly to live the gospel more fully, everywhere, without judging, but living more poorly, accepting misunderstandings and violence and loving those who criticise us. We need to live each moment in the hands of God, trying to create unity through our non-aggressiveness, drawing others into this life of poverty as we create communities which will be a link between the rich and the poor.[2]

Gandhi had recognised the need to follow his path with God as his only guide. The Mahatma had also admitted that, in the face of all the deception and suffering he encountered, he would have gone mad were it not for the sense of the presence of God in him.

In France Père Thomas did not share Jean Vanier's enthusiasm for starting l'Arche in India. He was a man of extraordinary compassion and openness of heart, but he was also a priest formed in the pre-Second Vatican Council Roman Catholic Church. For him l'Arche was an essentially Catholic community. Relationships with people of other faiths and indeed other Christian denominations were ultimately with a view to conversion to Roman Catholicism.

Nevertheless Jean Vanier went ahead. The signs that God wanted l'Arche in India were too strong and real. Within a week of Jean's first arrival in Bangalore l'Arche acquired a property with two hectares of land and two wells, thanks to Major Ramachandra and his associates who were committed to furthering education in the slums. A board of directors, made up of people who supported the spirit of l'Arche but who were also competent in human affairs, was equally swiftly established and by the end of 1970 the first Asha Niketan was opened. In no time at all Gabrielle had arranged for electricity and sanitation to be installed. The gardens flourished. A nearby factory provided basic work of the kind three of the disabled people could undertake for 1,000 rupees a month. Other Asha Niketans would follow. In 1972 a couple from the United States would start a community in Kotagiri, 2,000 metres up in the mountains, although this proved to be one of the few l'Arche communities that foundered. It happened too quickly, without sufficient preparation with the national board of directors. Within nine months of its inception it was compelled to close and the disabled people it had welcomed went to join the community in Bangalore.

In the United States Jean Vanier had met Mother Teresa when together they received the Kennedy Foundation Award. She identified him as a 'very holy man'. Her recognition of Christ in the poor, the spirituality of Thérèse of Lisieux and her gritty, determined practicality in being a 'carrier of God's love' to the rejected of the world formed the basis for much common ground, and the occasion marked the beginning of an ongoing if not always totally smooth relationship. She invited him to come to the city where she had been called to serve and live amongst the poorest of the poor as one of them. Jean Vanier was very moved by the prospect of visiting Kolkata, or Calcutta at it was known at the time. He saw it then as 'the centre of suffering in the world with its ten million refugees and its vast slums'. Once again he was frightened of all the misery and yet mysteriously attracted to a place of suffering and death which was simultaneously one of life because Jesus had transformed death into life, the 'true life which rises up from death'.

In 1971 in Mother Teresa's company he visited the refugee camps formed in the wake of the Bangladeshi war, went into homes for the dying run by her Missionaries of Charity, and met the people who lived out their poverty-stricken lives and died on the filthy pavements of Calcutta. On the back of Brother Andrew's motorbike he rode through the teeming traffic to Howrah train station and saw the families sleeping on the platforms, old people with scraps of paper and cardboard for a bed, abandoned children begging to survive. Their destitution and yet their capacity to share and love, their dignified faces and fullness of life, inspired him to write at the time: 'Is it possible that Jesus will come back from Calcutta, rising from Calcutta, the "tomb of Calcutta"?' He was deeply touched too by the poverty, courage and beauty of Mother Teresa, Brother Andrew and the Missionary of Charity Sisters and Brothers, recognising that he still had much to learn about 'how to live poorly'. The encounter with so much suffering seems to have tempered the energy and dynamism of the beginnings of l'Arche with a deeper sense of his own limitations but also more markedly with the desire to be poor and through that poverty to trust in the Holy Spirit.

As he moved increasingly between the material affluence of Europe and North America and the poverty of Third World countries, between the people of power and influence and the 'little' people, he became more acutely aware of the gulf between the two and felt his own hypocrisy when he found himself introduced as someone who had 'dedicated himself to the mentally deficient' or dined with the Governor of Bengal while others starved in the streets. Yet there was justification for this apparently dual role: 'Everything I say,' he wrote in 1972,

> I can say because I want to work in silent and hidden identi-
> fication with the little people, but at the same time I know that
> I must try and work within society, speak, spur others to act,
> manipulate money, act externally, use contacts, chair adminis-
> trative councils, meet governors, etc.

His notes written during a visit to India that year refer to:

> The two worlds which exist outside and within me ... the
> need to be really transformed by the grace of Jesus ... by the
> Holy Spirit ... to become poor not externally, but poor intern-
> ally because I am possessed by the Spirit, transformed by it ...
> to discover the security of God's love ... if not, these divisions
> between rich and poor will continue to bursting point, to the
> point of hatred and destruction. Unity must come between
> those who are entrenched in the world of wealth and human
> security and those who are in the world of poverty, but it can
> only come when the rich start to abandon their security to live
> the security of God and thus really draw near to the poor and
> the little ones.

Yet in all the suffering Jean Vanier encountered, in fact precisely
in those situations where human solutions no longer seemed
possible, he discerned the works of the Holy Spirit wrought little
by little in the hearts of men.

In August 1972 Gabrielle Einsle visited Calcutta for the first
time and fell in love with the 'City of Joy'. With single-minded
determination she set about creating the right conditions for a
home. That same year Jean Vanier returned to Calcutta and stayed
with Cardinal Picachy. Jean arrived late at night but the cardinal
came down to talk to him. He was deeply interested in what his
guest had to tell him about Asha Niketan in Bangalore and the
very next morning offered him the use of an almost empty two-
storey parish house located between all the noise and bustle of
Sealdah station, where some half a million people arrived and
departed daily, and St John's Church with its adjoining cemetery.
The substantial basement to the church was provided as a workshop and in time a contract with Philips India Ltd made it
possible to give the men at Asha Niketan, Calcutta, work adapted

to individual capacities. In their basement workshop they cut, twisted, stripped, soldered and counted radio wires. Their earnings enabled the community to pay for daily food.

Communities in Madras would follow in 1975, and in Calicut in Kerala in 1978. Nearly all of them came into being in a way which suggested that they were in some mysterious sense meant to be, but perhaps none had more extraordinary beginnings than the foundation near Calicut, the city of coconut palms beside the Arabian Sea. On a train between Calicut and Bangalore, a Mr Premanand read a newspaper article about the l'Arche foundations in India. He arrived at Asha Niketan in Bangalore with a strange story of how his father, a devout and prayerful Hindu, had owned a soap factory in the south of India until the military authorities closed it down. Having relinquished ownership of the factory, Mr Premanand's father had chanced upon a beautiful property by the sea in Calicut which he felt immediately he must buy. The price was 500 rupees but he had no money. On the very day, however, on which he was due to pay for the property, the sum of 525 rupees, the cost of the property plus travelling expenses, arrived by post accompanied by a letter from a man in Mysore who had had a dream telling him to send the money. On the newly purchased site Mr Premanand senior once more started up a factory, this time to produce furniture wax, but when the Communist government came to power in Kerala, despite Mr Premanand's father's warnings that this was a property given to him by God and that if the government took it over the venture would fold within three weeks, it did so. Sure enough, within three weeks the factory folded. Mr Premanand's father had written a document which Jean Vanier subsequently mislaid. He remembered the uncanny nature of its contents, however:

> He wrote of how he saw on one side of this property a place that would welcome people with leprosy and people with disabilities. There would be no drinking of tea or coffee. Nor was there for a while in Asha Niketan in Kerala, although there is now. He had had this Gandhian vision of welcoming the poor, and in recognition of this Mr Premanand offered us forty or fifty acres of this huge and beautiful property that his father had regarded as belonging to God.

The full estate was too large for l'Arche, but the community gratefully accepted five or six acres of land which remained unused for a while until Chris Sadler, an English woman who had been living and working with the *harijans* in South India, began a community there. In time Asha Niketan at Nandi Bazaar became an 'incredibly beautiful' community – beautiful in the gift of its people, of Mitran who called others to look afresh at the frog which he called a chicken, the lizard he named a mongoose or the banana he insisted was laughing; beautiful in its physical setting of golden beaches and natural silence, which Jean Vanier did not fail to appreciate; beautiful too in its fragility.

In India centuries of a lack of separation between life and religion meant that there was great spiritual wealth to be tapped. Everything was a religious act, and prayer came very naturally in a land which, despite the gradual influence of Western materialism, was still steeped in a sense of the sacred. There was something about the culture and climate, especially in rural settings where people lived in close contact with nature and its daily and seasonal rhythms, that was conducive to the recognition of the deeper meanings of life. The very simplicity of existence – the dependence on earth and sky, sun and rain, to meet the fundamental necessities of eating and drinking, bathing and washing – called upon people to relate more fully to the reality of matter, to each other and to the source of life itself. Indian assistants did not rebel, as assistants might in the West, when invited to pray twice a day. Yet only a tiny minority among both the assistants and the people with disabilities were Christians. The majority were Hindus, some were Muslims, and the Christians themselves included not only Catholics but Protestants and Syrian Orthodox. Finding a prayer life acceptable to all was not unproblematic. In Bangalore the community quite spontaneously elected to have a prayer room in which Gabrielle Einsle put an icon. A Christian assistant subsequently added a cross he had made. Then a Hindu member of the community added a picture of Ganesh, the elephant god. Some of the men went home to their families for the weekend and returned with pictures of other Hindu deities. The room came to contain a number of pictures of various gods. It had seemed right that if people wanted to display representations of their gods they should do so, that their way of worshipping should be respected, but there were Christians who were shocked to find a room where the image of Jesus was just one among several.

Diversity of religious faith was inseparable from diversity and complexity of culture. Furthermore, in India it was a question of expressing the vision of l'Arche, not so much in terms of the national culture (in itself a difficult task for community leaders who were initially all European) as of the Indian cultures, which varied not only between different states but also between castes. In Bangalore, many of the mentally disabled people who came to the community were Brahmins, possibly owing to widespread intermarriage, possibly because their families were better educated and therefore most likely to hear of the existence of Asha Niketan. The Brahmin caste was a culture in itself, one accustomed to subservience from others and not one well suited to showing ways of tending the country's poor to Europeans ignorant even of the complexities of Indian eating habits or of cultural beliefs, of the fact for example that it was a mortal sin to step over another's body, even over his legs. What was acceptable in Bangalore, which had been subject to strong Western influence, might not be acceptable elsewhere in India. This was apparent at the most fundamental level: in Bangalore, partly no doubt for climatic reasons, people wore shoes everywhere. Elsewhere, in Madras for example, it was unacceptable to enter even a rich man's house without removing them.

It became swiftly apparent also that in a country of such extreme material poverty it would be a particular challenge not to appear rich in relation to the majority of people and very rich in the eyes of the poor. 'Calcutta is not India. India is the villages. India is united families. India is the faces of the poor whose smiles radiate peace', wrote Jean Vanier, but he was not one to disregard the fact that Calcutta existed, Bombay existed and so too did the lepers, the street dwellers and the inhabitants of the asylums in numbers too vast to contemplate. It would be difficult to retain a sense of the meaning of l'Arche's existence here and easy to despair at the smallness of the four tiny communities, each made up of no more than a dozen people, in relation to the magnitude of India's need. In the context of that need it was indeed folly to choose to live with and love a few individuals deeply, but perhaps it was that each Asha Niketan was meant to be a small sign of what the world could be if only each person sought to live as a child of God open to the Spirit.

India was only the first of many countries in which l'Arche had to face a particular challenge in relation to its poverty and simplicity, together with other problems which the attempt to lead a life integrated with local people and their culture inevitably presented. Very soon a community was begun on the Ivory Coast where, as in most 'Third World' countries, there was no government funding. L'Arche was entirely dependent on money raised locally through the board of directors and by the community's own labour, and on gifts from abroad.

In Africa, as one of the first l'Arche directors on the Ivory Coast, recalled, traditional beliefs about people with disabilities appeared initially to make it virtually impossible for non-Christians to join. On the Ivory Coast some disabled children were not kept in the family because they were believed to bring bad luck, and the interests of the group took precedence over the individual. Some parents would take their child to a witchdoctor who would abandon it in the bush and afterwards inform people that it had turned back into a snake. A pregnant woman would not eat at the same table as a person with disabilities for fear of her unborn child being contaminated. In general there were strong fears about taking meals in the company of disabled people, especially those with epilepsy. How could the people of the Ivory Coast be persuaded of the mysterious value of their wounded and rejected children?

> How do you articulate l'Arche in a culture like that? Even the whole way of running a meeting, of working through a conflict is different. There are all those rules of African tradition and when you don't know them, even if you speak the same language, the words don't necessarily mean the same thing. In France a thing is black or white. In Africa it can be both.

There was much that Africa had to teach l'Arche. The quality of the welcome it afforded its foreign guests was one illustration among many of the hospitality and warmth of the materially poor. In time the small family in Bouaké and another in Ouagadougou flourished as witnesses, in a world of extreme material poverty, to the value of the person with mental disabilities. But the young assistants who came from Europe were at times accused of having large eyes but seeing nothing.

Communities swiftly followed in Haiti, Honduras and a rapidly increasing number of other countries where material poverty was an all too evident source of suffering yet, remarkably, not of bitterness or resentment. Often these communities were born as a result of invitations to Jean Vanier to talk or take retreats. He would arrive and grasp the essentials of the political, cultural and religious climate with extraordinary speed and energy. A need, an opportunity, a call would be perceived by him or others and – through meetings with health ministers, psychiatrists, religious and a multitude of others with or without influence – the means would be found to meet it in some small and frequently precarious way. Often too, the call to l'Arche would find its incarnation in a particular disabled person whose cry for love and relationship was articulated in his very flesh.

L'Arche in Haiti began when Robert Larouche, at one time a philosophy teacher in Quebec, accompanied Jean Vanier on a trip to Brazil and Haiti. They had gone to Port-au-Prince, recognising that the model of community established in Europe and North America could not necessarily be reproduced there and uncertain whether l'Arche really had a place in Haiti. For three months Robert stayed on in a poor neighbourhood on the outskirts of Port-au-Prince, finding out more about the place of people with disabilities in Haitian society. The disabled person there was perceived to be a heavy burden and consequently excluded and shut away in much the same way as in North America or Europe, only their attitudes were less camouflaged. People with disabilities were openly jeered at and mocked, and often turned into buffoons, clowns and beggars. In this way they could contribute to the financial upkeep of their family but lost all sense of personal dignity in the process. Institutions, usually run by the government, were reserved for those in extreme need or those who had been abandoned altogether.

In one psychiatric centre Robert Larouche met Yveline, an emotionally disturbed ten-year-old who used to run up to people in the street, singing at the top of her voice, until eventually she was placed in an institution. When Robert first encountered her she had been there for a year, the only child in the ward. No one had succeeded in tracing her family. The director asked whether she might not have a future in l'Arche. L'Arche had not previously taken in children but Yveline's predicament made it clear to Robert that a house should be opened in Haiti. The child psychiatrists in another hospital offered their collaboration and, together with several others, helped to form a board of directors to support the new community. In time there would be three different homes, a small school for the children of the community and its neighbourhood and a workshop, producing among other things, exceptionally good peanut butter.

In Honduras it was Nadine Tokar, a young French woman who first went there to pave the way for Jean Vanier to give a retreat, and was made painfully aware of the plight of the poor and their evident 'hunger for the good news'. Arriving in the capital, Tegucigalpa, eager to know more about the country, she climbed aboard a bus and found herself in the poverty-stricken suburb of Suyapa on a hillside overlooking the city. There an inordinately large number of *estancos* (shops) selling the national liquor provided the men with a much-travelled route to oblivion. There too an incongruously imposing basilica erected to the glory of the patron saint of Honduras formed the focal point for numerous pilgrimages. Further up the mountain was Nueva Suyapa, a district even poorer than Suyapa itself, born in the wake of Hurricane Fifi, when large numbers of refugees, whose houses had been swept away by one of the greatest natural disasters to strike Honduras, made their way to the capital in search of work and housing. On the mountainside behind Suyapa they were reduced to making their own shelters out of cardboard, wood and whatever else they could find. By the time Nadine arrived there, there was still no water or electricity supply and no tarred roads.

The extreme poverty of the people, their simplicity and struggle for life called to her, as did their spirit and faith. Entering the local church, a much more modest building than the basilica of Our Lady of Suyapa, on that first chance arrival in the square, she was moved by the old women she discovered reciting the rosary. When Jean Vanier came to give his retreat they returned together one Saturday night to a Celebration of the Word. The experience of hearing those virtually illiterate local women struggling to read the Word of God was one that would remain with her for years to come.

In Honduras, as in Haiti, a particular need had been identified among the young people, who in their poverty dreamed only of escaping to the material affluence of North America. Nadine returned to Honduras to organise another retreat with these young people specifically in mind. She visited psychiatric hospitals and asylums. One institution in particular filled her with horror: 'a terrible, dirty place where all kinds of people were just waiting for death: mentally sick people, old people, anyone who was abandoned or rejected'. There she met Marcia, who had been abandoned at the age of three and had spent 20 years within its walls before coming to live in the l'Arche house Nadine was to found in Suyapa.

In a hospital where she asked to see any abandoned disabled children, she was directed to a room set apart from the main wards with the warning that its occupant was dangerous:

> In an empty room was a cage and Raphael was in there. He was completely naked with nothing in his cage but a fragment of food. He was severely disabled and epileptic and had been abandoned as a baby. He had been born in the hospital, left there and grown up there. He had never had a relationship of any kind and was quite violent, incapable of touching or being touched, but with the face of an angel. I spent half an hour trying to play with him and touch him and during that half hour I felt deeply that he needed a home and that he was calling l'Arche, and it became clear that that call was my call.

Nadine had been happy in Trosly-Breuil but at that moment, regardless of all personal considerations, she found herself saying 'yes' to Raphael and Honduras.

It was equally clear to her that it was not just a question of transporting a French community to Honduras. Before doing anything else she must live there for a while and try to understand the language and life of the Honduran poor. For a year she lived in Nueva Suyapa with Dona Maria and her family in a small room with two beds, a fire and a table. It was not easy at first. When she entered the house the men and any visitors would go out. The colonisation of Honduras had meant that any foreigner was perceived to be educated and clever, a person of power, money and influence. The men of Honduras often suffered from a sense of inferiority and a lack of their own national identity and dignity. They made up for it with *machismo*, the resort to excessive alcohol and violence. In the congested houses of Suyapa, however, people soon realised that this particular *gringita* (young foreign girl) had nothing to give them in the way that they had expected and everything to receive and learn:

> I was like a little child. They taught me how to speak. Each night we would all sit on the two beds while Dona Maria cooked corn to make tortillas which she sold next morning to make a little money, and they would point to my nose or my mouth and I would repeat the words after them. They taught me how to wash my body, how to go to the bathroom when there wasn't one, how to wash my clothes in the river or buy food in the market.

For that year before opening Casa Nazaret, a blue-and-green painted wooden building that had once been a tiny seminary and subsequently a school, as a home for Marcia, Raphael and a handful of others, Nadine herself learnt how to live as a poor person in Honduras. She came to know the local families and visited the many who were disabled because of malnutrition and desperately poor medical facilities. It was hard to be amongst strangers and have an image of power and wealth thrust upon her when that was not what she wanted to live, hard too to feel the eyes upon her as she walked alone in the dusty streets, but it enabled her to touch upon the feelings of the poor: 'the mixed-up feelings of rejection and curiosity, something very strange'.

If l'Arche had entered into a broader and deeper understanding of the needs and nature of the poor and disabled of this world, so too had Jean Vanier. He had been journeying: journeying to give talks and retreats, journeying to help found and nurture the small communities that were springing to life across the continents. As the communities grew in number, he too was growing. 'To grow', he would write some years later in *Community and Growth*, is to emerge gradually from a land where our vision is limited, where we are seeking and governed by egotistical pleasure, by our sympathies and antipathies, to a land of unlimited horizons and universal love, where we will love all men and desire their happiness.

He was manifestly emerging from some of his own 'antipathies'. The young man who during his time in the Navy had had such a clear understanding of who and what was good and bad – 'There were the Allies and the evil ones' – who during his university studies had worked on the basis that 'Aristotle was right and Plato was wrong', and who had come to l'Arche still with the conviction that the 'right and the wrong were outside me' was progressing towards a more subtle understanding.

He had hitherto been an outspoken critic of the 'normal' who failed to treat the disabled as people, one who was not afraid to stand up and state in the baldest terms that, 'normal people, not the handicapped, are the strange people. It is they who are the ones with the problems.' By his own admission, there had been a time when, in his compassion for disabled people, he had been ready to point an accusing finger at parents and families who had, albeit sometimes unconsciously, added to their wounds. Had some of them not rejected their children? Was it not because of their cultural values and lack of competence that their son or daughter felt unloved, unworthy and useless? Yet in the same way as he would come to recognise that he had been insufficiently aware of the needs of the villagers of Trosly-Breuil and the importance of co-operation between l'Arche and people outside it, based on mutual respect for each other's gifts, so he would come to a greater understanding of the suffering and needs of parents of people with disabilities and to the realisation of the importance of working in co-operation with families.

It was during a pilgrimage to Lourdes, that 'very physical reality' to which so many people came in their brokenness, the place where at the age of 19 Jean Vanier had somehow known that he would leave the Navy, that in 1971 Faith and Light, an international Christian association for the mentally disabled, their families and friends, came into being. The seed of the idea was originally sown at a meeting with Marie-Hélène Mathieu,

General Secretary of the 'Christian office for people with mental disabilities' in Paris. Marie-Hélène had visited Trosly-Breuil in 1967, OCH (as her organisation was known) helped l'Arche financially, and she herself had become the coordinator of the burgeoning communities in France. She had also been deeply touched by a meeting with the parents of two severely mentally disabled sons who wanted to organise a pilgrimage to Lourdes in which their boys could participate. In those days parents with disabled children in Lourdes – as in hotels, beaches and holiday resorts elsewhere – could find themselves hurt and isolated. Yet l'Arche's experience of previous pilgrimages to Lourdes, La Salette, Fátima and Banneux had shown how disabled people were transformed by these journeys, how unity was cemented en route by their sensitivity to water, light, processions and all the other signs that spoke to their hearts.

With Marie-Hélène Mathieu l'Arche decided to organise an international pilgrimage for people with mental disabilities, their parents and friends. It was an important occasion for celebration and joy, a time of discovery for many parents that they were not alone, that their child was not a source of shame and that they could celebrate together. For many of the young people there it was an opportunity for real commitment to mentally disabled people, and for many of those with mental disabilities it was a moment of joy and a meeting with God.

Five days together in Lourdes brought so much hope that when the time came to leave it did not seem possible that the experience should end there. 'Do whatever the Holy Spirit inspires you to do to build up a world of love around the disabled person', was Jean Vanier's directive. The Faith and Light movement, which he described as a 'kind of first cousin to l'Arche' was born. By the same mysterious process of people with disabilities bringing people together, Faith and Light would spread throughout the world. These 'communities' each made up of 30 or so people – children, teenagers or adults with mental disabilities together with their parents and friends, particularly the young – would meet regularly for sharing, prayer and celebration. They were centred on the discovery of the mystery hidden in the disabled person, who was so often close to the spirit of the Beatitudes, and whose frailty broke down the barriers in people's hearts. They were also centred on the awareness of the immense suffering that the birth of a disabled child could bring. Parents too were wounded and, in their pain, tended to isolate themselves. More and more, therefore, the Faith and Light communities would gear themselves to mutual help and the dispelling of loneliness between meetings, to looking after a child for an afternoon, inviting disheartened parents for a meal, organising a holiday camp or simply keeping in touch by telephone. The 'Christian office for people with mental disabilities' also contributed to the cementing of these links, not least by producing a magazine entitled 'Ombre et Lumière' (Shadow and Light), for which Jean Vanier regularly provided articles. In time its broad message about how to live with a son or daughter with disabilities would reach far beyond its some 15,000 official subscribers.

Through Faith and Light a number of people discovered their vocation actually to live with disabled people and joined an existing l'Arche community or founded another – in Rome, São Paolo, Switzerland and elsewhere. Through Faith and Light, Jean Vanier would be able to state some time later, thousands of mothers and fathers were 'beginning to dance and laugh with their children'. He recalled a mother in the then Yugoslavia who had four children, three of whom had mental disabilities. 'My three disabled children are so beautiful,' she had told him, 'The one who's normal has a lot of problems.' In a multitude of other instances a total inner transformation was brought about.

Meanwhile the growth towards a 'more realistic and a truer love' was to take Jean Vanier into the enclosed and pain-ridden world of prisons. He found himself invited to talk even in maximum security prisons and, as he spoke of the pain and the brokenness of the mentally disabled people with whom he lived, he found he was speaking too of the pain of the prisoners he was addressing.

> One of the most moving moments for me was when I was talking about our people and their pain and depression and rejection and a man got up and screamed, 'You know nothing about our pain. You've had it easy.' He explained about his life, about how he had seen his mother raped when he was four, how he had been sold into homosexuality so that his father

could drink. Then, when he was thirteen, the men in blue had come. Finally he really screamed at me, 'If one more person comes into this prison and talks about love, I'll kick his bloody head in.' You can imagine the sort of silence that followed. I knew that for me this was a make-or-break situation.

Jean Vanier sought to remain peaceful in the face of this explosion and was able to acknowledge that he had indeed had it easy. He asked whether he could repeat what the prisoner had said to others who did not know what he was going through. 'He said I could and I said, "If people outside need to listen to you, then it might be important to listen to what those outside have to say to you."' When the talk was over he went and shook the distraught man by the hand and asked him where he came from and whether he was married.

> I asked about his wife, and his eyes filled with tears. I still remember him saying that his wife was in a wheelchair. At that moment I saw his immense wound, his cry for love. Here was a guy coming to talk about just what he needed, and this immense explosion had been because I had touched his wound.

In one prison in Western Canada Jean stayed for several days and had his own cell. By day he led the prisoners in quiet reflection and prayer. At night as he looked at the moon and the stars through the barred window, he felt a deep solidarity with all the men and women in prisons around the world. He was invited to spend an evening with Club 21, the club for men convicted of murder who were serving prison sentences of 21 years or more. A great number of them talked to him of their experiences. Contact with them brought with it the recognition that had he been born into a different family and had a different education and had the kind of experiences that those men had, he too might well have done what they had done.

Entering the prison world was for Jean Vanier an 'incredible revelation'. It taught him more about himself and more about people in general. It dispelled some of the naïvety of which he knew he was capable. 'Instinctively when you're in prison the guards are the baddies, but reality isn't quite like that.' He remembered, not without laughter, the prisoner who had acted as his secretary during a retreat at Calgary prison. They had talked a good deal together, and as the man had nearly completed his sentence he asked the retreat leader for some addresses to contact on his release. Jean Vanier obligingly gave him some. A few months later he received a succession of letters from people across Canada informing him that a friend of his had been and stolen their stereo, television and a whole series of other items.

More significantly, contact with people who occupied a world of cells and locks and metal doors revealed to him that the most fundamental characteristic of a human being was a heart crying out for love. It was a characteristic common not only to the person with disabilities or the prisoner but to all humanity. What was more, so much depended upon the response that cry received.

If that heart is listened and responded to then people don't create barriers but if the heart and the cry for communion is wounded at a very early age the barriers are stronger, so strong that it can cause psychosis in people. If the heart receives love it flowers, but if it is hurt it becomes angry and seeks revenge. It resorts to anti-social behaviour.

Exposure to different forms of poverty and a growing recognition of his own was blurring the boundaries. 'The world in l'Arche, the Third World, the prison world – they all seemed so close together.' Like the barriers between people with disabilities and the 'normal', or between the First and the Third World, in Jean Vanier's understanding the barriers between the wounded inside and outside prison walls were dissolving. At times that dissolution was manifested very concretely. In Ottawa he took part in a weekend gathering in a disused prison in which prisoners, ex-prisoners, police, prison guards and directors, psychologists and government officials came together for two nights and two days without anyone knowing who the others were or what their usual role was. They slept together in dormitories, not knowing whether the man in the next bunk was the director of the prison or one of its inmates. The idea did not, as Jean Vanier had hoped, lead to other similar gatherings. It was nonetheless a much valued experience. Another Canadian prison linked its prisoners with severely disabled people. Once a week they would go out together for a picnic. The 'beauty of those men from the prison, their kindness towards those very disabled people, the bringing together of the marginal of society for a picnic on the beach' would not be forgotten.

At the very beginning of l'Arche, the community at Trosly-Breuil had itself welcomed two men who had been condemned to death but subsequently reprieved. As a way of rehabilitating them into society, the arrangement had worked quite well; after ten years they left to work elsewhere. From the point of view of community life, however, it was less satisfactory. They were, Jean Vanier acknowledged, 'a bit too wounded'. Thereafter he was reluctant to take people directly from prison. The demands of community were too similar to those of prison. They should first spend time in the outside world doing what they wanted, rather than opting for community life whilst still in a state of weakness and vulnerability. He himself never found it easy to go into prisons. The experience, though life-giving, evoked in him fear and revulsion. He had difficulty too in going into hospitals where there might be 20 or 30 disabled people smelling of urine, or picking up a child and then having to put it down: 'When you touch a child who has never been touched other than for func-tional things, when you hold him close to your body and play with him, the child immediately starts to open and blossom out, and then you put him down …' Similarly he had difficulty going into prisons, meeting men with whom he got on well, and then leaving them to the clang of metal doors.

'What people do to people in prison and what people do to people with disabilities is a measure of what society is, of how hard and broken it is.' To Jean Vanier it was in fact an indication of how deeply society too was wounded. For him there was a strange similarity between the man told by his mother when he was eight years old that, if only the contraceptives had worked, he would not be here, who subsequently took part in the kidnap-ping of a child; and the director who, though less wounded, was sufficiently hurt for the growth of his heart to be stunted and threw himself into activity seeking admiration because he could not believe in communion. The prisoner's wounded heart had turned him to anti-social behaviour; in the factory director, bent on competitive work and unjust to his workers in the pursuit of his own project, the wounded heart drove him to apparently social but in reality anti-social behaviour:

> The two poles seem to be the same, just as in the gospel the prodigal son and the elder son are the same reality. In a way it's easier for the prodigal son because the truth about him becomes more visible, whereas the elder son doesn't know the truth about himself.

Jean Vanier had come to the understanding that we are all Pharisees, thinking we are good and knowledgeable, thinking we have power and the right to dictate what others should do. In reality we are crushing the little people with our imposing ways. 'That is the mystery of the two poles of humanity: at the heart of each is the wound.'

SEVEN

TOWARDS COMMUNION

'ONE OF THE THINGS I discover more and more is that it takes months and years to build community', Jean Vanier claimed, long after the surging energy of 'take-off'. The creation of new communities had continued, each one slightly different in roots, orientation and character. In North America a considerable number had been born out of the Faith and Sharing retreats or through affiliation with Daybreak. In general, the 17 communities founded there between 1972 and 1977 subscribed to two patterns. There were those modelled on Trosly-Breuil and Daybreak, wanting to be Christian communities centred on the poor. These were financed, supported and controlled by the State and sought to take full advantage of any professional resources available; they also had solid and reliable boards of directors. There were other communities, however, that sought to be closer to the poor by sharing their insecurity and declining State assistance and control. They set themselves up in poor urban areas or in the country, close to the land, and often took in other marginalised people as well as those with mental disabilities. Despite slight differences of orientation, nearly all the communities took in people from large institutions, many of whom had suffered as a result of long years of separation from their families. There were consequently times when the burden on fragile communities was almost too great.

In France, most of the communities were modelled on Trosly-Breuil and received a grant from the State, although two later communities chose not to be State-subsidised but to live instead off the proceeds of their own agricultural labour and the pensions and salaries of the disabled people and assistants who worked outside the community. Other communities were born out of Faith and Light pilgrimages, including two in Scandinavia, which had some difficulty rooting themselves in the country's social and church fabric. Another, in Belgium, had already been established as a home for people suffering from cerebral palsy but, having taken part in the Faith and Light Pilgrimage to Lourdes in 1971, its founder had asked that it be recognised as a l'Arche community. His request was accepted, and in time a total of six Belgian l'Arche communities would be established, two of which were Flemish. L'Arche in Africa had begun in Bouaké on the Ivory Coast, largely because the prior of a Benedictine monastery wanted it and offered his help and support. There, as in Haiti, Honduras and other Third World countries, l'Arche was characterised by the clear option to live in the poorest neighbourhoods and welcome people who had been completely abandoned. Also, because there were fewer regulations in these countries, it was easier to welcome adults and children with disabilities together, a fact which gave foundations a very particular character.

Looking back on the 1960s and 1970s in general Jean Vanier identified three different community models: the religious life, exemplified by Mother Teresa's Missionary of Charity Sisters and Brothers, the Taizé Brothers and others; residential homes for people with disabilities which began in the United States, Canada, the United Kingdom and Scandinavia with a professional vision of 'reinsertion' into society; and the new-style communities that sprang up, particularly in North America, as a reaction against the consumer society, large impersonal institutions and legal rigidity. Friendship House and Benedict Labre House were among these last. So too were all the communities that sought to live close to nature and the 'communes' which often had very high human and spiritual ideals reflecting a desire to live simply, without the constraints of society, and sometimes in greater proximity to the poor. The various l'Arche communities founded during that period inclined to different degrees to these three models. Their different characteristics brought to the broad banner of l'Arche all the richness of diversity. They also meant that communities sometimes suffered from a lack of clarity about their own identity.

There were, Jean Vanier discovered, always plenty of courageous people prepared to be heroes, to sleep on the ground, work long hours and live in dilapidated houses. The problems arose when it came to living with brothers and sisters who had not been chosen but given, and maintaining fidelity in the simple things that made up the daily round. After the beginnings that were so evidently given, some communities came very near to closure. In most there were times of tension and trial, related not only to the problem of integrating l'Arche into different countries and cultures – to such very practical questions as whether meals should be taken at table or on the floor; the establishing of appropriate wages for assistants in Third World countries; and the maintenance of the right kind of simplicity of life in relation to the poverty of those amongst whom they lived – but also the very spirit of communion which must be nurtured and sustained if communities made up of people from diverse backgrounds were to live, grow and belong together. Most of the early foundations came about because of personal contact between their individual founders and Jean Vanier. They did not necessarily know each other. In the early years there was little support other than from Jean himself. Nor was there any means to ensure a common vision. In 1972, in an attempt to establish and maintain greater unity between the individual communities, all the founders gathered in Ambleteuse for what was to be the first meeting of the Federation of l'Arche Communities. Those present began to put the vision of l'Arche into writing. This draft was in time reworked and amended to become the International Charter of l'Arche. In time also a small International Council, of which Jean Vanier was initially the coordinator, was formed to watch over and guide new foundations. Even that guidance, however, was not always enough.

Australia was the first country in which l'Arche began without strong support from Trosly and was in many ways in the words of one of its founders, 'a folly of a foundation'. In 1974 Eileen Glass, an Australian, met Jean Vanier at a retreat he gave in London and subsequently spent six weeks at Trosly. A couple of months later she continued her travels in North America and ended up spending nearly two years in l'Arche Winnipeg, a community very much in its foundational stages. Returning to Australia, she joined forces with a couple in Canberra who had a son with a mild mental disability and were eager to do something for people like him who were 'falling through the gaps' in existing services. When in April 1977 Jean visited Canberra he encouraged Dr Dick Bromhead and his wife, Margaret to make a beginning – this despite the fact that they still had six of their ten children living at home – and asked Eileen Glass, who had no experience of Boards whatsoever, to set up a Board of Directors. The Archbishop of Canberra offered the use of an old convent for the community and early in 1978 the Bromhead family moved from their comfortable home in Canberra to Bungendore, a village about 30 kilometres to the east of the city. In April they welcomed the founding member and an assistant and l'Arche Genesaret began.

After three years at Bungendore the decision was made to relocate the community back to Canberra. At that time the family moved into a home of their own and a community household was established for the other members. In time there would be three such households in Canberra, a second foundation would open at the end of 1981 in Milton, a small town on the south coast of New South Wales, and 1983 would see the beginning of l'Arche Sydney. Milton would be obliged to close in 1986 in part because the priest who had been strongly supportive of its opening moved on, in part because a condition of government funding was that the people with disabilities attend a 'government approved' workshop and the nearest such facility was 40 kilometres away. That same year, however, a new community in Hobart would benefit from the Tasmanian Government's initiative to move people with disabilities out of institutions wherever possible.

In fact these first four Australian communities were obliged to operate in a climate of emerging professionalism and government standards and to grapple with many of the issues which would only later have to be faced by l'Arche in France. What was more they had to do so in an atmosphere of isolation. From the beginning l'Arche communities in Australia had to live with their geography. They were far removed from the centre of the l'Arche world and were not 'on the radar' of the wider l'Arche family in the way that foundations in Africa or Honduras were. They had one visit from the international coordinator a year and it was not until 1981 that Eileen Glass was invited to the International Council. Even the telephone was not then as effective. The positive side of this isolation was that they developed a strong regional life and knew each other's communities well. In the early years they even took holidays together.

Another consequence of the combination of this isolation and changing government standards was that the Australian communities looked rather different from l'Arche in some other parts of the world at that time. The l'Arche communities in Australia were not able to develop their own workshops as legislation prohibited a service provider from taking responsibility for more than one aspect of a person's life. Consequently an organisation could only provide work, or education, or housing, a reaction to the 'womb to tomb' model of care provided by institutions. This meant that the people with disabilities all went out to work in different settings. When they had good jobs this was an excellent experience of integration into society. It could also mean, however, that it was not always possible to ensure they had appropriate, meaningful full-time work.

Despite the differing outer forms of l'Arche that were beginning to emerge, despite the external pressures to meet varying government requirements, it remained nonetheless clear that internationally, nationally and at the level of individual communities what was being sought after if not always fully experienced was something more profound, subtle and durable than collaboration. Jean Vanier spoke often of 'communion', a form of relationship central to l'Arche, his own understanding of which was to deepen with the years. In 1989 he said of it:

> Generally speaking communion is a sense of unity deeper than working together. It is more on the level of being, and somewhere it breaks down the barriers of loneliness and gives people a sense of freedom. It has a very deep respect of difference. It is very close to the things of God. It is frequently deepened in silence and is linked much more to the body.

He had begun l'Arche in the desire to live the gospel and follow Jesus more closely. He was a man of prayer grounded in a sense in the mysticism of Père Thomas and in oneness with him. For him relationship with disabled people, with the poor with whom Jesus had identified himself, was an essentially religious experience. Often he referred to gentle moments lived with the profoundly disabled, to bathtime with Eric for example, who was almost completely blind and deaf:

It was an occasion when a deep communion could be established; when we would touch his body with gentleness, respect and love. In hot water Eric relaxes; he likes it. Water refreshes and cleanses. He has a feeling of being enveloped in a gentle warmth. Through water and the touch of the body there was a deep communion that was created between Eric and myself. It was good to be together. And because Eric was relaxed, it made me feel more relaxed. He has complete trust in the person who gives him a bath. He is completely abandoned. He no longer defends himself. He feels secure because he is respected and loved. The way he welcomed me, the way he trusted me, called forth trust in me. Yes, Eric called me forth to greater gentleness and respect for his body and his being. He called forth in me all that is best. His weakness, his littleness, his yearning to be loved touched my heart and awakened in me unsuspected forces of love and tenderness. I gave him life; he also gave me life ... These moments of communion are the revelation that God has created deep bonds between us.[1]

Asked once in what way disabled people were religious, Jean Vanier referred to such moments of peace and contentment at bathtime and went on to raise the question of how they could be 'held on to'. In some way, he maintained, this touched upon the way in which all who lived in l'Arche, regardless of any professed creed or world-view, were religious. Those who stayed in l'Arche were responding to the cry of the disabled person for communion which, whether perceived as such or not, was 'very close to the things of God'. 'L'Arche', Père Thomas insisted, 'brings together all people of good will, whatever their country, age, race or culture. Without knowing his name, they sincerely and loyally seek the Saviour.' Most people in the communities, be they atheist, agnostic, Hindu, Christian or – as would increasingly be the case – barely informed about the nature of religious faith, could sooner or later identify with those quiet moments in which deep bonds were created. The desire, even the need, to hold and nourish those moments could, moreover, lead naturally to prayer. The early recognition of the right to 'choose in freedom', brought about by Philippe's timely questioning as to why he had to go to Mass every day, meant that there was no obligation to hold any religious belief or to participate in the daily prayer or worship of the various communities. Jean Vanier had been obliged to recognise that whilst he had wanted to create a Christian community, this was not Raphael and Philippe's primary concern. What they needed, above all, was friendship and security. The religious foundation of a community was not automatically present. Many communities did not have a spiritual guide, priest or minister, but in the experience of most, relationship with disabled people had a way of awakening individuals to the spirit of prayer which many saw as essential if that 'deep sense of unity' was to be nurtured and sustained. One Muslim assistant, who when he first came to Asha Niketan felt that prayer was meaningless, nevertheless joined the others for the house prayer because he could see that it had value for them. Over the years he was, in the recollection of another community member 'transformed'; 'I feel he really prays and it's through his relationship with one of the disabled men who does not speak that something has opened up in him.'

Even, perhaps particularly, where the pull towards meeting the requirements of the State and away from the spiritual dimension was particularly strong, where the pressures of an achievement-orientated society and the demands of a rapid pace of life over-taxed energies and allowed little time for those gentler moments, the need for prayer was felt. If the community in Erie reflected what Father George Strohmeyer, a priest there described as the 'beautiful blend in l'Arche between the French vision and the North American sense of how to go about things', its strength lay in its competence and capacity to meet State requirements as opposed to the community dimension of caring, spending time, appreciating the mystery of the person. Increasingly the need was felt for a spiritual centre to the community's life. In time Erie set aside a building called the 'Waterspring', along similar lines to Daybreak's 'Dayspring', a place of prayer, quietness and worship to which people could come for spiritual nourishment. They also welcomed a young man who felt his particular vocation as a lay person was to be a man of prayer at the heart of the community.

In Choluteca, the second tiny Honduran foundation on a dusty *barrio* not far from the Nicaraguan border, the first instinct of its Mexican founder was to set aside a tiny corner for prayer in which the Blessed Sacrament could be reserved. She was a young woman about to live alone amongst people with disabilities, but if the Blessed Sacrament was there in the middle of the community she felt sure that her neighbours would understand. They did, as did intuitively the disabled people who came to live with her. Not wishing to impose her own desire to pray upon her companions, she rose early and went quietly to the chapel until one day Santos enquired why she did not invite them. Collectively they decided that each morning they would go together to the chapel to offer the day to Jesus and take part in a liturgy at which they could receive Communion. 'Felipe did not know Jesus at all before he came to live here, but little by little he understood that in the small tabernacle was someone who loved him.' With his wasted legs he could only pull himself along the rough ground by his arms and often succumbed to frustration. 'He would go to the chapel when he was angry with me or with whatever other cause.' In the evening when the community gathered once again for prayer Felipe would murmur over and over again, '*Padre in cielo, Padre in cielo, Padre in cielo*' – 'Our Father who art in heaven'. Sometimes at night he would cry out his suffering with Jesus. In the same community Sulema used to bang her head to the point of creating an open wound, but she too seemed to experience relief simply by being in the chapel. When she was very angry she would go there to shout, and afterwards emerged strangely at peace.

The actual experience of communion with disabled people proved to be a point of profound unity. In communities founded upon the spirit of the Beatitudes, unity also sprang from the idea that, as Père Thomas pointed out, 'all those who truly believe in the Spirit are attracted to the Sermon on the Mount'. Disabled people themselves, it was found, had a way of cutting across barriers potentially created by diversity of religious faith and denomination. Asked by a visitor to the community which God he worshipped, Viswanathan at Nandi Bazaar near Calicut responded unhesitatingly, 'I don't know which God I worship. Can that be known? There is a little light and in that we pray, that's all.' Most disabled people taken to any church would respond not according to whether it was in the Roman Catholic, Anglican or United Church tradition but, as Père Thomas had early realised, according to the faith and love that went into it. When they listened to Père Thomas' homilies they were not responding to his Thomist theology but to the tone of his voice, and they would relate to any voice with the same quality regardless of the language it spoke. For others, for whom tradition and ritual were an indispensable part of their faith, however, the issue was less straightforward. At the point of the profoundly religious act of l'Arche, the act of meeting people with disabilities, person to person, there was union of all diversity, but at the point where that experience was given articulation, for those who needed articulation, tensions arose.

L'Arche had begun in France, founded by members of the Roman Catholic Church. At Trosly-Breuil the language, vocabulary and values were, despite the insistence on respect for other religions and other Christian denominations, very French and very Catholic. There was a growing appreciation of the value of married members of the community in terms of what they could contribute in helping the community to become part of the wider local community, and of what might be called the 'naturalness' of their children in relationships with people with disabilities. Some married people at Trosly-Breuil, however, still felt that they did not quite fit into the scheme of things, in which celibacy appeared a higher form of life. There were also those who felt that, even in the absence of any tangible imposition of the Catholic faith, not to be Roman Catholic at Trosly was a serious limitation. If there was an ongoing tension in the Catholic Church between openness to helping people become Catholic and openness to helping people become themselves, in the early days of l'Arche there were some who felt that, especially in Catholic countries but elsewhere also, it was unduly inclined to the former. Jean Vanier's 'tent' might have 'broadened' with increased exposure to other nationalities, faiths and traditions but as the spiritual son of Père Thomas he had been very traditionally Roman Catholic and had begun l'Arche approaching Protestants as people to be converted rather than sisters and brothers with whom he was called to live and grow in Christ.

In India, in the early years, despite the endeavour to find a form of worship that would speak to Hindus, Muslims and Christians alike, and at the same time give space to the celebration of each one's personal faith, the assistants who came from abroad tended, albeit innocently and blindly, to dominate the life of the community with their Christian faith. The celebration of Christmas, for example, far outweighed that of any Hindu festival. Yet for a while this domination passed unnoticed, precisely because Hindus were so open and disinclined to be upset by it. A similar unconscious domination, some non-Catholics found, existed in predominantly Catholic communities, and even where communities were made up of a number of different Christian denominations, the tensions were far from negligible.

The founders of Daybreak were Anglican and married. Many of the first disabled people to come to Daybreak were also Anglican. Links were accordingly established with the local Anglican churches. A very high proportion of the assistants, however, were Roman Catholic. They, in their turn, forged links with the local Catholic church. There followed, in the words of one of the early members of that community, 'the tremendous pain of living so intensely together and then on Sundays going up the driveway in two different directions'. The pain was all the more acute for the fact that everything about l'Arche tended to be articulated in terms of relationship, family and love, in a way which made the revelation on the seventh day that these qualities no longer prevailed shocking. Furthermore, the pain was even more intense if it was not quite mutual, if you were in the minority and 'out of step, not quite as good and not quite as religious'. Even in the United States the majority of people in l'Arche were Catholic. Not surprisingly, sensitivity to other religious traditions was at times slower in its actual practice than some might have wished – to the point where one community director at a retreat in Winnipeg was reduced to exclaiming, 'I feel like I'm a member of a Roman Catholic club.'

L'Arche had not set out to be ecumenical in the sense of consciously bringing together people of different Christian denominations or religions, any more than its founders had envisaged communities outside France. Nevertheless, in a number of different contexts the l'Arche journey became an ecumenical one because of the needs of its people in different countries, and perhaps nowhere was the call to become ecumenical clearer than in the United Kingdom, where the majority of the people with disabilities belonged, at least nominally, to the Anglican Church.

In 1971 Dr Thérèse Vanier, who had by then studied medicine at Cambridge and become a clinical haematologist on the staff of St Thomas' Hospital in London, took part in the Faith and Light pilgrimage to Lourdes. Having spent the very first Christmas at Trosly with her brother, she had been, somewhat discreetly, involved with l'Arche since its very beginnings. As someone of great compassion and understanding but equally considerable competence as a doctor, she had found herself intrigued by it but at the same time distanced from it by her professional training and certain reservations about its incompetence. When she first visited Trosly-Breuil she had been both attracted and repelled:

> The attractive thing was and still is the very simple attitude of just bringing people together who are very different and saying, 'This is actually possible.' What to me has always been the repelling side is to assume that you can go on doing this without more space for everybody, and I would include the disabled people. People need space and silence and other aspects to their lives apart from a constant movement from work to meals to celebrations.

Her pilgrimage to Lourdes was undertaken as a doctor in a group of people for whom she was medically responsible. In the course of it she found herself very occupied with a 50-year-old Welshman called Billy and his mother who was in her eighties:

> Between them they must have weighed about 30 stone. Billy had the most appalling asthma and his mother had chronic heart disease so both of them were in wheelchairs. I saw quite a lot of them and not just medically. It didn't take me long to discover that Billy's one prayer was not to have to go back to hospital and that his mother's one prayer was that Billy would die before she did, because if she didn't outlive him nobody would ever visit him.

At the end of the pilgrimage Thérèse saw them both off on a train to Wales and for a time, in the process of getting back to ordinary life at St Thomas', she almost forgot about them. A couple of weeks later she was informed that Billy was dead. He had arrived back in Wales too late to return to the hospital until the following day and during the night had suffered a fatal asthma attack. After the initial shock, his mother had realised that both their prayers had been answered. Furthermore the meeting with mother and son had touched Thérèse in some indefinable but enduring way.

She started working together with Ann and Geoffrey Morgan, a couple who had previously been at Daybreak, towards the opening of a community in England. At the same time she took up part-time work for two days a week at St Christopher's Hospice. The two roles proved to be complementary:

> It wasn't just remembering Billy and his story. It was the whole question of being with powerless people, people whose defences have gone or are going, who are confronted with reality and who confront you with reality. Just as the disabled person is stripped of many sophistications and concealments and adornments, the same is true of someone who is seriously ill and indeed of their family. Also in terms of the meaning of these people in present-day society or in the Church today, there are many common factors. Our experience in l'Arche and the hospice experience is that just as very needy people, very powerless people, can be a tremendous source of disruption with pain around them, so they can also be an incredible focus of unity when you begin to really care for their needs and when you begin to see the value that is there. The caring for their needs and the appreciation of their value really go together, because it's making a big demand to see the value of something that is alien, like death or like someone who is mentally disabled, until you actually enable people to meet it. We all need to be able to give if we're going to receive.

To Thérèse Vanier, with all her professionalism and expertise, the greatest gift of the dying or the disabled person was the way in which he or she could teach her her own incapacity.

At the same time, her work as a highly capable physician in the hospice was a relief and support to her in relation to life in l'Arche in which she professed to have no idea what she was doing. Thérèse herself was a Roman Catholic, as was Geoffrey Morgan. His wife, however, was Anglican, and the first l'Arche community began at the very heart of Anglicanism. Jean Vanier had been contacted by a French woman living in Paris who owned a house in Canterbury which she wanted to sell specifically for the use of people with disabilities. His sister went to view it and considered it unsuitable, sited as it was between a busy road and a housing development. Nevertheless, struck by the strangeness of the unexpected contact with the unknown house owner and uncertain of her own judgement, she asked Jean to come to England and help with the decision. Meanwhile the same woman had once again been in touch with the suggestion that if l'Arche was going to establish anything in Canterbury, they should first of all go and see the Archbishop.

On a cold and snowy New Year's Day in 1972 Thérèse and Jean Vanier visited Archbishop Michael Ramsey at his home in the cathedral close and told him what they were trying to do. The Archbishop, eager to help, put them in touch with the Anglican authorities who would give them first refusal on any church property that came up for sale. Eventually they bought what had been the rectory at Barfrestone, a small village with an old Norman church ten miles from Canterbury, and 'Little Ewell' was initiated. 'We had been led to make contact with the centre of Anglicanism; we found opening up before us a whole series of friendships with members of the Anglican Communion and the hierarchy of that Church', Thérèse Vanier recalled. 'Curiously, it did not spell out to us at the time that of course our people would be members of that Church; we discovered that as they came to live with us. It is the only house in the United Kingdom l'Arche communities in which we built a chapel.'

A greater awareness of the ecumenical dimension of the new foundation, and the questions it would have to face, arose when a Roman Catholic priest, who wanted to spend part of his sabbatical year at Little Ewell, offered to celebrate Mass for the community. There were other l'Arche communities made up of different faiths where the issue of division at the Eucharist did not arise. In India, where the majority of community members were not necessarily Christians, the difficulties of finding a form of worship in which all could share would with time, patience and forgiveness resolve itself around the need to simplify what faith was really all about and link it to daily life. Prayer tended to centre on times of trial, when for example the community was without water, and times of rejoicing: the appearance of the first cashew nuts or mangoes. When water was first drawn from a new well, that water was drunk as part of the worship. People brought to the prayer the fruits of nature and their labours – a harvest of yams or a bunch of bananas – giving thanks to the One who had prospered the work of their hands as he had prospered the work of their hearts. Without seeking a superficial syncretic oneness, it became possible to speak of a profound unity which grew through the meeting of hearts in the little moments of the day, the shared experience of the love, forgiveness and mercy of God, by which they were forgiven and learnt to forgive and respect each other. In communities where not everyone participated in times of prayer, celebration was often found to be a source of unity – the celebration of local fiestas, of the gift of members of the community on the anniversary of their arrival, of birthdays – occasions which lifted people out of their daily routine, their fatigue, their tension and their worries.

In communities, however, where people belonged to different denominations of the Christian Church, each of which would normally look to the Eucharist as a focus of shared thanksgiving, forgiveness, repentance and reconciliation, and where the similarities in eucharistic celebration became increasingly apparent, inevitably the Eucharist featured prominently in their concerns. The initial vision had been of 'a Christian community', and one of the declarations of the Second Vatican Council had been that no Christian community could be built up 'unless it has its basis and centre in the celebration of the Most Holy Eucharist. Here, therefore all education in the spirit of the community must originate.'[2]

Jean Vanier's own more recent words reflect a similar train of thought although, significantly, related to that particular religious experience at the very heart of l'Arche: 'It is very clear to me that the Eucharist is at the heart of every community that is body-centred, and maybe every community should be body-centred.'

He was speaking of another of those 'gentle moments' involving a man who came to l'Arche in a very disturbed state:

> He couldn't stay still. We were using a lot of words with him, but then we discovered that he had athlete's foot and the doctor told us to wash his feet three times a day. There was a transformation. His language became more coherent when we were washing his feet. There is something about the touch of the body, holding the body, respecting the body. That is the initial communication. We forget that, and yet that is at the heart of everything. Somewhere that brings us very close to the whole relationship between the Word and the Eucharist. Then, as you touch the eucharistic body you touch the division of the churches, the pain, but then maybe you're touching the whole mystery of the broken body of Jesus.

At Little Ewell in England, with the gradual arrival of disabled people who were all Anglicans and the simultaneous appearance of a Roman Catholic priest prepared to celebrate Mass, the question of the position regarding Anglicans receiving Communion arose. In the French communities, with the permission of the bishop and local priest, Christians of other denominations could receive Communion if there was no church of their own communion accessible to them. At Daybreak in Canada, in the climate of experimentation that followed Vatican II, all kinds of solutions were tried, including that of a Catholic priest and an Anglican priest concelebrating the Eucharist. Some at Daybreak, however, found it hard to let go of the old order and join in the spirit of experimentation. There was also a general reluctance in l'Arche to pursue a path within the community which did not match what was happening outside.

To Jean Vanier it was part of the mystery which made the impossible somehow possible that within seven years of its foundation, without even wanting it, l'Arche had become ecumenical and inter-religious. In his covenant with Père Thomas and by his baptism Jean himself felt linked to the Church, born and reborn in it. In the Church he had been nourished by the flesh of Jesus and the Word of God: 'All that is good and holy in me flows from the covenant with Jesus in the Church.' As early as 1966, when l'Arche first went on pilgrimage to Rome, Pope Paul VI had welcomed the people with disabilities as people for whom God reserved a special role in the Church, and from 1972 onwards Jean visited the Pontifical Council for the Laity regularly. It was clear to him that l'Arche must not become either an exclusively religious community or a specifically Roman Catholic lay community. At the same time, he sought to ensure that it did not become another church in itself. When, therefore, it became apparent that in England, a country which was not predominantly Roman Catholic, permission from the Roman Catholic Church for Anglicans to receive the Sacraments at a Roman Catholic Mass would not be readily forthcoming, it was decided, with a certain frustration and sadness, that the idea of no intercommunion should be accepted.

There were other factors involved in the decision to conform to the rules of the Roman Catholic Church. There were potent arguments relating to the attitude and understanding of the disabled people themselves: people with mental disabilities could not comprehend the differences, difficulties, and regulations. Left to themselves they would disregard them. Why therefore impose incomprehensible rules? Why not follow their simplicity and directness? After all, they were leading the assistants in their own need for unity. Why not follow them? Offset against these was the fact that the path along which disabled people were happy to lead was sometimes determined by factors as random as which assistant they liked accompanying them. Monsignor Richard Stewart, who advised on ecumenical affairs in the Roman Catholic diocese of Southwark, raised the question of whether the families of Anglican disabled people who had permission to receive Communion at a Roman Catholic Mass and chose to do so, would approve of the idea. Might they not see it as a 'Roman Catholic take-over'? Shouldn't people with disabilities have a choice as to whether they wished to attend Eucharist in the Anglican Church if that was their Church? In the experience of l'Arche, disabled people needed to *belong*. Might this not include for many of them a sense of belonging to their own Church, the Church of their family?

The importance of building relationships between disabled people and their sometimes estranged families was recognised. Such links could bring healing to families who had often

undergone years of suffering and guilt because they had not had
the resources to care for the person with disabilities at home and
had 'abandoned' them to a hospital or institution. Sometimes too
the disabled person could be a source of reconciliation, drawing
different family members together. A similar idea of the place of
the poor, of people with disabilities, in creating unity between the
churches was germinating. In 1971 the World Council of
Churches had published a Study Encounter entitled 'The Unity
of the Church and the Handicapped in Society'. In l'Arche it was
felt that if disabled people had a role to play in church unity, it
was not for others to take steps on their behalf, but rather to look
to their needs within their own Church and then help them to
be the leaven within that Church.

To l'Arche in general it was becoming increasingly clear that
ecumenism was not just a melting pot, and that it was important
to help each person to be rooted in his or her own tradition. As
to the families of the people with disabilities, for some it was
important that their son or daughter belonged to the Church of
their origins because it confirmed their value to that Church. For
others whose own break with the Church related directly or
indirectly to what they had experienced as its rejection of their
child, a path to healing and reconciliation might be opening.

In Little Ewell it was agreed that Anglicans and Roman
Catholics would go to their different parish churches on Sundays
and that once a week there would be both an Anglican and a
Roman Catholic Eucharist in the community chapel. All would
be invited to attend both but there would be no intercommunion. Other communities followed in the United
Kingdom with other questions. In 1973 l'Arche was offered a
house in Inverness, Scotland. The decision to open a community
some 800 miles from the first United Kingdom l'Arche community might again have been considered foolhardy but an
American Roman Catholic working in l'Arche, Trosly-Breuil,
took up the challenge of initiating a community in a city where
the people with disabilities would belong to the Church of
Scotland, a reformed church with Calvinist roots. Expressed in
the simplest terms, ecumenical arguments there could rest on the
question of whether or not to pray round a lighted candle, let
alone the much more delicate issue of the Eucharist.

Very soon after coming to England, l'Arche had recognised that it would be inappropriate simply to translate into English the prayer of l'Arche in the form in which it had said by people gathered round the table in the first small house in Trosly-Breuil. The original prayer, largely addressed to the Virgin Mary, was rewritten for England in such a way that it was addressed to God, the Father, through Jesus, but still accorded a place to Mary. In Presbyterian Scotland even that small place was conceded to the Holy Spirit:

> Father, through Jesus our Lord and our Brother,
> we ask you to bless us.
> Grant that l'Arche be a true home,
> where the poor in spirit may find life,
> where those who suffer may find hope.
> Keep in your loving care all those who come.
> Spirit of God, give us greatness of heart,
> that we may welcome all those you send.
> Make us compassionate, that we may heal and bring peace.
> Help us to see, to serve and to love.
> O Lord, through the hands of your little ones bless us,
> through the eyes of those who are rejected, smile on us.
> O Lord, grant freedom, fellowship and unity to all your people;
> and
> welcome everyone into your kingdom.

Liverpool in 1976, London in 1977 and Bognor Regis in 1978 all saw the opening of other l'Arche communities. Their respective ecumenical journeys varied. In London, before the community opened, the decision was made that there would be no community Eucharists. People would go to their own parish churches. This decision was subsequently altered but at the time no one had the courage to impose or have imposed on them the pain of division at the Eucharist.

Amongst all the suffering and the sometimes negative reactions to decisions taken along the way, there was much that was positive. L'Arche in the United Kingdom was able to see its beginnings near Canterbury as an important sign. There was a constructive aspect to the need to find means of expressing community unity throughout the Christian year other than through the Eucharist. Celebrations and pilgrimages were prized as a means of expressing and living the spiritual values they shared. The creation and use of symbolism became a tool to express deep truths.

In the struggle to express Christian unity without individuals divorcing themselves from their own Churches, many l'Arche communities discovered the importance of a blessing during the Eucharist for those not actually receiving Communion. That the healing of this gesture could be extended beyond l'Arche communities was brought home to them in 1985 during a retreat given by Jean Vanier in the crypt of Canterbury Cathedral. During the Anglican and Roman Catholic Eucharists people came up for a blessing. Thérèse Vanier subsequently wrote[3] of how the Bishop of Dover had been touched by the fact that not only Roman Catholic lay people but priests were doing so:

> I remember also a mysterious little intervention by Robert from Liverpool l'Arche. Robert is Anglican and knows and values this because he goes regularly to his own local church. He is also used to mixed gatherings when he may ask for a blessing at one Eucharist and communicate at another. On this occasion, at the Anglican Eucharist which was presided over by the Archbishop of Canterbury, Robert presented himself apparently uncertain whether he was asking to receive Communion or a blessing. The Archbishop waited and had just decided that Robert was asking for a blessing when Robert suddenly put out his hands. He received the host, looked at it lengthily and broke it in two, handing one half back to the Archbishop and eating the other half himself. He then came back to sit in a totally different part of the crypt. I know this because he came to sit near me, where there was a vacant place at the end of the row on the central aisle. At the end of the liturgy, the Archbishop, visibly moved, came down the aisle near Robert.
>
> After the Eucharist Robert was taken to meet Lord Runcie, who was also on the lookout for him. Holding out a small quivering hand, Robert introduced himself: 'I'm Robert, Robert from Liverpool.' The Archbishop bent his 6ft 4ins

down to Robert's 4ft 6ins and replied: 'I'm Robert too and I'm also from Liverpool. Today we are brothers.'

Afterwards Thérèse Vanier reflected on the incident as one of both pain and healing:

> Few if any of us are likely to extend a hand to an Archbishop who is visibly moved, whether in compassion, solidarity or friendship. Maybe we need to ask ourselves why ... but for Robert from Liverpool, who had broken the host and given half back to the Archbishop, it was no problem. For the Archbishop I suspect this was a gift.

Some time later Bishop Stephen Verney remarked on how the inability of members of l'Arche in the United Kingdom to receive the Eucharist together had led him to some 'exciting insights' on how otherwise their people could be a eucharistic community:

> What Jesus said is, 'Do this in remembrance of me.' Did he mean just do the Eucharist in remembrance of me? He did not die upon the cross in order that there should be hundreds of thousands of Eucharists performed all over the world. He died on the cross in order that the truth of the Eucharist might be set free in the world. What he did in the Eucharist was actually take the bread, or as the Greek word says 'received' it, gave thanks for it, held it up to God to be blessed, then broke it and gave it. I wonder whether when he said, 'Do this in remembrance of me', he didn't mean us to do as he did, in the sense that we should take, or receive from him our whole selves, offer them to God in thanksgiving so that God may transform us, then break us and give us. To be a eucharistic community would then be to be people, not hiding behind the Eucharist, but saying, 'We're actually challenged to do these four things.'
>
> St John in his account of the Last Supper did not mention the Eucharist but rather the washing of the disciples' feet, as if to imply that this was the actual truth of what Jesus was doing. So perhaps the washing of the feet, or some other simple human action through which 'we take, give thanks, break and give', could actually represent the inner truth of the Eucharist.

While people in l'Arche obeyed the Church in the realm of ecclesiastical ritual, nothing prevented them from offering these ordinary actions to God to become extraordinary.

Jean Vanier and l'Arche had turned Bishop Verney's understanding 'upside down and inside out'. He was once asked to take a retreat for disabled people and wondered how on earth it would be possible. Afterwards he found himself wondering how on earth in future he would give retreats without them.

> For months beforehand we tried to think of themes that would be intelligible to people with disabilities and to do that I had to get closer and closer to the heart of the truth. During the retreat they mimed some of the gospel stories, and their mimes brought a freshness and an actuality to the humanity of Jesus. Then, after the Eucharist we danced. Seeing all these disabled people dancing and us dancing one realised somehow what Heaven should be, that we should all be set free to dance together. Whether we were disabled or not, clumsy or graceful, somehow didn't matter.

Slowly the importance for the churches of having disabled people in their midst became apparent. Canterbury Cathedral was never quite the same after a pilgrimage of l'Arche communities from Canada and the USA joined the huge Easter congregation at a sung Eucharist in 1974. This was one contribution to a general shift of attitude to disabled people in the Church of England, as in other Churches. Such contributions did not, however, need to be on the Canterbury pilgrimage scale. Paul, in the London community, was largely responsible for the introduction of the 'sign of peace' in the local Anglican parish church, because he consistently disregarded the provisional decision not to adopt it. In a multitude of ways the weak and the broken were potentially a reminder – to Churches inclined at times to lose sight of the gospel of the weak – that the poor could be a focus and a source of unity and love.

Doris, a strong-minded woman who was hemiplegic and had survived nearly half a century of hospital life and remained resilient, full of life but angry too, reminded Thérèse Vanier of an essential aspect of ecumenism:

Above, left: Jean Vanier in naval uniform
Above, right: Jean Vanier on board HMS *Vanguard*

Members of the Vanier family

Above, left: The village of Trosly–Breuil

Above, right: Eau Vive, Père Thomas' 'international work of the heart'

Far left: The Farm

Left: The foyer de l'Arche

Above: L'Arche Sydney on pilgrimage to Uluru *(photo courtesy of Cameron Cutts)*

Left: Maureen, Elaine and Kathy gardening in l'Arche Bognor

Below: Gordon and Jo of the Edinburgh community pegging out the washing

The meditation room at Asha Niketan, Kolkata
(photo by James Dodds)

Left: L'Arche in
Tegucigalpa, Honduras

Left: Jean visits one of the African communities

Right: Sharing a meal in the Erie community, USA

Left: The founder members of the Trosly community at Jean's birthday party in 1988

Above: Jean with Pope Paul VI

Right: Jean with Pope John Paul II *(photo courtesy of L'Osservatore Romano)*

Below: Jean with the Mufti during a visit to Syria in 2004

Left: Père Thomas with Mother Teresa

Right: Jean with Little Sister Magdeleine of Jesus

Left: Jean working with Kathryn Spink

Right: Henri Nouwen with Patsy, Elizabeth and Sue at Christmas in Daybreak *(photo by Paula Keleher)*

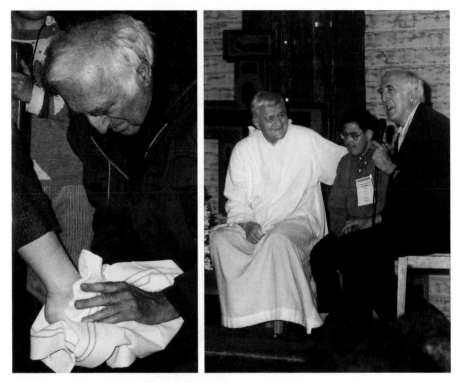

Above, left: Washing feet at a Faith and Light celebration
Above, right: Jean with Brother Roger of Taizé at Paray-le-Monial, 1999

Left: Cardinal Walter Kasper, Archbishop Rowan Williams and Jean Christophe Pascal at the International Federation of l'Arche meeting in Assisi in May 2005

She did not always know where to fix her anger and we were not always sensitive to her fears and wounds. She did not like people to hold her paralysed hand. One night at prayers we joined hands to say the Our Father and a new assistant tried to take Doris' paralysed hand. She had not been warned – that was our fault – she was too insistent. Doris got angry and stamped out shouting, 'I don't like the way you Catholics pray.' The focus was wrong. The anger was right. So much hurt within and between the churches as between people, has more to do with insensitivity than doctrine.

The need for sensitivity of this kind impressed itself with varying degrees of immediacy and intensity upon l'Arche communities throughout the world. In Erie Father George Strohmeyer acknowledged that it was only as the greater l'Arche discovered its ecumenical life that the Erie community began to pay attention at home to the fact that whilst the majority of assistants were Roman Catholic, some of the disabled people were Protestants. The Waterspring in Erie had both an oratory in which the Blessed Sacrament was reserved and a larger chapel in which the daily liturgy was held. That larger chapel was adorned only with a plain cross on the wall and an icon. On the table which served as an altar the Word was enthroned. 'Symbolic small beginnings for us, but we have to be constantly vigilant because we don't have any Protestant assistants and it's really hard for Catholics to think ecumenically for others.'

In a subsequent week of prayer for Christian unity, daily prayer services at Erie gave expression not only to different Christian traditions, but also to Hindu, Islamic, Buddhist and Jewish, 'in a real attempt for us to find our deepest communion'. 'Roman Catholic with growing ecumenical mission and vision' was the description to which by the end of the 1980s the Erie community most comfortably laid claim, but that description did not fit every l'Arche by any means. In time Jean Vanier himself referred to 'non-homogeneous communities'. Any attempt at definition even of l'Arche in London needed to accommodate the presence of people who were not necessarily Christian.

By 1985 a Dutch Buddhist in the Lambeth community experienced no difficulty in living Buddhist teachings in the day-to-day life of l'Arche: 'The teachings of Jesus and those of Buddha are very close together, so in that way I can feel that I can live a very harmonious life.' She had experienced a period of difficulty related to her need to find personal space and establish what time she could take out of community life for her own faith and in what ways it was appropriate for her to respect the Christian life of the community. She had left for a while but after a period of working in institutions and hospitals in Holland without the support of a community with a spiritual life, came to the conclusion that l'Arche was one of the few places where she could live out what she believed. It felt right for her to take part in the evening prayers in the house and often she joined in with her own form of Buddhist prayer to the beat of a drum. Her faith was treated in a very respectful way by the community as a whole, and especially by the people with disabilities:

> Most people in Western society ask what is Buddhism, why do you beat the drum and why do people shave their heads? – and before they have the answers to those questions they can't really support it, let alone join. But people who need no worldly explanations are very supportive.

There were those who saw the danger of the 'melting pot' as ever present, but l'Arche in general retained a sense of what the Churches were doing. Despite his earlier experiences of its human imperfections, the Church continued to be vitally important to Jean Vanier, essentially because it was the mystery of Jesus, Jesus rendered present in a particular way through Sacrament: 'The Church is what Jesus wanted for the communication of the mystery.' Ecumenism, he maintained, could not be divorced from the growth to wholeness within the body of Christ. L'Arche's position would always be unique in that it was, as one Canadian put it, 'not at a theological place but at an experiential place'. L'Arche members were trying to live the deep unity that is communion on a day-to-day basis. They were helped along the way by 'their people' – by Sulema in Honduras for example, who, by repeatedly placing one person's hand in that of the next and insisting that they greet each other, made lack of communication or forgiveness almost impossible.

At the same time they were not allowed the relief of avoiding confronting the questions, the escape into collaboration. There were always those who tugged at their hand and their heartstrings when the time came to walk in a different direction. Yet talking to long-term members of various l'Arche communities, again and again I encountered the sense of privilege at their close proximity to the poor whom they recognised as a path to unity, and if there was suffering in the search for communion in diversity, then suffering and the wound and its mysterious power for effecting communion was at the source of life in l'Arche. For those who wished to see it, the mysterious relationship between the broken bread and body upon the altar and the broken bodies of the poor and the suffering was ever present, and if there was pain in the division of the mystical body of Christ that is the Church, and pain in their own broken hearts, then that in itself was surely a form of communion. 'Slowly I discovered', Chris Sadler claimed of her life in Nandi Bazaar, 'how deeply I carry in my own yearning for God, the yearning of each one here, and as we become more one body, I sense a little bit of the great groaning of the universe.'

The extent to which l'Arche was being called to live in communion with the wider community and the world was becoming apparent in all kinds of ways. For the community in Choluteca there was something missing if the discovery of the spiritual treasure of the poor was not shared with their neighbour. From l'Arche's first arrival in the *barrio* the poor people in the parish made it clear that if the community was coming to Choluteca they wished to involve themselves in it. At the foot of the altar in the church, where once a month a priest came to say Mass, they placed a small basket with a piece of paper on it marked 'For l'Arche'. The parishioners had hardly anything themselves but what they had they wanted to share. With the pile of tiny coins collected during the first month Casa San José bought Felipe a pair of shoes, and the people of the *barrio* were proud of their achievement. The occupants of the other tiny houses viewed the community's comings and goings initially with a certain guardedness, but eventually they visited and gradually came to see in the life of the l'Arche house something to which their own families could aspire.

It was important that in Casa San José the community made

their own tortillas and cooked them over a wood stove rather than buying them ready made, because that was how others in the *barrio* had to live. It was important that despite the heat they did not have a fridge, because that gave a privileged neighbour, who did have one, the opportunity to offer them the use of his. It was important that, although in time, with the help of the board of directors, they could have bought a little car, they did not do so because when Santos, Sulema, Vilma or Felipe travelled on the local bus to the nearby town they met and talked to others who could in their turn see that the life of the people with disabilities at Casa San José was not out of reach of their own disabled children. In a society of broken families where men often had several common-law wives and children that were all too frequently disabled, the neighbours watched the little community living amongst them and saw a tiny model of what family life and the place of the person with disabilities could be.

In the small courtyard of Casa Nazaret in Tegucigalpa, amongst a number of frail and often underwatered fruit trees, there grew an avocado pear tree. In the early days of the house Nadine had been joined by Régine, another French assistant from Trosly-Breuil who had also felt a special call to Honduras, but they had had to wait interminably to obtain the legal recognition from the government necessary before they could take in children. While they waited, one night the neighbour's wooden house caught fire and with it much of Casa Nazaret. It was, Nadine was able to perceive, providential that the children had not been in the house at the time – the board of directors had been right to insist they wait – and she planted the stone of an avocado pear in the arid ground as a symbol of new life.

Not long afterwards, with the necessary repairs carried out and with government endorsement, the house welcomed the children Régine and Nadine had been visiting regularly in hospital. The small community had started with a fervent desire to be part of the life of the local people, but the presence of Raphael who had spent so long in a hospital cage, and of Claudia who was blind and autistic and who screamed day and night for a year, absorbed so much time and attention that the community became more enclosed. After a while it was realised that something was disappearing from their special relationships with the neighbouring people. Then Raphael, for whom the community had been founded and for whom they had waited so long, became more seriously ill. The tiny community had to live through his gradual deterioration and eventual death, but his funeral was an occasion of extraordinary communion between the community and its neighbours who carried it in time of trial, and between the rich and the poor who so rarely otherwise met in the tragically divided capital of Honduras. Raphael's death, and that of Sulema a short while later in another house built a little higher up the hill overlooking the city, brought communion with the community in the wider sense of the word.

Although other deaths and other sources of pain and suffering were to follow, the avocado pear tree grew and flourished. Like the increasing number of other l'Arche communities throughout the world, the occupants of the two houses in Nueva Suyapa with their tiny school and busy workshop became increasingly aware that they were being called in a very concrete way to recognise both that there was a universality in the call to drink from the cup of suffering and that they were being shown the mystery of death and resurrection. To Jean Vanier both of these realities were part of the path to unity and communion of hearts. If even the would-be followers of Christ could not drink from the same eucharistic chalice, all could still drink from the same chalice of suffering: the sufferings of division, woundedness and brokenness in our world. Unity for him would come round the treasure of the body of Jesus: his broken, risen body hidden in the Eucharist and the broken body of Jesus in the poor. And if at times little light was shed upon this mystery, there was always the example of Jesus' disciples who saw and felt only pain and failure and to whom it was not obvious how his brutal death could bring healing and hope. Sometimes, when intellectual processing did not help it was just a case of living with the questions and accepting the mystery, and in this too, as Thérèse Vanier was to write in *One Bread, One Body*,[4] the people with intellectual disabilities often led the way:

> The ability to 'accept' mystery is a sure way of finding meaning to life. Only by the acceptance of mystery can one possibly reconcile faith in a loving God with, say, the death of a child or young person. It is a matter of accepting something which is a

scandal and needs to be recognised as such, while trusting that somehow, at some time, the meaning of this mystery will be revealed. Those who have been able to integrate experiences of loss into their lives alongside their experience of dependence have acquired a certain wisdom and peace. They have acquired an exceptional ability to trust and to relate to God and others.

EIGHT

SERVANTS OF COMMUNION

> Jesus is the 'Good Shepherd' leading us all into oneness with God. He is also calling each one of us to grow in responsibility to care for others and to become good shepherds: servant leaders. This is a sign of spiritual maturity.[1]

JEAN VANIER'S UNDERSTANDING OF authority was based on the role of Jesus as a good shepherd as described in the tenth chapter of St John's Gospel. 'The qualities Jesus gives to this good shepherd are truly those that every shepherd of a community needs. Shepherds lead the flock and give direction. They must also "know each one by name".' In the biblical vision the *name* signified the person's gift and call or mission. Shepherds must therefore have a personal relationship with each one. They must know an individual's particular gifts in order to help them grow, and know their wounds in order to give strength, comfort and compassion, especially in times of pain. Shepherds must be bound to people with bonds of love and be ready to give their lives for them, sacrificing their own personal interests. Pressed to identify his own strengths, Jean Vanier referred to his faithfulness to people, the fact that once he had entered into real personal contact with someone it was something he rarely broke. He spoke too of the capacity to trust and listen. He also had a gift for drawing out the abilities and sense of responsibility in others, and giving them the confidence to follow the call of God into places where they might otherwise fear to tread.

From the early days of l'Arche he had tried to give others a role in the direction of the community. Early on at Trosly-Breuil he had formed a community council of six people to share his responsibilities and nominate heads of houses and workshops. He had also set up a board of directors which he later acknowledged he had regarded at first as a necessary evil but which in time he had come to value and honour:

> At first I just wanted to get on with it, and there were these guys asking awkward questions. Gradually I saw that I needed them for finance, for contacts with governments and so on, that I couldn't do it alone. Then I saw that as a community we needed them, that they could bring wisdom to the community and another understanding to the way we were dealing with situations. They were not just useful when it came to financial matters but also, in many instances, really knew what community was about.

The establishing of a good board of directors became an essential part of the formation of any l'Arche community, not simply as a body legally responsible for property, finance and other such issues but also as people who, if they exercised their authority with a real understanding of the vocation of l'Arche, could help the community to work through crises, define and set up structures and enable it to be clear about its established goals. As an external authority with an outsider's eye they also had a role in relation to leaders of communities. They were there to confirm, give support and encourage. They were also there to supervise and challenge when necessary.

The safeguarding balance of what Jean Vanier called the 'triple authority' of the priest or minister, the doctor/psychiatrist and the community leader or director, built itself quite spontaneously into the fabric of the community at Trosly-Breuil. The role of the priest was based very largely on Père Thomas's understanding of his place, not as a director and decision-maker in the community but as a defender of the interests of the poor. In a sense there was a parallel to be drawn between his role and that of the psychiatrist/doctor, for he too was there to defend people's well-being. Together they were responsible for the physical, psychic and spiritual health of individuals, which obliged them at times to adopt a position counter to the movement of the community as a whole, a movement which did not always allow an individual what was in his best personal interests. A further tension was moreover inherent within their own particular roles, for whilst they must protect the interests of individuals they were also the community priest and the community psychiatrist/doctor. The health of the individual was also to a large extent dependent on the well-being of the community.

There were at times uneasy complexities associated with each one of these roles. Although a priest who was answerable to his bishop might have slightly greater independence than the psychiatrist who was paid by the director, not all priests trod the path adopted by Père Thomas quite so willingly. Whilst, with the passage of the years, in many parishes and dioceses the presence of disabled people came to be appreciated as a gift and the influx of energetic young people welcomed, priests and pastors were not always supportive of their local l'Arche communities. Part of the difficulty arose because l'Arche communities did not fit into any preordained categories. If the community was not Roman Catholic, then what was it and under whose jurisdiction did it fall? To the problems of religious identity was added the fundamental challenge of the person with disabilities, who could be noisy and disruptive in services and with whom people outside the community might well feel initially ill at ease. There were priests who were themselves shy of people with disabilities, who could not open their hearts to them. Then, for the secular Roman Catholic priest the whole concept of a community, particularly one in which men and women lived together under the same roof, could represent an uncomfortable challenge to his personal experience.

Many priests and bishops of various denominations who grew close to l'Arche claimed that they found in it something which not only challenged but actually affirmed their priesthood. The ecumenical dimension, the simplicity, the way in which communities touched the heart, the relationships involved, the manner in which people with disabilities saw beyond the cassock and remembered them as individuals, the fact that people were hungry to be affirmed in the gospel, to be told that they were leading a Christian life – all these factors could give meaning to the vocation of priests. They could also be very demanding. Furthermore, to respond to l'Arche's desire to share the Sacraments and Word might be something radical. It was also something very small, based simply on relationships with little people. The unpretentious role of the priest or pastor as servant of the poor was one to which some subscribed more readily than others.

Yet the desire to be a Christian community had meant that, in 1965, almost immediately after approaching a secular authority and forming an association, Jean Vanier had gone to the then Bishop of Beauvais to speak about l'Arche and express his desire to be in communion with him. He had subsequently been greatly touched and encouraged by the bishop's friendship and eventual retirement to a small house in Trosly. Thereafter he made similar approaches to the local bishop each time a new foundation was being formed. Invariably the response was one of interest and support. Some communities were actually founded by priests, but although l'Arche gradually discovered a more active model than the hidden, contemplative, mystical one set by Père Thomas, it always encouraged priest-founders in time to leave the role of community leader and assume a more spiritual role. It was Jean Vanier's belief that,

> … to live in l'Arche we have to espouse gospel values. That means a *metanoia*, a conversion at such a depth that it isn't just a question of knowledge of Christ but rather of espousing the vision of Christ. This is so contrary to anything of this world that we need the Holy Spirit. The role of the priest as a man of God, who is close to each person and who brings the Sacrament, is to be a constant reminder of the spiritual dimension to our lives. And where there is a priest who really understands the gift of the poor as people who receive with the greatest simplicity the message of Christ, he has a very specific role.

In 1978 two former assistants were ordained in Compiègne to be priests in l'Arche but also to have a ministry in the diocese. Both experienced some difficulty in finding an appropriate role within their respective l'Arche communities. Thereafter other bishops in France and Belgium accompanied other young people in their preparation for the priesthood in and for l'Arche. These ordinations were taken as a welcome confirmation of the Church's acceptance of l'Arche. The role of the priest in l'Arche, however, remained one subject to evaluation and discovery. In time a distinction was drawn between priests 'of' l'Arche and priests 'for' l'Arche. Priests of l'Arche were those whose main ministry was in a l'Arche community. Priests for l'Arche were those who exercised a ministry in l'Arche in a limited way for a limited time. Priests of l'Arche were called upon to help other priests in the region find an appropriate place within the communities. They also frequently took part in events, meetings and retreats organised by l'Arche. Some priests in l'Arche were also members of their community council and participated in the working out of the priorities and fundamental orientations of the community. In general, however, theirs was a rather hidden role at the service of the spiritual growth of individual members and of the community as a whole. It was sometimes difficult for priests to be accountable to the community and be called by it to growth and progress. Their area of responsibility was not clearly defined, and tensions could arise in communities between the priest and the director, the parameters of whose authority were also complex.

Because of the double identity of l'Arche, both as a community 'espoused to gospel values' and an establishment responsible to public and government authorities for the welfare of disabled people, the role of director was at very least a dual one. The very term 'director' reflected the need to denote a function with recognisable standing in the eyes of public authorities from which l'Arche received financial support and relatives who entrusted their people to the communities. At the same time this 'director' must also serve as shepherd and servant of the community. It was not always easy to find the balance between directing and ensuring a level of efficiency on the one hand and, on the other, the more pastoral role of listening, being attentive to those who suffered most and were not perhaps happily settled, and watching over the spirit of the community. There were times when it was almost impossible to unify the two aspects and it was not unknown for a director to sign himself 'director' in some correspondence and 'community leader' in letters to the bishop.

In essence the three roles of priest, psychiatrist/doctor and director were complementary, overlapping and subject to tensions both between one another and within themselves, in a way which safeguarded against overemphasis of any one aspect of life in l'Arche, against abuse of authority and against authority becoming too onerous, especially as communities grew in size. It might also be said, however, that the result was authority that was only weakly grounded. Ultimately its effectiveness depended on trust, respect for the other person's ministry and good personal interaction and relationships. It depended on each person who exercised authority recognising that authority in the light of the role of the Good Shepherd.

Although in the earliest years Jean Vanier did not articulate his understanding in quite that way, somewhere at each level of authority and responsibility was the idea of authority and responsibility exercised as a servant of God's plan of communion. In *Community and Growth* (1989 edition) he rendered that idea explicit:

> Yes, the leader's role is to facilitate communion: a community is fundamentally more a place of communion than a place of collaboration. If the leader or prior is a servant of communion, then he or she must be a person of communion, seeking communion with the Father and communion with people. Then the leader will create space for communion in the community. We must remember that all of us, and not only the leader, are called to be servants of communion.

Within this framework there was, even in the 1960s and 1970s when Jean Vanier was often absent from Trosly-Breuil for six months of the year or more, still scope for his charisma and personal authority to carry considerable weight. Despite his early formation of the community council, by his own admission he had known how to weigh up the balance on the council even in relation to differences of opinion between himself and Père Thomas and ensure that what he felt was right for the community was implemented. The structures at Trosly had remained fairly vertical and hierarchical, and people still referred directly to him and found their support and authority in him. It was Jean Vanier who drew up the agendas and ran nearly all the meetings. Consequently, when he was away the community awaited his return to settle most of its problems, and when he was in residence such long queues formed outside his room late into the night that he took to sleeping in a cubby-hole in his office. Finally, in 1974, in recognition that the director could not, while he was so active in other parts of the world, also direct the Trosly-Breuil community entirely on his own, a special meeting of the council was called to study how to provide for more collective decision-making. The meeting was approached with a certain nervousness. After all, it was to touch upon the role of the community's charismatic and much loved founder, and if sometimes people in l'Arche suffered from too much dependency, they were aware that they also found security in him. As if to confirm the need for greater provision for the future, however, shortly before the meeting the news was announced that Père Thomas had come close to a life-threatening cerebral haemorrhage.

For 24 hours the elderly priest had lived in the present moment, but could not remember what had happened on the previous day and had no grasp of the future. He had asked Jacqueline d'Halluin to go to Paris to get him a ticket for Lourdes but, when she telephoned to tell him that no tickets were available for the requisite day, he had no recollection of his own request. So normal was his behaviour at the time that the friends with whom he had just eaten a meal noticed nothing wrong. Nevertheless Jacqueline d'Halluin alerted a doctor. Père Thomas was treated immediately and the clot on his brain was dispelled. The incident was sufficiently serious, however, to bring home to the community the fact that their founders would not be with them for ever. The need for a deputy director to share in the director's responsibilities was confirmed.

A new constitution was set up in January 1975, stipulating that the council would consist of 15 members instead of six. All of these would now be elected by the core of permanent assistants, whereas previously the appointment of half the council had fallen to Jean Vanier as community leader. In time this constitution too was subject to change. In 1976, for example, a new stage was reached with the decentralisation of the houses into geographical areas. The main principles introduced in January 1975, however, held good, the general movement being away from a 'vertical' to a more 'horizontal' constitution, in the sense that at each level of community decisions were taken collectively, from within the group concerned.

A similar process was undergone on the international level. The second meeting of the International Federation in October 1973 brought together 35 representatives from a dozen communities. During that meeting two charters were confirmed: the specifically Christian Charter born out of the first Federation meeting and the Indian Charter. The Indian government had made it a condition that Asha Niketan have a charter before it could be formally opened, and it had of necessity provided for inter-religious communities. At the 1973 Federation meeting it was decided not to try to agree on one Charter which would remain vague at the Christian level in order to be acceptable to everyone. It was also decided to create a structure to sustain the links between the increasing number of communities. To this end a small council was formed around Jean Vanier, the 'international coordinator'. In reality, however, this council was never able to meet: the unity of the Federation was still maintained almost exclusively through Jean Vanier's regular visits to America, Europe and India and his personal links with individual communities.

At the third meeting of the Federation, at Shadow Lake in Canada in 1975, there were almost a hundred delegates representing some 30 existing communities, including the new foundations in Haiti and Africa. At this meeting Jean Vanier announced his decision to step down as international coordinator. Work began on an international constitution creating eight regions in the Federation, each with a regional coordinator elected for a three-year term. These eight coordinators, along with the international coordinator, a vice coordinator, and Jean Vanier as founder, formed the international council of the Federation which was to meet once or twice a year.

Essentially l'Arche was trying to feel its way towards structures which allowed for the decisions, vision, mutual aid and support to be dependent not on one person but on the group. For the person who first had to assume the role of international coordinator in place of Jean Vanier the step was far from easy. Sue Mosteller found herself suddenly not only director of Daybreak, having succeeded the Newroths, but called upon at an international level to step into Jean Vanier's shoes. She was satisfied that she was a good community leader but the international role filled her with a sense of inadequacy: 'I hadn't travelled very much. I'd been a nun in a convent. I hadn't read widely. I didn't know anything about other cultures. I was afraid of aeroplanes.'

Père Thomas was terribly anxious about Jean Vanier's decision to step down as international coordinator – so much so that he came to dissuade him from leaving and when that failed, went to the bishop to request that he tell Jean not to relinquish his position. Despite their differences, Jean Vanier's leadership still represented a form of security for the priest. Yet even with hindsight Jean continued to believe that the fact that he had stepped down and worked with Sue Mosteller was 'salvation'. For the first couple of years he continued to steer the international coordination from behind the scenes whilst trying to keep Sue Mosteller in the forefront:

> He was always pushing me into the centre. I couldn't speak French and I'd have to go and give talks in France. I would be so scared I was weeping. Jean told me the first thing we had to do was get the international constitution written, so we worked on it together. He would suggest where I should go and visit, and I just went.

Jean Vanier had a strong and exceptionally attractive personality and an understanding of what community was all about. He was caught up in a vision to the extent that there were those who felt that if they trod too closely on it he simply did not hear them. But hand in hand with that went the gift for engaging others in the same vision and a growing capacity to listen to others, rooted in his early discovery of the gifts of the weak. He had developed the ability to be extremely patient. Some might say that he was too patient at times with the wrong people, but his patience was based on a ready acceptance of the way an individual was at a given time and on an awareness of the fruits of waiting. Experience had shown him how people and situations could change. In general he had outstanding ability at every level. To those around him he seemed invariably to know how to go about things and, if he did not, he knew how to find the person who did. He himself, however, recognised relatively early on in the history of l'Arche (at least in principle), the need to take a step backwards and give others authority as part of easing one of the classic difficulties in the history of most communities: the transition from a charismatic founder. Looking back, he was also aware that almost inevitably he had gathered about him a lot of 'yes' people. Perhaps it had to be like that during the founding era but it had its shadow side.

By 1976 Jean Vanier was still director of the community in Trosly-Breuil. At a gathering of the more permanent assistants that year, however, Odile Ceyrac found herself nominated deputy director to assist him in the overall leadership of the community. She had been in l'Arche since 1969, had been previously put in charge of the Val Fleuri and had managed, whilst an assistant at Trosly-Breuil, to undertake more formal studies outside the community in the psychology and education of people with mental disabilities. All the same, she considered herself hardly competent to become responsible for a community which was by that time made up of more than a hundred people.

On the very day that she was appointed deputy director, Jean Vanier left once more for India. On his return she collected him from the airport, still looking to him to make decisions and give advice, but Jean fell asleep in the car. This was something he was easily inclined to do, but on this occasion he was ill. During his ensuing two months of hospitalisation and a further two months of convalescence, the community went through a period of unrest. Hitherto, even in his absences Jean had been very present. Whatever his official title, he had still been the person on whom everybody relied. His illness, following the period of Père Thomas' ill health, was very much an endorsement of the already recognised need in Trosly-Breuil to find a way of going forward and taking decisions as a community, if necessary without him.

Internationally also, his illness might be said to have achieved what his more deliberate attempts to prepare for that ultimately inevitable transition could not. As a consequence of it the Federation assumed a new responsibility. It was significant that despite Jean Vanier's absence the meeting due to take place in Africa at that time was not cancelled. It was he who had initiated l'Arche in Africa; the other Federation representatives knew little about what was happening there. Nevertheless the international meeting in Africa passed off successfully without him and it was probably crucial for future development that it did. Sue Mosteller remembered a point in the year 1977 when she realised that she did not have to be Jean Vanier, that her calling was to be different and that she could be accepted in her own right. In a multitude of other ways people were forced to get to work and assume responsibility regardless of how timid and apprehensive they were.

Following his illness Jean Vanier returned briefly to the directorship of the community of Trosly-Breuil, but in 1980 stepped down as director and asked Odile Ceyrac, who took over the position, if he could take a sabbatical year during which he would have no major responsibilities in the community. Someone at one of the subsequent community council meetings contrasted his leadership style with that of his successor: 'When you were here as director you would bring the problem and the solution to it and your role was to convince us the solution was right. Odile brought the problem and was silent.'

Jean's influence remained considerable but he did not again return to the role of director, nor indeed to any other specific role on the international plane. 'God,' he recognised, 'is giving me other things to do, moving me in other directions.' There were those who, even in 1989 when I travelled round a number of communities, still questioned whether he had really 'let go' emotionally. Although in the United Kingdom, for example, he tended to be known as Thérèse Vanier's brother, and although the dependence on him might be hidden, it remained real. Be it in Canada, the United States, Honduras or France, l'Arche had its own vocabulary which was all the more distinctive because it sounded slightly strange in English. Undoubtedly it reflected a community experience and undoubtedly language, as Jean Vanier himself was quick to point out, is an evolving entity, but the vocabulary of l'Arche was very much that of Jean Vanier: of 'journeys', 'passages', 'breakages', 'accompaniment', 'formation' and 'celebration'. Just as I met again in a multitude of subtle ways the hidden presence of Père Thomas, so I rediscovered Jean Vanier's words, his thinking, his mannerisms and even his distinctive laugh. And if there were those whom I met who had light this was still, it was suggested to me, very largely reflected light.

The transition to the new structures at Trosly-Breuil was not easily made by all. Père Thomas was a Dominican who thought most readily in terms of religious orders. He continued not to approve of Jean Vanier's efforts to assume a less obviously authoritative role. In his old age he could not make the change to the community's new way of living without some difficulty. He had always occupied a position on the council, but the larger numbers represented a greater trial in relation to his deafness. He found meetings in general difficult. There was also a generation gap for him to contend with and, in a community where a growing number of people belonged to different Churches or did not profess any specific belief, the whole question of the attachment of l'Arche to the Church he represented was not entirely clear. His role in relation to the community, though vital, was becoming even more hidden.

In 1971 l'Arche had acquired what had been a farm in the village, and Jacqueline d'Halluin, whose artistic and creative talents had been repeatedly called upon to refurbish and furnish successive houses, had informed Jean Vanier that she was tired. As an artist, she had never felt particularly drawn to community life. The moving from one house to the next and the constant new challenges had given her a degree of personal space that had made life in community more acceptable, but the time had now come, she felt, to create a place of rest for herself and Père Thomas. The farm's old buildings surrounding two shingled courtyards were turned into a complex of accommodation, library, oratory and chapel in which to welcome the many guests coming to Trosly-Breuil.

Since coming to the village Père Thomas had rediscovered his ministry. With his appointment by his religious order to l'Arche Trosly-Breuil all censure by the Church authorities had ceased. He had always been by nature a teacher, of theology in particular. For him to be able once more to give homilies was in itself a great gift. His years of suffering had fed his charism and this together with his own deafness had also made him approachable to all kinds of people who found in him one who listened with extraordinary compassion and was ever ready to lead them to Jesus, the Holy Spirit and the Sacraments. His message relating to the centrality of the Annunciation, Mary's openness to the Holy

Spirit, and the incarnation, what he referred to as the 'theologal' life in her, which all were called upon to allow to develop, was sometimes expressed in the kind of vocabulary which some found difficult to understand. Père Thomas felt so comfortable with Jesus and Mary that he spoke of them almost as if they were part of his family, and he did so in an unusually high-pitched voice which some could find off-putting. But beyond the words many sensed a message. They caught a glimpse of an inner life, a deep, mystical union with God and gleaned from him a greater sense of peace. Henri Nouwen once described how having talked with Père Thomas four or five times during a year he spent at Trosly-Breuil, he had found his vision immensely stimulating and learnt some good ideas about which he could write sermons, but how it was only later, when Henri was going through a deep spiritual crisis, that he really met the French priest. In a state of anguish Henri attended a retreat for the priests of l'Arche:

> Père Thomas spoke for a week and every day he wanted me to come to be with him, and suddenly I knew that in his presence some healing took place that had very little to do with any of these great ideas. I suddenly knew that he knew anguish as nobody else did and that he was no longer talking about how to deal with certain things but that he became the source himself, the place where grace was given; that he was so empty that when you were in his presence you were in the presence of God. I was in the presence of a holy man, a man who radiated the presence of Jesus in a way that, whether you were a believer or not, you knew you were there.

One of the founders of l'Arche in Erie also spoke of how following two interviews with Père Thomas through an interpreter, he had realised that he was best understood as 'enlightened', as one capable of passing on that enlightenment which is a spiritual and not mental, cognitive formation.

> It was a week or two later that I realised he had talked only in terms of Thomistic, scholastic philosophy and theology, in terms of what I had learned half-heartedly as a student of philosophy and theology. I had learnt it, but I hadn't appreciated it. Suddenly Père Thomas spoke in the same terms and gave it

all heart. For the first time I understood, because Père Thomas
was living it.

When the elderly priest moved into the Farm there were many
who sought, as Jean Vanier had done, simply to be in his presence
because he was in some mysterious way a powerful reflection of
the presence and love of God. It was hard for l'Arche to let
assistants go when they were found not suited to life in communion with people with disabilities. It was hard to part with a
person with disabilities who set fire to one of the buildings. But
for Père Thomas, whose heart was as large as all the world and
who always put the person first, it was impossible. The Farm
became a possible alternative for such people.

It may be true that what Père Thomas still wanted for Jean was
ordination and that he would have liked to see l'Arche develop
more along the lines of a religious order. Certainly the
Dominican priest in his habit, who was firmly rooted in the
Church of the pre-Second Vatican Council, for whom the religious life was the ultimate way to follow Jesus, and for whom
relaying the Word of God was the role of the priest, drew to the
Farm many Church people who were experiencing difficulty
with the upheaval and renewal occasioned by the Second Vatican
Council. These people were not always at one with what was
happening in l'Arche either. If, however, the Farm was set up in
a state of some tension with l'Arche's failure to welcome marginalised people apart from those with mental disabilities, with
l'Arche's ecumenical and inter-faith role, the need for professionalism, the role of the laity and indeed Jean Vanier's own position,
it also had a very positive and complementary role in relation to
it. L'Arche was what it was and Jean Vanier was what he was
because Père Thomas had brought to them his spirituality and
compassion, and in the atmosphere of peace and spiritual intensity surrounding the converted stables and outhouses, Père
Thomas continued to be 'eaten up' by people and constantly
engaged in those 'little conversations' which he recognised
without a trace of egoism, 'could go very far'.

For his spiritual son, greater maturity involved sacrifice and
renunciation in a number of respects. His departure from the role
of director brought difficult moments when his susceptibility and

egoism were bruised, although not, he insisted, too much suffering. Living the example of the shepherd who must be 'ready to sacrifice his own personal interests' and taking every opportunity to express his confidence in those who were in new positions of responsibility, he embarked upon a passage which would bring 'liberation' for his heart and mind.

NINE

MORE EARTHY AND MORE
HEAVENLY

THE PLAN, ACCORDING TO WHICH everything had happened so
swiftly, had also made use of 'the fragility of the person in it'. That
was the way God worked, Jean Vanier recognised – 'through what
is clean and what is dirty'. His own fragility was very complex.
He could easily become the naval officer, but behind the capacity
of the naval officer was vulnerability. Power in people invariably
hid vulnerability in a way which gave him occasion often to
speak with curiously vivid imagery of 'the wolf at the door of the
wound'. The wolf in each person was frequently orientated to
efficacy. What in his case, the vulnerability was behind the wolf
he was not quite certain. He sensed only that

> … in each of us there is immense anguish, a fragility which can
> come out in different ways, confronted by relationships that
> could lead to anguish, by people whose anguish reveals our
> own anguish, our fear of contradiction … You're never quite
> sure what is a power that is given you to go forward which
> shouldn't be contradicted and what is the fragility that should
> be contradicted.

In everyone's journey there were inevitably moments when he or
she went through 'breakages' or 'passages' in the process of bringing together the poor and the rich person inside each one. His
illness in the spring of 1976 was one such moment in his own
life. With hindsight he could see that he had been moving at a

speed that was much too fast for his body. The frequent air travel, the nights spent at times on airport benches, the contact with suffering in all its multifarious forms which he found himself 'carrying a little in my flesh', the strains of being constantly available to people, of being the bearer of the message of the poor to the sometimes reluctantly receptive rich, of sleeping in different beds in different climates had finally taken their toll. 'I wasn't listening sufficiently to Jesus in my body, and so at one moment my body said, "Stop".'

L'Arche had a way of calling for the body to be given appropriate recognition: in the understanding of the Church, in the formation of community, in the lives of individuals. It was as if Jean had in some way to live that recognition in his own flesh. He had contracted amoebic hepatitis, together with a secondary infection to which the doctors did not put a name but which was undoubtedly related to exhaustion and the failure to take proper medical precautions in tropical climates. During the two months he spent in the Cochin hospital in Paris he discovered in a more personal way the path of death and resurrection. There he experienced also, and possibly for the first time, what it was to be assisted rather than to be an assistant. He learned new lessons in patience, for the doctors were unable to tell him how long he would be confined to bed, and he very soon realised that it would take time in his weakened condition before he was able to walk let alone fly again. Jean Vanier professed not to have too much difficulty in accepting illness any more than any other 'breakage' in life:

> That doesn't mean to say there haven't been difficult moments, moments when I've touched anger and so on, but I can't say I am someone who has suffered a great deal. I've matured I think but I can't say I have difficulty accepting. I think there is something in me which gives me the possibility of advancing peacefully.

When he looked at the suffering of others he sensed his own limits:

> My capacity to bear inner pain or anguish is probably less than many others, so God can't give me too much. Of course he

can, but I think we each have our psyche which permits us to go only a certain distance. It has always been very gentle for me.

Confined to his sick bed, he did not lose the ability to exclaim, 'Alleluia', a much used exclamation in l'Arche, at the smallest intimation of good fortune. His capacity to find humour wherever there was the least potential for it did not fail him. The fall of the mercury after it had nearly burst the thermometer was cause for amused satisfaction. So too was the fact that his height had induced the hospital staff to provide him with the bed in which General de Gaulle had slept when undergoing treatment in the Cochin hospital: 'It's just a simple hospital bed, only longer than the others. Praise the Lord!' Nevertheless the message of the experience, namely to rest, was undoubtedly a sacrifice for him in which the regular presence of Père Thomas at his bedside was a necessary source of support. It was the first time in 12 years since l'Arche had begun that they had spent so much time together. 'He helps me to abandon myself, to be more inwardly silent', Jean Vanier wrote at the time. He also wrote to the l'Arche communities asking them to pray that he remain faithful and able to take advantage of this period of inactivity to discover a new 'activity' because this was perhaps the time to discover the Jesus who 'dwells in our hearts and asks only that we remain in his love'. In the sleeplessness of those hospital nights he had time to think of all those who were alone, and to recognise how fortunate he was to have so many brothers and sisters who loved him.

> There are so many people who are alone, hidden in hospitals, prisons, flats and rooms, so many rejected, wounded, unloved people. Let us pray together for them, and give thanks for all the love and peace that Jesus gives us, which unites us and which we are called to share. And at the heart of this unity and peace for all the 'Raphaels' of this world in whom the hidden Jesus is a source of peace and joy.

Jean Vanier appears to have emerged from the 'breakage' of this illness in a state of greater equilibrium than had previously been his. Thérèse Vanier was certain that the doctors advising him told him a few home truths of a kind that no one else could. The experience prevented him from pushing himself to quite the same extremes, from spending nights without sleep and completely disregarding his own fatigue. It also pointed him towards a more reflective role. It did not, however, prevent him from continuing to rush round the world.

New Year's Eve of 1976 saw both Jean and Thérèse Vanier knocking on the door of Stephen Verney's house in Sussex. Books had a way of finding their way into Jean Vanier's hands at a time when they were likely to strike a special chord of recognition. On this occasion the book was Stephen Verney's *Into the New Age*.[1] The title was a translation of the Greek words *eis ton aiona*, which occur like a refrain through St John's Gospel. Stephen Verney had written of how as humanity stood at the edge of a new epoch he believed that the new age could be entered for good rather than ill through the discovery of interdependence.

> It was a time when we were seeing the dawning of ecology, a time when new scientific insights were emerging. One was beginning to see the universe in terms of energy and matter being two ways of talking about the same thing. We seemed to be moving into a new world on that side; and on the Church side there was a feeling of great hope and renewal. In the Roman Catholic Church there was all the aftermath of the Second Vatican Council. There was the Pentecostal movement and all kinds of renewal in the Anglican Church. I was trying to write a book that would bring together the vision of a renewed earth and a renewed heaven with the idea that we at the heart of it could be very earthy and very heavenly.

In his foreword to the book Canon Verney wrote of how good and evil were interlocked in everybody and everything, and chiefly within ourselves. As people discovered their potential for good, they uncovered at the same time their potential for evil. The way out of this predicament was through death and resurrection. There was, he acknowledged, nothing new about saying this. What was needed in the crisis of this generation was a new courage in choosing it, new depth in feeling it and a new perspective in understanding it.

Deeply moved and excited by the book, Jean Vanier wrote a

note to its author that was 'so charming and so gracious' that Canon Verney felt he must somehow 'get to know this man'. They talked late into the night and saw in the New Year of 1977 together. Many things had struck a chord of recognition in Jean. There was the fact that the book had been born out of the author's personal experience of the death of his wife and was a witness to the life that is born out of death. There was the vision it offered of a new Church. There was also the assertion that at the heart of Christian community lay forgiveness and that part of the role of the leader was to assume the anguish and aggression of those he was leading and to be a leader in forgiveness.

If when faced with aggression or servility, Stephen Verney had written, the leader aspired to enable the group to live the life of the new age, then he must be

> ... one step ahead of the group in this very process of forgiveness which is its essence. That is to say, he must become more aware of the good and evil that interlock both in himself and in the group, and he must pass through the experience of death and resurrection by which they may be unlocked and transformed. This he will have to do not once, but continuously. As Jesus puts it, hyperbolically but realistically, he must 'take up his cross daily'.

The passage had sufficient impact on Jean Vanier for him to quote directly from it in his own book *Community and Growth*. What moved him above all was the statement, 'We are more earthy, and more heavenly, than we have cared to admit.' The sentence touched on all that was at the heart of l'Arche: upon the relationship between the body and the Word; upon the relationship between the poor and the presence of Jesus in them; upon the challenge and the gifts of scientific knowledge and the call to spirituality; upon the interlocking of good and evil in terms of both the community and personal experience. With hindsight Jean Vanier commented, 'I'd read quite a lot of theology, but somehow in that book human experience and the gospel message was being intertwined in a very beautiful way.' At the time, the relationship between the human experience of l'Arche and the theology and spirituality of the gospels seemed to him to be becoming more defined.

In 1978 a new house, La Forestière, was opened at Trosly-

Breuil, to welcome ten people with severe disabilities. None of them could talk. Their autonomy in general was extremely limited. L'Arche had begun with people who had a certain degree of ability. They had been able to work in the workshops. Some had even left to live independently in their own apartments in Compiègne. However, as group homes and workshops began to develop in France under the influence of various parents' associations, l'Arche came to a greater appreciation of the pain and rejection of those who were more severely disabled, those whose abilities were too limited for them to fit into any workshop programme or be part of a group home.

The welcoming of the severely disabled was a project which had long been close to Jean Vanier's heart. Fortunately, as he himself later acknowledged, his original plan to have eight buildings on the edge of Trosly to which l'Arche could welcome 80 people, was overruled by a group of permanent assistants. It was replaced with a more modest undertaking to have one house in Trosly and one in Cuise or Pierrefonds which would permit better integration into the existing community. The occupants of the newly-built and carefully-designed La Forestière brought to l'Arche a fresh recognition of the presence of God in those who could not speak and who could barely move their inert limbs.

It was in La Forestière that Jean Vanier requested permission to spend his sabbatical year. There he lived many of those 'gentle moments' with Eric, Lucien and the other men and women who, though severely restricted on the verbal rational level, and though physically almost totally dependent, still had a capacity for relationship. Though poor in many other ways, they were extraordinarily rich in qualities of the heart, yet really to recognise this required in itself a certain openness of heart. In their company Jean came to appreciate more fully that, in order to perceive all the treasures of Eric's heart, he must himself become poor. He must move into a slower pace of life, become even more attentive and ready to listen, be more centred and contemplative. Eric, whose loneliness was reflected in the tension of his whole body and who relaxed only when he sensed that he was loved, called Jean Vanier to greater love. Eric, who was completely blind and deaf and unable to speak, invited him to interior silence and to receive him in his silence.

After dinner, in the evening, the assistants would help the disabled men and women into their pyjamas. Then they would all meet in the living room for a time of quiet and sharing. Some of the men and women would sit on the assistants' laps; others on the floor beside them. They would sing, pray or simply be there silently, content to be together. If the rush of activity of the years of the community's rapid growth had left Jean Vanier less time than in the earliest days to pray in the little oratory or chapel, he was still in the habit of taking advantage of any given moment to find a contemplative stillness. He could, as another member of the community recalled, stretch out by the fire at La Forestière and manifestly be 'resting in God'. In such moments Jean Vanier loved having Eric on his lap. The man's slight form became more peaceful and sometimes a faint smile would pass across his face. As Jean acknowledged in *Our Inner Journey*:

> Eric revealed to me the mutual openness which is at the heart of l'Arche. He opened his doors, his person to me, to my person, to my touch. I opened my doors, my person, to his presence. He gave himself to me and I gave myself to him in service and a spirit of communion. We trusted one another. His weakness touched me and called forth love. These moments of communion are the revelation that God has created deep bonds between us. For 'to love is to win over, to establish ties'. As the Little Prince says: 'We become responsible for the one we have won over.' It is such a gentle thing to discover this covenant which unites us; to know that we are made for one another in order to communicate life to one another.

Yet there were also darker moments in their relationship. There were times when Eric or the other men and women at La Forestière would yell in their distress or hit themselves, refusing all relationship. Lucien's screams had a way of penetrating the very core of his being, awakening his own inner anguish. Initially hurt by the rejection, it was as if a part of his being that he had learned to control was exploding:

> I too became anguished. His closing up on himself would make me do the same. His violence and aggression aroused my own. And I was horrified to discover the sources of violence

within my own self, to discover that in certain circumstances I myself could do harm to a weaker person. At certain moments, I touched the sources of psychological hatred within me. I could understand how a human being could try to hurt and destroy another. I saw how the weak person can draw out what is beautiful in me but also what is worst.

The men and women of La Forestière were able to call him forth to new life, to tenderness, openness and patience, but they also made him discover the world of blockages, fear, hardness and even violence that was in him: everything that was an obstacle to mutual trust. Their wounds, he found, revealed his own wounds. He had known he was capable of anger. Once at a meeting he had really exploded. He could hold himself back until he came to bursting-point, but that was very rare. As a younger man the danger had been more that of cutting people off. Patience meant 'bearing with people who made you fed up' and he was aware that he could become impatient with people who had that effect on him. The experience of his own darkness as a consequence of living at La Forestière, however, was a revelation of a part of his being at which he really did not like to look. It was humiliating. But it was also part of progress to greater self-knowledge and led to the recognition of the importance of how people reacted when a relationship was no longer apparently a source of life, when it exposed instead their fears and defence mechanisms. He knew that it was vital that they did not flee it but continued rather in the knowledge that they needed the help of God and others:

> I can only continue if I recognise that God has created a covenant between Eric and myself. Because of these bonds we are responsible for each other. And if it is God who has established them, it will be he also who will help us to deepen them. He will give me the grace and the patience to accept my darkness and, even more deeply, he will help me to trust that it can disappear in his time.

The confrontation with his own poverty and wounds brought home to him, not for the first time but possibly in a more profound way, the impossibility of feeling superior to the person with disabilities. Brought back to the deepest reality and truth of his being, where divisions no longer existed between the 'carer' and the 'cared for', or the 'educator' and the 'educated', he felt he could come to be himself. He did not have to be the 'adult', to strive to be important or powerful:

> I no longer need to pretend to be someone. I can now accept to be the child I am, a child of God ... And now that I have become more realistic, and I hope more humble, I can enter into a truer relationship with the disabled person. I am his brother, a brother responsible for his brother.

Writing of his experiences during that year of living with the most severely disabled, he emphasised the importance for any human being of not denying the darkness within, and of the forgiveness which he had discovered more than ever before was crucial to l'Arche. He had also discovered how demanding l'Arche must be in encouraging growth: the growth of others and his own. It was not just a question of living the bonds of affective communion: the community must grow together towards greater autonomy, truer identity and stronger hope. At the beginning of Jean's time at La Forestière, Edith, one of the severely disabled women, had thrown herself out of her wheelchair. An assistant had insisted that she got back into the chair herself and a minor struggle ensued. Jean acknowledged feeling that the assistant had been too severe. Then, however, Edith had begun to make an effort and once she had done so the assistant helped her. Reflecting on the incident, Jean Vanier found himself asking whether he was as demanding with himself for his own growth, as he was with people with severe disabilities. 'I do not want to elaborate too much on this question of pedagogy and growth,' was his conclusion, 'but I am convinced that we have no right to expect so much from others if we are not just as demanding with ourselves. Each one of us has to grow in love and in fidelity.'

The 'passage' that followed the 'breakage' of his illness had brought him to a state of greater wellbeing, psychologically, spiritually and in every respect. He had come to recognise a need to be more completely present, not only in body but also in mind and heart, to the people with whom he lived at La Forestière, and subsequently at the Val Fleuri. He had also come to a new valuation of the simple, hidden life. The first disciples of Jesus – the twelve apostles who were possessed of a very creative spirituality and travelled from place to place proclaiming the Good News, healing the sick, creating communities of prayer and sharing – were not, it seemed to him then, models for life in l'Arche. Rather he felt called more and more to live what Jesus, Mary and Joseph had lived, and to deepen his life of simplicity and littleness. Jesus had lived for 30 years in Nazareth before he began to announce the Good News or perform miracles. Before entering into the struggle, he had lived like others around him – a life of work, celebration and prayer in a small town. He had loved the people and suffered with them. He had not exercised any special charism.

There was, Jean Vanier realised, immense value and even healing in the unspectacular. This was why at times he felt hurt when members of the Charismatic Renewal Movement wanted to pray over people with disabilities for healings to take place in l'Arche. He did not deny the value and importance of charismatic healing. Nor did he deny that healing took place in l'Arche. Certainly, he knew of assistants who had been healed of 'wounds in their sexuality' through the touching of the bodies of people with disabilities and through experiences of deep communion which, whether acknowledged as such or not, related to the flesh and the Word. But he sensed that the way of healing in l'Arche was through daily life together, through the covenant that existed between the assistants and 'their people', through a love that accepted all, believed all and bore with all.

He had confronted some of his own wounds at La Forestière. That same year he heard Fred Blum, a psychotherapist, give talks to a 'renewal' gathering of assistants who had been in l'Arche for more than five years, on the subject of the 'wounded healer'. Blum maintained that only the healer in contact with his own wounds could be an agent of healing for another person. Only if he had touched his own vulnerability would he be able to welcome the vulnerability of another. Jean Vanier's understanding of healing, like Blum's, was based on a common experience and recognition of a certain value in vulnerability. There were those who cited the example of psychotic children who became university teachers and directors of banks as instances of healing. That worried Jean Vanier:

… because there are plenty of directors of banks who are not actually labelled psychotic but who are so caught up in their own project that they are unable to be truly open. The only healing which seems to me to be true healing is the gradual opening up of people to other people in true relationship. It's not pedestal healing. It's not integration. There are integrated psychotics, people in our society in whom the barriers around their vulnerability are so strong that they are unable really to listen to other people or be peaceful.

A gradual deepening of his consciousness of the wound was to take place, in relation to that of other people and in relation to the Word made flesh as a source of life in the broken bodies of humanity. 'Can it be that as we touch the discarded, entering into communion with them, we are healed?' he asked some time later.

Can it be that in the bowels of the earth and in the mud of life we find the Word made flesh? Can it be that in all that is apparently ugly and sinful and painful we find a secret source of communion, a touch of God? Can it be that the Word made flesh is hidden in our broken bodies and flesh? Must we ourselves be broken so that the source of life, the spring of water may flow from our very brokenness?

In touching his own brokenness and shadows Jean had experienced in a profound way the truth of the claim that 'we are more earthy and more heavenly than we have cared to admit'.

In all this I feel very vulnerable, for on one side I have seen, I have caught a glimpse of the kingdom and the new vision of Jesus. I have even tasted it in my flesh and heart, but yet I am so aware of my own barriers and inner fears and am sometimes paralysed. By what? I do not know. I am frightened maybe by an inner world too broken, too terrible to be brought up into consciousness, where madness and agony and pain are intertwined. But yet I believe too that under all that pain there is a yearning for the kiss of God, a communion where we can drink from each other's chalices, and from the chalice of Jesus' delicious wine of the kingdom but also the wine of his blood and pain.

Whilst living at La Forestière, he was given a letter by the analytical psychologist Carl Jung to a young Christian woman in which, referring to the words of Jesus in Matthew (25:35–36), he wrote of how he admired Christians because they saw Jesus in someone who was hungry, thirsty, naked or a stranger (someone who is 'strange'), but that Christians never seemed to recognise Jesus in their own poverty, in what was 'strange' inside them, in the violence and anger that were beyond their control. Yet they were called to welcome all this poverty, not to deny its existence but to accept it and meet Jesus there. Jung's letter helped Jean to recognise that he could not welcome and receive Jesus unless he could welcome his own weakness, poverty and deepest needs.

The confrontation with his own vulnerability had drawn him closer to the mystery of the vulnerability of Jesus, which moved him deeply:

> The whole tension in the life of Jesus is his bigness and his littleness. The words around the Eucharist reveal that he wants to give his body to eat, which is impossible. People say, 'We want a good prophetic leader and here we have someone offering his body to eat', so they all leave him as of that day. Then there is the incredible revelation that Jesus is a lover and vulnerable …

Years previously, after taking part in retreats conducted by Père Marie-Dominique in 1958 on St John, he had been inspired to read John's Gospel from beginning to end, and gone on to read St Luke's in a similar fashion. There had long been a special value for him in relating experience to the gospels. Already in 1965 he had given talks on the Gospel of John, although their contents were a far cry from what he would write later in *Drawn into the Mystery of Jesus through the Gospel of John*. At Trosly-Breuil he often led a weekly sharing on the gospels. If the Word touched people it was firstly because Jesus was in that process but also because of the relationship of life to the gospels. Jean Vanier was wary of too much symbolic interpretation but profoundly struck by the way in which they were 'so incredibly human, so historical, so true'. Behind them was such an anthropology, such a vision of what it meant to be human. A 'blueprint' of reality was not quite the right expression but they fitted so clearly into what people were.

So it was that from the intertwining of human experience and the gospel message he drew his reflections on love, paternity and a multitude of other themes that had a specific bearing on life in l'Arche: on growth, on the yearning for God and the cry of the poor, on the importance of spiritual nourishment, on the welcoming of the vulnerable and of vulnerability, on the sharing of weakness and on celibacy. Contemplating Joseph in his love for Mary, it seemed to him that those who had been called to the celibate life had much to learn about the quality of their love for one another. It was important for disabled people, many of whom were unable to marry, to live and celebrate with assistants who had accepted this gift of celibacy in order to be able to create a family life with their people. By choosing celibacy these assistants were identifying more fully with the struggles and the suffering of people with disabilities. Through the quality of their love for one another, as exemplified by Mary and Joseph, they were called to strengthen and sustain each other in their choice. Joseph and Mary also had much to teach married couples. They were a model of a privileged and unique relationship which was also very necessary in l'Arche. Couples and families not only helped to integrate communities into the town or neighbourhood, they also brought to l'Arche a witness of stable faithful relationship.

Jean Vanier saw in Joseph a particular model of paternity, as the father of Jesus not 'according to the flesh' but through his love:

> He is more of a father than any father who has adopted a child. He accepted the responsibility of this fatherhood even before Jesus was born, from the day the Angel told him to take Mary into his home and to call the child 'Jesus'. Joseph became responsible for the Word made flesh, Jesus, so that he might grow and accomplish his mission of love.

The paternity of Joseph was of course unique and special, but it could still provide a model for those to whom disabled people had been entrusted. Many people with disabilities had suffered rejection by their fathers. It was up to people in l'Arche to call them forth, to be responsible for them, to liberate them through love, and to give them confidence in themselves by having confidence in them. In a way which reflected his own relationship with a father who had trusted him at a very early age, Jean went on to reflect upon paternity:

> It is an extraordinary gift. It implies a communication of life, a liberation of what is deepest within another ... A father (or the father figure) loves the other with a personal, unique love and desires his growth. There is a relationship of mutual trust between the two. They love each other. The father sustains, encourages, counsels, confirms and when necessary corrects. He knows the personal gift of each child and helps each one to find his/her place in the community and in society. A true father also knows that no one is perfect. He realises that in each one there are wounds, fragility, anger and depression. He is patient. He prepares, sustains and encourages growth. He knows how to forgive and comfort; he also knows how to call forth and challenge.[2]

The process of dying a little to his own project, of becoming more aware of the way in which good and evil were interlocked in himself as in everything, of touching the darkness within and living the truth of the resurrection – all these experiences enabled him to put the right words on the experiences of others, not only orally but in the form of numerous books and articles. Personal and community realities were given expression in his talks and his writing, invariably in the light of the gospel message, and especially in the light of 1 Corinthians 13:

> Though I speak with the tongues of men and of angels, and have not charity, I am become as sounding brass, or a tinkling cymbal. And though I have the gift of prophecy, and understand all mysteries, and all knowledge; and though I have all faith, so that I could remove mountains, and have not charity, I am nothing.

Jean Vanier had heard the cry for love that flows from the heart of people in need. He had seen that that cry was often mixed with pain and anguish, that the appeal for communion could unleash not only the love in those to whom it was addressed but also their hardness of heart and their fears. He had also recognised that even in communities that strove to develop relationships of communion there was loneliness. In particular, people who carried final authority were always in a sense alone. Many people maintained that Jean Vanier knew them well; not so many that they really knew him well, and there were times, some suggested, when he did not perhaps share what needed to be shared. Jean Vanier himself was not sure about the truth of such an assertion, but in any case perhaps it was part of the necessary reality/mythology of a man in his position.

He had never felt called to marry. Celibacy had been part of his original option for the priesthood which was subsequently endorsed by the realisation of how important it was for people with disabilities to have about them not only the secure relationships provided by married couples but also models which revealed an alternative to marriage. It was important to show that celibacy could be not simply a negation but something very positive. In marriage or outside it, men and women were called to love each other in a relationship of affective communion and not just to be collaborators: 'Where there is affective communion, fecundity and life flows from them, but where there is division between men and women all kinds of breakages follow – there is a breakage with the child.' Men and women towards the end of the twentieth century were moving into a world of collaboration rather than communion. Jean Vanier was not sure that people were really conscious of the gravity of the problem, but it was one which he began to sense deeply.

His vision of 'family' had grown to embrace communities and people throughout the world. The constraints of long distance air travel for someone of Jean's physique were undeniable, but he took to relating his own discomfort to the suffering endured by a Tibetan nun incarcerated in dreadful conditions, about whom he had read, and the people and the warmth that awaited him on his arrival justified the journeying.

As to his relationships with brothers and sister 'in the flesh', perhaps as a consequence of their all being 'rather self-contained', they had become 'close but distant'. As a child he had been very close to Bernard. They were close in age and had been the two mischievous ones, but Bernard had embarked upon a different spiritual path. He was an artist who had lived for many years in the village of Marcoussis to the southwest of Paris. They would meet sometimes, but the conversation had a way of running out. Michel, the youngest, over whom Jean had at intervals kept a watchful eye on his parents' behalf when the Vaniers' 'Benjamin' was a young man, had taken a degree in the field of education which had always been his great interest, and taught at university level. Married for a second time, he lived and would eventually retire in Montreal. His eldest brother, Benedict, who had become a Trappist and whom Madame Vanier saw as in some way the power-house behind Jean, he described as 'incredibly holy and God-filled but not a communicator'. For some years he was chaplain to the Sisters in a Cistercian convent near Quebec, but returned to the monastery thereafter.

With Thérèse Jean shared the commitment to l'Arche. He had also come to recognise the common ground between the care of people with disabilities and care of the dying. Underlying both was a profound respect for the person and recognition of the importance of listening to their needs, and it was to Thérèse and her experience of working in palliative care at St Christopher's Hospice that he attributed much of what he knew about the tragedy of many people dying in hospitals. In a way, however, they had always retained their big sister/younger brother relationship and both would acknowledge that they were very different in temperament.

'In a community', Jean Vanier maintained, 'you have a lot of deep relationships' and if the loneliness of people with final authority was their cross, he also wrote[3] of how it was a 'guarantee of the presence, light and the strength of God. That is why they, more than anyone else in the community, must have time to be alone with God. It is in these moments of solitude that inspiration is born in them and they will sense what direction to take.'

In the opening chapter of the same book he wrote:

> My people are my community, which is both the small community, those who live together, and the larger community which surrounds it and for which it is there. 'My people' are those who are written in my flesh as I am in theirs. Whether we are near each other or far away, my brothers and sisters remain written within me. I carry them, and they, me; we

know each other again when we meet. To call them 'my people' doesn't mean that I feel superior to them, or that I am their shepherd or that I look after them. It means that they are mine as I am theirs. There is a solidarity between us. What touches them, touches me. And when I say 'my people', I don't imply that there are others I reject. My people is my community, made up of those who know me and carry me. They are a springboard towards all humanity. I cannot be a universal brother unless I first love my people.

TEN

PART OF OUR BROKEN WORLD

THE QUESTION OF HOW TO articulate the assistants' commitment to loving 'their people' and living the mystery and gift of l'Arche arose out of a letter written from Haiti in March 1977 by Robert Larouche. The letter was born of his need to put his own relationship into words, and find out how others reacted to how and why he wanted to do so. He had reached a point where he wanted to tell Yveline, Joliboa, Bernadette, Raoul and Jean Robert, with whom he shared his life in Kay Sin Josef, that he wished to commit himself to them more fully. He wanted to respond to his call to the poor at a fixed moment in time: 'I would almost say a solemn moment when I can realise the depth of the commitment, seize it in all its fullness and then say "Yes" to it.' To answer the call of Yveline, Joliboa, and other poor people around them who were hungry for the Good News was to answer the call of Jesus. At the same time, Robert went on to acknowledge, he needed Jesus in order to answer that call with increasing fidelity. In the relative isolation of Haiti, he also felt the need for a sense of unity with others answering the same call:

> Through meetings and visits I feel closer to many of you who make a similar choice each day: the choice of a radical sharing and gift to the poor within the heart of l'Arche. I feel more and more dependent on you, and at the same time I need to associate myself more and more with that which each of you is receiving and living wherever you may be. I feel the need to be very close to you, not only as part of a spiritual community

(created through our mutual desire to live the spirit of the
Beatitudes in l'Arche) but also as part of a tangible community
which gives strength to each person and which makes us trust
each other more and trust Jesus who is guiding us.

Assistants from different communities were touched and challenged by what Robert Larouche had written. At the end of a
retreat led by Père Thomas' brother, Père Marie-Dominique OP,
prior to the international meeting of l'Arche in 1978, about 30
of these assistants gave voice to the bonds which they felt Jesus
had created between them and the poor, and their desire to
remain faithful to them. It was not a question of taking vows, or
of forming a group amongst themselves as in a religious order. It
was simply a public announcement of a deep call to give themselves to Jesus and the poor in their different communities and
their 'yes' to this call. It was a recognition of a certain spirituality,
that for them the poor were a privileged way to enter into the
heart of Jesus, the heart of the gospel and so into the heart of the
Church.

The word which Jean Vanier felt best reflected his relationship
with Raphael and Philippe was that of a 'covenant'. Exodus
(2:23–24) described how 'the children of Israel sighed by reason
of the bondage, and they cried, and their cry came up unto God
by reason of their bondage. And God heard their groaning, and
God remembered his covenant.' Then Yahweh revealed himself to
Moses (Exodus 3:7–8) and said,

> I have surely seen the affliction of my people which are in
> Egypt and have heard their cry by reason of their task masters,
> for I know their sorrows. And I am come down to deliver them
> out of the hand of the Egyptians, and to bring them up out of
> that land unto a good land and a large, unto a land flowing
> with milk and honey.

The covenant between God and the poor remained, Jean Vanier
insisted in *Community and Growth*. Communities continuing the
work of Jesus, in that they were sent to be a presence to the poor
living in darkness and despair, were entering into a covenant with
Jesus and the poor. Furthermore,

> ... when we know our people, we also realise that we need

them, that they and we are interdependent. We are not better than they are – we are there together, for each other. We are united in the covenant which flows from the covenant between God and his people, God and the poorest.

So it was that after Père Marie-Dominique had given his endorsement as a theologian to the idea, those who wanted to give expression to the relationship which they felt existed between themselves, Jesus and the poor he entrusted to them, were invited to answer 'Yes' to the question '… *(name)*, you are invited to live a covenant in l'Arche with Jesus and with all your brothers and sisters, especially the poorest and the weakest. Do you want this?'

Bill Clarke, a Jesuit priest who had spent a period in l'Arche and remained close to it, sometimes conducted specific retreats in preparation for those who wished to announce the covenant: 'There comes a point in a friendship when you and I recognise the relationship and determine to be faithful to it. By articulating this something happens to our relationship.' Until 1986 covenant retreats in Europe took place in France or Belgium and in the context of a daily Roman Catholic Eucharist. When ecumenical covenant retreats began, during which Anglican and Roman Catholic Eucharists were celebrated on alternate days, inevitably the question arose as to at what point the covenant, which had been recognised as closely linked to the Eucharist, should actually be announced. A solution seemed to lie in St John's account of how before he died Jesus washed the feet of his disciples. In ecumenical retreats, therefore, the covenant was announced on the last day during a paraliturgy of the Washing of Feet. As Jean Vanier would later write in *Drawn into the Mystery of Jesus through the Gospel of John,* having knelt down and washed his disciples' feet, Jesus left them his spiritual will and testament (John 13:34–35):

> In the Law of Moses, the Hebrews were called to love God
> with all their soul, heart, mind and strength
> and to love their neighbours as themselves.
> Here Jesus is calling his disciples not only to love others as they
>   love themselves

but to love as he – Jesus – loves them.
That is what is new. He is creating a holy sacred covenant
  between them.
They are called to live in communion with each other,
to share with one another,
to serve one another in simple acts of love and caring,
never judging or condemning but forgiving.

'Covenant' and even 'communion' were not, however, words that would strike a ready chord of recognition with later, less religiously instructed generations or people of other belief systems, and even for those well versed in the Christian faith there was something very elusive about the underlying vision of l'Arche: identifying and holding on to the subtle connection between the Word and the flesh; between the hidden Jesus and the broken bodies and wounded hearts and minds of the people with disabilities; between the silent presence and the necessary doing. It was a problem to which some of the assistants gave expression: that of retaining a real sense of the relationship between the poor as prophets for our world, as paths to unity and wholeness, and the small, humdrum and sometimes even distasteful tasks of their days and nights spent with disabled people.

Jean Vanier had from the very beginning stressed the importance of 'living with', of *living* rather even than experiencing, for somehow experiencing implied too much detachment. Living l'Arche was as elusive as the twinkle in Maurice's eyes as he accentuated his disability to win the sympathetic and supportive embrace of well-intentioned ladies. It was as tangible as the bathmat found each morning stuffed down a lavatory. Living l'Arche was the sudden appearance in the night of one of the 'folks' who had completely ignored you all day but who chose just as you were falling asleep to sit companionably, if unspeaking, on the end of your bed with no evident intention of leaving. Being stared at as you walked with Johnny to share a bottle of Coca-Cola bought with his hard-earned money from a Honduran street stall; the envious preoccupation with a visitor's wedding ring; the cooking of meals balanced to suit the medical and dietary requirements of people with disabilities; the careful administration of medication; hours spent assisting with exercises designed to foster the tiniest step towards autonomy; the launder-ing of clothes soiled because of limbs and mouths that defied control; deriving pleasure not only from a chocolate but from the shiny coloured paper in which it was wrapped; the endless repetition, at first welcome but gradually more irritating, of 'She's my friend'; seizures, sudden floods of tears and unpredictable rushes of anger or affection ... all these were part of living l'Arche, as were the broken chairs and glasses, the concrete reflec-tion of less visible damage to rejected hearts and restricted minds.

As Jean Vanier was at pains to emphasise, the poor could be a 'pain in the neck', not to be idealised: 'They come up to you and ask you the same question for the 150th time and they're touching your weak spot. They're weakening your walls and making you discover how beastly you are. And that nobody likes.'

Those who came to be assistants in l'Arche, be it in Brussels or Brazil, came for an almost infinite variety of reasons. They were drawn to the idea of community, to disabled people, to Jean Vanier or Père Thomas. They had read Henri Nouwen's, Odile Ceyrac's, Bill Clarke's, Thérèse or Jean Vanier's own books, or were in the process of rejecting all reading in the pursuit of 'first-hand experience'. They had drifted there almost by accident, reacting against something that had gone before or searching for something they could not really define or, in countries where jobs were scarce and money short, they identified in it some sort of security. They came with definite ideas of what their life in l'Arche should entail and they came without the slightest notion. They came for a week and remained for life; or they came for life and left after only a month. They stemmed from the country in which the community was founded or they were called there from the other side of the world.

The need to find local directors and assistants in non-Western countries was increasingly recognised, and in time in poorer countries the reins were gradually handed over. Globalisation, the opening up of the former Eastern bloc countries and increased opportunities for travel meant that assistants in the West could come from virtually anywhere. In London the assistants were English, German, American, Lebanese and a multitude of other nationalities entering a very different culture. In India and Africa and countries of extreme poverty there was fever and diarrhoea and physical discomfort with which to contend. Showers could take the form of buckets, meals could be beans three times a day. In other countries where l'Arche was counter-cultural there were the pressures of disappointed families and lost friends and the isolation born of the failure of others to comprehend. Among the assistants were students, religious, linguists, former teachers, psychiatric nurses, bankers, law graduates and people potentially capable of achieving the kind of professional status outside l'Arche which the world would more readily applaud. Some came with the approval and support of their families; some were indulged in what, it was felt, must be a passing whim; some had to face a barrage of criticism or silent disinterest when they returned home. Few found it easy to explain the full significance of life in what was neither a religious order nor an institution that could supply them with a good salary and job security. Often even approbation took the form of praise for a son or daughter who was wonderful because he or she was 'working with the mentally handicapped'. Many experienced the tensions between life in l'Arche and the world from which they came in quite a painful way.

When assistants arrived they were thrown in at the deep end, some never having had much if any previous contact with people with disabilities. There was the fear of hurting them, of not being able to cope with their needs once they had been identified, or simply of being rejected. There was the challenge of being suddenly required to cater for twelve or more people when there was little time in which to do the cooking, and starch and a number of other ingredients could not be used because the disabled people could not eat them. There were the complexities of living in close proximity to people of both sexes, the difficulties of choosing between a life of celibacy and that of marriage and, if an individual wanted to marry, the problem of finding the opportunity to build relationships not necessarily within the community which might lead in that direction.

There were particular pressures on women in male-dominated cultures and additional pressures on men in societies which measured people in general, but particularly men, in terms of their achievement, position and earning power. It was easier on the whole for women to find fulfilment in l'Arche than for men, perhaps because compassion was a primarily feminine quality but also because the lack of identity, the 'disappearance' entailed in a life made up of simple daily household chores and joys, in which choosing what coloured socks to wear could represent a major decision, tended to be more difficult for men. In general, there were the difficulties of relating to the other assistants in the house, which in the long-term was often more difficult than relating to people with disabilities, and to the community as a whole.

In time in many communities a system of trial periods in which the new assistant and the community could decide whether they were mutually suited was introduced. There would also be a system of accompaniment and support in which a more long-term member of the community was assigned to listen to and guide and share experiences with a newcomer. In time also l'Arche came to see that not only individual members but also individual communities needed 'accompaniment', someone who in a relationship of trust would listen, pick up the anguish, reassure and probably find meaning in the pain. Eventually it recognised the need for accompaniment of assistants ideally on three levels: work accompaniment to enable assistants to carry out the daily tasks entrusted to them, community accompaniment to help them put down roots and advance along the path of love and gift of self within the community, and spiritual accompaniment by a priest, pastor or lay person to help them to discover their call from God and deepen their life of prayer and communion. There was a time, however, when the need for assistants was so great that people simply asked to come, arrived, were welcomed almost irrespective of their suitability for such a life, and were then left largely to find their own way.

Inevitably assistants were often themselves deeply wounded people. They came as part of a broken world. Still there was a limit, as Jean Vanier had recognised almost from the beginning of l'Arche, to the number of people who had difficulty in relation-ships any one community could carry. In the words of one community leader, 'It is hard but there is something about recognising our limitations. We just can't be a boat for everyone.' At the end of the 1980s on average the London community houses were called upon to welcome two new people a year, who would affect the way the entire household inter-related. Usually people were taken from the age of 18 upwards but caution had to be exercised with those over 40, who were often idealistic and needed change but were not actually flexible enough to fit into households that demanded an enormous amount of pliancy. Eighteen-year-olds had to be fairly mature but could sometimes inject life into a community where the other assistants were predominantly in their thirties. Often they knew they were only there for a year before going up to university and for that year gave themselves unreservedly.

Older people with disabilities, however, did not always appreciate the presence of unbridled youthful vigour. Fifty-four-year-old Doris did not particularly want to live with the pace and enthusiasm of an 18-year-old bounding with energy. Nor was a person not yet in her twenties necessarily aware of what was appropriate for Doris. It was Doris' dream to be someone's child again. Her yearning was reflected in her taste for pink frills and bows. Older assistants tried to encourage her to buy more serious clothing as part of an attempt to encourage her to acknowledge that her mother was dead and she was herself an older woman, but when an 18-year-old took her shopping she came back with a bright yellow and orange flouncy dress. The complexities of people of different generations, dispositions and backgrounds try-ing to live under one roof were by no means confined to those of appropriate fashion.

Irrespective of all such considerations, people who came to l'Arche as assistants were sooner or later called upon to confront their own wounds. Most spoke of a period of euphoria, and possibly naïvety, during which the discovery of the gifts of the disabled people was paramount; many referred to a period of darkness, breakage and disillusionment with community that followed: 'You have really to be hurt by l'Arche, not just to be fatigued but to hit a wall of something you can't penetrate and then to say, "What does this mean and where am I?"' Often it was only then that what Jean Vanier had to say about suffering, growth and community gained a deeper relevance. There were those who did not remain to work with that experience, who left still dis-illusioned. For those who stayed, invariably it was a relationship with a disabled person which helped to surmount fears, which was in some way compelling and which called to change. 'When you enter into a relationship with someone, washing the dishes is different', claimed one assistant who came to l'Arche having 'discovered herself' when faced with the suffering caused by the 1982 Israeli invasion of Lebanon. She had previously been used to having a maid and a secretary. 'When you are doing the cooking you think of each one and his likes and dislikes, when you make his bed it is specially for him. My mother couldn't believe it – me making beds!'

What was it that wrought such a change? What was it that made Maria Conchita continue to give her time and services to l'Arche in Honduras? The first time she went to cook at the Casa Isabella, Brenda gave her a black eye and bruises. Instead of cooking she spent her time cleaning up the mess after Brenda had defecated on the floor, yet there was something so strong between them – she did not know quite what. At La Forestière Edith, who came to l'Arche, Trosly-Breuil at the age of 16, having spent all her previous life in institutions, touched the lives of many who had contact with her, not least Jacques, one of the men with disabilities at La Petite Source, who had a history of violence but who, as her godfather, valued and fostered the relationship between them with regular visits and invitations to meals, and extraordinary delicacy and protective kindness. Severely disabled, Edith had been given away at birth and, deprived of affection and attention other than for her most basic needs, she had resorted to vomiting up her food, tearing things or trying to poke her eyes out with a spoon. When first she came to La Forestière she used to beat her head. At times it had to be bandaged and her hands restrained even while she slept. And yet, in the experience of one assistant who coordinated the different houses in the region at Trosly-Breuil, she had the capacity to transform:

> Edith is a very affective person, a very calling person. She awoke all the violence there was in me. She would yell and scream with such anguish. It took two of us to look after her and I remember once I had been away for a week or so. When I returned I was supposed to be taking care of her, but all she did was resist and yell. She just wouldn't help herself and I got

really mad with her. Then suddenly I stopped, realising what I was doing, and started to speak to her properly. I took my time with her whereas before I had just been pulling her around. She became calm and she looked at me with a very deep serious look she has, and we started again. I found myself asking her forgiveness and she made the effort to help herself, and I had this overwhelming feeling of love for her.

Before I had been living a kind of inner revolt: Why them? One of them was only six days older than me. Why should he be the way he was? Why not me? Why Edith? What was the sense of their lives? To be successful you had to do things well, you had to get married. At least in the workshop people were doing something productive but not these people. Why did God permit it? Then suddenly I found myself loving Edith and with a love that was somehow very pure. You never know why you love people but this was pure in the sense that it wasn't because I was helping her or because she needed me but just like that, and in this very pure feeling for her I found that I could forget that she was disabled. We shared a sense of humour and I would giggle with her. That changed my life. If I in all my human weakness could love Edith then God must and, if God loved people like that, he could love me too. That was a very freeing feeling for me. For Edith it doesn't matter whether you're the Queen of England or a tramp. What she feels is how you are.

It was a gift which challenged, disturbed and made great demands upon assistants living with those who had it. In London, Paul too was highly sensitive and intuitive. For part of his life he had been completely out of touch with his family. By the time the l'Arche community brought him back into contact with the family about whom he had talked so much, his father was dead. His mother showed him pictures of her deceased husband in an attempt to make Paul realise that his father was no longer there and what that meant. One night during that period Paul came downstairs crying. 'I had never seen Paul cry,' Katharine Hall, one of the London assistants in the 1980s recalled,

> ... but he was crying his heart out. He came into the kitchen and said, 'I want my dad.' There were four assistants there at the

time and I said, 'I can't give you your dad, Paul. You know he's dead.' Then he said, 'I want my mum', and I said, 'There's no way you are going to see your mum at eleven o'clock at night. I can't give you your mum or your brothers and sisters', because he went through the whole string. His next words were, 'I want a glass of water.' Paul is much better now but then if he could get you to do something for him rather than do it himself, he would. So I said, 'You get the glass and the water.' He proceeded to fill his own glass which shocked me immensely. His face was still streaming with tears and he stood there and said, 'Can you heal my dad?' 'Heal' is not a word Paul often uses. I replied, 'No, I can't heal your dad, Paul', wondering where on earth this conversation was going to lead but he then said, 'Well, I know who can … Jesus will heal my dad'. He turned to one of the assistants and said, 'It's all right, Mary', and he went round and gave the four of us the sign of peace. 'It's okay, I'm going to bed now.' We were all so shocked, firstly at him crying, then by the question and really by the existential nature of the question that we couldn't believe he was going to bed, but maybe we needed it and that's why it happened.

It was good to face Paul's loss. Good too, to recognise that it was all right to be powerless in front of Paul, that it was not necessary to know all the answers. That part of those present which wanted to solve problems and be in control was being gently told that all Paul wanted was someone to be there. It was an important discovery: 'I cannot heal your dad, Paul. I cannot heal you, Paul. All I can do is be in relationship with you and be Katharine beside you.' It was also an experience which touched upon the value of the wounded healer.

Fatigue had long been a major and pervasive problem among assistants in l'Arche. Much of it was very understandably a product of the physical and particularly the emotional demands made by mentally disabled people who had been rejected or made to feel a disappointment by their families, who were not accepted by society, who suffered from a sense of having no value and who desperately needed relationships because that was the level on which they functioned. Living with people whose behaviour reflected their loss in the form of anger, aggression, depression and a multitude of other ways took its toll, as did an assistant's struggle with his or her own vulnerability. In some countries the ecumenical dimension produced stress, most obviously when two assistants were needed to see that the disabled people in the household went to three different churches while they themselves wished to go to a fourth, but also in less tangible ways. Finding appropriate space for personal prayer or intellectual nourishment required a strength and maturity of which not all were possessed, when the requirements to do other practical community work were almost constant.

Tensions arose because many assistants lived and worked in the same place. The lack of privacy in cultures where life in general was less gregarious could be a source of strain. Even if an assistant had his or her own room, the opportunities to be alone in it might be limited. Heads appeared round doors with small requests, anecdotes that must be urgently recounted, handiwork to be shown, beaming smiles or simply the need to re-establish the warmth of relationship and so fend off the anguish of thwarted desires and ingrown loneliness. Acceptance in such moments was sometimes a matter of salvation. It would be inappropriate and difficult to close the door, however great one's personal need for solitude. The door must be open wide to others too: to the visitors who came to the communities for a variety of reasons and not always with great understanding of what was going on around them. It was not always easy to muster one or more extra places at table, an additional bed and a welcoming smile.

One Saturday night at Daybreak springs particularly to mind. Brad Colby, the young houseleader, was left alone in the house with half a dozen of the disabled people, some of whom had decided they would like to watch a video. The video recorder would not work. Another had to be fetched from one of the other community houses. Popcorn and beer were an integral part of Saturday viewing. Brad set about making popcorn in the kitchen. A Japanese priest arrived from the airport for a few days' stay in the community. He was one of a group hoping to start a community similar to l'Arche in Japan and had come to see how things were done, but he spoke only half a dozen words of English. He was settled in front of the video while Brad went off to find him some refreshments. In between making popcorn and preparing a visitor's tray at the end of a long day, he was trying to make a stranger evidently confused by a very North American style video and a totally unfamiliar environment, welcome. It was at this point that one of the 'folks' decided to remove her clothes and carry them, naked but for her slippers, through the assembled company to the washing machine. Brad began tactful attempts at explanation to the newcomer, and all this under the watchful eye of someone who was there to write a book about life in l'Arche. I could feel only admiration for the way in which at eleven o'clock at night, over the washing up, he was still prepared to talk about what it was that kept him there.

There were the pressures from professionals. In the Erie community the people with disabilities were required to have 'goal plans' which set objectives for them and monitored their progress. Assistants had to complete paperwork for each disabled person every evening. They tried to do it when the 'folks' themselves were not present, but this often meant waiting until after they had gone to bed. Elsewhere, despite the value that many psychiatrists and psychologists placed upon l'Arche for providing the kind of care and support that flesh and blood families sometimes failed to do, there were tensions at times between them and those trying to lead a family life with the subjects of professional analysis in the houses. Many assistants felt that relationships should be natural. The professional who started to look closely at and label these affective relationships and at how the team of assistants related to each other could be perceived as a disturbance and a threat. Most assistants recognised the value of professional care but not all had great confidence in their own intellectual ability, and talk in terms of professional formulae could crush them. If the involvement of professionals was constructive in that they compelled communities not to turn in on themselves and forget the existence of other sources of inspiration, if they challenged communities in their support because they had other reference points and drew on other experiences, it was in the nature of challenges to be taxing.

The very structures designed to ensure the input and information of community members, not only in relation to what was happening in their own household but at the level of the International Federation, were also demanding. A Federation meeting held in Rome in May 1987 of 350 people from 82 communities, the highlights of which were a visit from Mother Teresa and a meeting with Pope John Paul II, adopted a new constitution which divided the regions into three zones. Two years later the number of zones was increased in order to bring better, closer support to the regions and through them to individual communities. All the same, the development of the common consciousness of a house, then of a community, a region, a zone and so of the extended international communities, took considerable energy and effort.

For some communities awareness of the international family was not really a factor. For Felipe in Honduras, who had never travelled beyond the nearest town of Choluteca, to grasp that he had 'cousins' in the community in Tegucigalpa was in itself a large step. For others in cultures more used to world travel it was easier to grasp the concept of an international community. The time and energy consumed by meetings on all the different levels could nevertheless be a source of pressure. Meetings were valued as opportunities to share and nourish, when each one had an opportunity to speak, and as times of listening, support, evaluation and reviewing each other's authority. They were also another demand on heavily overstretched resources.

Authority in itself could be a source of stress which some integrated more easily than others. In the early days of l'Arche in Trosly-Breuil, when new houses were being so rapidly acquired, and in other young communities, it was possible for people barely in their twenties to find themselves in charge of a household within months of their arrival. That meant not only being responsible for the welfare of the disabled people, budgeting for and ensuring the smooth running of the house, but also exercising authority over other assistants, some of whom might be considerably older or have been in l'Arche much longer than the houseleader. Authority in such circumstances, with the added dimension of the absence of the usual levers of kudos or financial incentive, could be an elusive and complex issue. The relinquishing of it, both for people who had held positions of authority in the 'outside world' and for those who had held authority in l'Arche, could be equally difficult.

L'Arche had developed a system of 'discernment' to appoint

the director for a given community. At Trosly-Breuil a discernment team was made up of the president of the board of
directors, the regional coordinator and three assistants elected by
the community. As founding members Jean Vanier and Père
Thomas were also included. This discernment team consulted a
representative group from all sections of the community –
disabled people, short-term and more permanent assistants –
firstly about the current needs of the community and secondly
for nominations. One nominee was then confirmed by the board
of directors who appointed the director for a mandate of three
years. At Trosly-Breuil the local bishop was also consulted and
invited to endorse the appointment.

This triple endorsement of the appointment could be, as one
director put it, 'a beautiful experience'. The more critically
inclined could view it as a cumbersome procedure which was the
necessary consequence of the inability to ground authority either
in the will of God or in more worldly bases such as finance or
the power and justification of the State. Certainly discernment
could be painful. Discussion of people, their gifts and weaknesses,
even when done in the name of the Holy Spirit, could feel at
times more like proceedings in Maoist China. Once his or her
mandate had been fulfilled, a person who had carried considerable authority could moreover find himself with none. Like the
servant who had been ploughing or looking after sheep in St
Luke's Gospel (17:7–10), he was then required not to expect
appreciation or rest but to feel only that he had done his duty.
Humanly speaking it could be very hard; children of fathers who
no longer held positions of authority could be cruelly uncomprehending. It was not easy to accept direction from one
apparently less competent than oneself, and even harder to accept
that he was more competent.

Hardest of all, no doubt, was the relinquishing of the role of
community leader on the part of founders who had felt called in
a special way to people and places of need, who had struggled and
made sacrifices to initiate tiny communities, who had been
through all the birth pangs, led the way through the early years
during which wounds of rejection and anguish had to be healed
before trust was born, and who were then called upon to die a
little to their own project. Yet it was recognised that the cycle of

change was important to any community. Each person had their particular style and gifts, and at different moments in the life of the community different requirements came to the fore. An outgoing director might still be young and far from ready to retire but, were he to remain director for the next 25 years, it would stunt other people's growth.

Underlying the cycle of change was the message that the individual's value to the community was based on who he or she was as a person and not on the role fulfilled or position occupied. It was, however, a difficult dynamic. On the one hand there was a challenge to nurture human growth and individual gifts, necessary if young assistants were to feel that l'Arche was something to which they could give their lives, and on the other there was the spiritual message that fundamentally l'Arche was about faithfulness to the relationships with the disabled people at its heart. Ultimately the poor in l'Arche were the 'elders', in the sense of the word as it was used in the early days of the Church. Based on the vision of Père Thomas and Jean Vanier of their own roles, there were no 'fathers' or 'mothers' in l'Arche, only 'brothers' and 'sisters'. The only real authority which attracted, as far as Jean Vanier was concerned, was 'moral authority'. Jesus had knelt at the feet of his disciples and washed their feet. By this simple gesture he had revealed the face of God and a new way to exercise authority. Because this way of humility and service was the mode of leadership to which Jean had aspired and leaders in l'Arche, after this model, were servants and because it was the poor who confirmed and everything should be done with reference to them, conventional lines of reasoning were frequently turned upside down. Ostensibly more capable was not better, city rather than country or vice versa was not necessarily better, nor was bigger automatically better.

This message was not always easily conveyed to people outside the community, even to boards of directors. In a country like Honduras, where the poverty was so great and there were so many mentally disabled people, it was understandably difficult to justify the need to remain small and in some ways 'inefficient' to the often wealthy people who would willingly exert their influence to raise funds to help many more people in a more conventionally efficient way. It was not always easy to convince people profoundly touched by the magnitude of the need of the importance of not sacrificing the quality of the relationships with the few in order to help the many, especially when many assistants themselves experienced difficulty in sustaining a sense of the value of such tiny, fragile symbols of an alternative way of living.

The value of boards of directors as pools of expertise was increasingly recognised and appreciated. In Toronto, when an institution for severely disabled children was due for closure, Daybreak was among the places approached to take the children concerned. Authority was given by the government to purchase what became the 'Corner House' in Richmond Hill but, having bought the house, Daybreak was subsequently told by the government that it was too expensive. L'Arche had purchased a house to provide accommodation for both the disabled children and the assistants who would live with them, but the government allocated funds per disabled person. From their point of view it was unnecessary for all the assistants to live in. The cost of the house in relation to the number of children it would take was thus too expensive. The possibility of selling it was mooted but the principle of 'living with' was not one on which l'Arche was prepared to compromise. An emergency meeting of the board of directors was called and it was they who were able effectively to convey this message to the government officials.

This issue was uncontentious. Others might be less so: that of the money spent on assistants travelling to international meetings of the Federation, for example. Board members sometimes did not recognise the need to foster the spirit of l'Arche and promote reciprocal support in this way, and contended that the money could be used in ways that the poor themselves would more readily understand. In the 1960s there was often friction between young assistants in scruffy jeans, who tended to be inclined to anti-authoritarianism and disinclined to cut their hair and shave, and board members of an older and very different generation. Those who came later were rather different. Even those who came in the 1960s, disclaiming the value of their degrees and skills, tended in time to rediscover the value of their qualifications in the context of community. Nevertheless tensions continued to exist. Boards of directors again represented the challenge of a different perspective. They were made up of valued, creative people who often had a very real understanding of the community and who, Jean Vanier felt, should be more honoured in l'Arche. They could also at times be a source of pressure.

If there were conflicts they had a way of resolving themselves through that same relationship with the people with disabilities. The passage of time revealed that the closer board members were drawn to the disabled people themselves, the more their lives were transformed. Professional people who had at first been worried by such considerations as the appropriate dress code for a meal in l'Arche and quite unable to relate to individuals in the community found themselves welcoming disabled people into their own homes and lives. Committee members sat through intolerably long meetings because they were eager to hear news of very basic personal relationships in the houses. Talented, capable people gave their services on committees for many years because even those sometimes laborious encounters offered a little vision which they carried into other corners of their lives.

If the assistants in l'Arche had a common denominator it was the desire to live an alternative culture in which the weak were not rejected but given dignity, combined with the desire to see this culture integrated into society. In other respects they were as diverse as the disabled people themselves. Not all who went to l'Arche experienced life with disabled people as a benediction; but perhaps it was true that those who remained must in some way at some time.

The question of who was going to live with people with disabilities and how assistants could be confirmed and deepened in their choice became a pressing one. It was arguably impossible to take on all that life in l'Arche entailed were it not for the fact that, in sharing the lives of disabled people, assistants came to witness the quality of soul which shone through their wounded bodies and the wealth of love which a poverty-stricken spirit could not hide. Perhaps it was that the assistants too were craving communion, that in each one of them also the poor person was crying out his thirst, pain and depression. In some mysterious way a reciprocal healing took place and at its most profound level it was possibly that healing which confirmed people in l'Arche. If assistants as part of our broken world were of necessity also wounded, then the question really amounted to, 'What is going to heal the wound in you and me?' It could be healed by a warm community, but even that was not sufficient. In the vision of Jean Vanier: 'Somewhere the wound can only really be healed or accepted in its reality through an experience of God.' People grew in the consciousness that they were loved by God and began to accept the broken body.

For assistants to be able to put down roots in l'Arche, Jean Vanier maintained, there needed to be a call from God, a call that gave them the energy to make the 'passage' from a society built upon values of power, status and riches, in which the weak and the powerless were cast aside as useless and disturbing, to a society, a community in which the values were those of love and total acceptance of others, and the weak and the broken were welcomed as friends.

Over the years l'Arche came to recognise the vital importance of renewals and retreats for assistants. Jean Vanier was fully aware of the danger of not giving them the space in which to discover anew that they were loved by God, that their lives had meaning and that the Father was with them:

> If the call is crushed by our work and by tensions, then the very energy which gives assistants power to befriend the poor and to see them in the light and presence of God will be lost, and they will no longer be able to live the mystery and the gift of l'Arche.

If many of the early assistants had discovered that they had been called by Jesus to do his work of love in communion with him, the challenge then was to retain the sense of that call and the mission given them and not to become too engrossed in the many things they had to do, not to become too caught up in their own project or in the need to prove themselves. Their challenge was to *remember* in a way which could transform the ordinary actions of the every day, through the process of taking, offering, breaking and giving, into something extraordinary: to remember that in the activity, the pain and the breakages they could turn anew to the Father; to remember that they were part of a plan of communion; to remember the truth of the Eucharist – 'Do this in remembrance of me.' When people touched their limits, Jean Vanier insisted, the opportunity was there to discover prayer, to cry out to God, 'Come', and to return to the plan of communion. The alternative was anger, depression and compromise. 'But to turn to the Father when we are broken and hurt,' he acknowledged, 'calls for a certain maturity of faith' and in an increasingly secularised Western world that maturity of faith could not be taken for granted in assistants. The man who maintained that it was not always possible to supply answers but that what mattered was 'walking with the right questions', was to walk with the question of whether l'Arche nourished this maturity of faith for a long time.

As the people with disabilities grew older it was often they who trained the young arrivals, they who illuminated the way. Of course there were still times when Marcia took to her bed and refused to get up, when Sam shut himself in the bathroom in a tantrum, swiftly followed by loud appeals to the Lord to help him cool down, or when people simply withdrew into themselves, unable for a while to laugh and share; but most of the disabled people seemed with the passage of the years to find a certain peace, a home, maturity. It was, in the words of Patrick Mathias, only 'natural not to like being disabled' but with maturity people with disabilities could find a 'very agreeable form of life, a good life'. Henri Nouwen, writing of his life at Daybreak, pointed out unhesitatingly: 'The weakest members in our midst are, in fact, the assistants. We come from different countries and our commitments are ambiguous at best. Some stay longer than others, but most move on after one or two years.'

As increasingly assistants came without previous knowledge of 'traditional family life' or even of what it meant to sit and chat over meals, it was the people with disabilities who moulded a motley group of strangers into a family and taught them the true mystery of community. 'Covenant relationships' were not one way but mutual. Relationships in the l'Arche houses, expressed through banana-telephone games at the meal table and quiet sharing at prayer times, quite often helped those with little previous experience of religion to perceive a real presence of God. What was more, as one community leader pointed out, to talk of the weakness, vulnerability and powerlessness of people with disabilities was by no means the whole story. In time the l'Arche communities in the United Kingdom would make subtle alterations to the l'Arche prayer in an attempt to reflect this fact. 'O Lord, through the hands of your little ones bless us' was changed to 'through the hands and eyes of each other'. What the leader of l'Arche Lambeth wanted to say about and to and on behalf of people with disabilities was: 'You are powerful people, strong people with gifts that are not just rooted in your vulnerability.'

ELEVEN

THE MUSIC BEYOND THE WORDS

IT WAS AFTER ONE OF THOSE long and leisurely lunches at the Val Fleuri. The conversation at the tables in the three spacious reception rooms had ranged haltingly but with animation from Madonna and her music and proposed costumes for a forthcoming fancy dress party to the progress of the crops in the vegetable garden and a healthy grumbling about a hard morning's work. Jean Vanier had outraged his fellow diners by pinching the last grape. The washing up had been done amidst much jostling and jollity and we had gathered to relax over coffee and a visitor's gift of a box of chocolates.

What did the men of the Val Fleuri feel should be said in a book about l'Arche, enquired Jean? 'Tell about our anguish,' responded Girard, 'about the suffering that is in my heart. About how hard it is when I can't sleep.' 'I've been in l'Arche for 25 years at the Val Fleuri,' interjected Jean-Claude, 'I came with my mother who thought I would be happier here. L'Arche is my real family.' There was a general chorus of agreement: 'L'Arche is my place. The Val is my home.'

'Write about Josiane's death' (the reference was to an assistant who had not long previously been tragically killed in a car accident). 'I'm afraid of death', commented Girard. 'For me it's hard,' said Dédé with a deep sigh, 'but the greatest joy of my life is my godchild.' 'Write about our anguish,' directed Marc, a talented artist, having reflected long and solemnly over his pipe, 'but also about our hopes.' 'About celebrations,' another voice appended eagerly, 'we have a lot of celebrations and birthdays.'

There were those who chose not to talk in front of the more than 30 others present, but over the next few days they sought me out and spoke of what was important to them: their families whom they visited or did not see; the mobiles they made in the workshop; holidays past or yet to come; the assistant who had moved to another house but whom they telephoned every day … and all, it seemed to me, not so much in the spirit of wanting to unburden themselves but of support and giving. Lulu's need to do something for others was the same as everyone else's. People who had known what it was to be constantly on the receiving end of attention, not always gladly given, were happy to be supportive. 'It must be hard to write a book about us', were recurring words of sympathy.

I learned to value the repeated requests for progress reports and the spirit with which people struggled with evident difficulty but enormous good will to articulate their thoughts about what they were living into my tape recorder. It was good to hear Pete in Toronto talk of his activities in the local church choir or bowling club; to be part of Ann's constant word games and to become her 'Kattee', to have breakfast in Erie with Andy who, prior to coming to l'Arche, had been one of numerous children adopted by a woman interested only in the government cheques they brought with them and who had consistently deprived him of food; to fold the laundry with my room-mate, Mary, and listen to her admonishing the community dog in the night; to hold Adam's head in my lap in the car to Orangeville because the journey had caused him to have a seizure. I found myself wordlessly appreciative as I was shown people's paintings, their knitting, their trophies for horse-riding or bowling, the pictures of them with the Pope or in Disneyworld, the photographs of past assistants or much-loved nephews and nieces.

For me one of the most memorable experiences of l'Arche was that of watching two young men eating a meal together. They were both in their early twenties, both dark-haired and bearded, but one was bright-eyed and in this world's terms good-looking. The other, with wasted limbs and a body that did not hide his suffering, was physically a distorted reflection of the first. Severely disabled, he could not so much as swallow without a guiding hand to close his mouth and tilt his head backwards. Throughout that long and difficult meal, what passed between those two was very much more than the small spoonfuls of food so gently delivered and so silently but appreciatively received. For me at that time it brought a new and potent actuality to the word 'communion'. Some years later, in a very different context, I ran into the young man who had been doing the feeding. He had left l'Arche and embarked upon a demanding and competitive career, but he carried a photograph of his disabled friend in his wallet and told me that he turned to it whenever he was feeling low or lost. It had taken him time, but now he knew how much this friendship was a source of nourishment to him.

It had taken time for Jean Vanier too to assimilate intellectually what he and others in l'Arche were really living in terms of the components of community life. So much had happened spontaneously, almost in ignorance and had only afterwards been discovered to be right or wrong. His was, he claimed, an 'integrating but slow mind'. In 1976, however, he had been asked to give four talks for four consecutive weeks on the theme of 'community'. The large church was packed on every occasion and he had begun to realise that l'Arche had something to say on that subject. All his early books, with the exception of *In Weakness, Strength*,[1] had really been created out of talks he had given. As early as 1964, when he had been teaching at St Michael's College in Toronto, someone from Griffin House had approached him to write a book. Jean Vanier had simply handed over his lecture notes. The result was *Tears of Silence*,[2] a work in his own distinctive kind of blank verse that came from deep within him, which he would years later describe as 'quite a lovely little book of meditative prose with pictures'. Similarly *Followers of Jesus*[3] had really been a typed-out and edited version of talks he had given to Jesuit provincials and other religious superiors in Toronto at a time when he was beginning to give retreats and become better known. *Be Not Afraid*[4] again evolved out of a series of talks given in Ottawa. All of them had been essentially on the theme of the poor person as a gift to be welcomed. They had sold well and been found to be useful during a period in the Roman Catholic Church between 1965 and 1980 which others frequently referred to as critical. Jean Vanier himself had not been particularly aware of the explosion that occurred within the Church following the

Second Vatican Council: 'I knew people were leaving but I didn't see it.' What he had been aware of was a hunger for the kind of spirituality which the life of communion with the poor in l'Arche was feeding.

Out of the four talks he gave in 1976 on the theme of 'community' had evolved the first draft of what he considered his first real book, *Community and Growth*. It was shown to the French publishers, Laffont, who liked it but suggested that parts of the final chapter be rewritten. Jean Vanier did not get round to doing so for two years, and when he did return to it he found it 'absolute trash'. Over the intervening years his thinking had matured. In 1978 he travelled to Fátima by bus. During the three-day journey there and the three days back he dictated for eight hours a day little snippets about community to different people who wrote them down in relays. Those dictated thoughts became the basis for the actual book which he subsequently began to order into chapters. In 1989 he worked on a revised and extended edition[5] which he was satisfied was much clearer. Jean Vanier's writings were very much the result of his life and commitment. As he grew and his understanding of what he was living deepened, so his books reflected that evolution. By 1989 over 20 years of living with people with disabilities had provided him with a deep well from which to draw when others were confronted with similar 'breakages' and 'passages' to his own, and from which to pass on the message that living waters flowed not just from the heavens and places of light, but also from the broken earth.

Fifteen years later the author of *Community and Growth* predicted that it would remain a reference book for some years to come. It was read everywhere, especially by novices in religious orders although, paradoxically, as was the case with many of his books, not very much in l'Arche. He supposed that was for two reasons. The first was a 'fear of the written over and above the oral' because of the insistence in l'Arche on the importance of learning through the process of 'living with'. It related to the understanding that at the heart of l'Arche, the real 'founders' were the people with disabilities. L'Arche was not like a religious order where everybody was obliged to read what the founder had said, and there was something very good and positive about the unconscious and mysterious vision that it was from people with disabilities that others must learn and not from 'above'. As communities sought more and more to integrate with their own particular cultures, there was also a touch of 'We don't want to be like Trosly and Trosly is Jean Vanier.'

Man and Woman He Made Them[6] had been written in 1984 because so many questions about sexuality were being raised both in and outside the community. A well-known figure in French literary circles who had a child with Down's syndrome had written a book which was somewhat critical of Jean Vanier, and stated in particular that his daughter was now happy because she had access to contraception. Jean went to see him and eventually felt inspired to write a book exploring the relationship between men and women from a Christian and community standpoint. Tackling questions in relation to whether love necessarily implied sexual relationship, how people could live with anguish and loneliness and how they reached emotional maturity, it reflected the way in which men and women who were often unable to develop sexual relationships could demonstrate what true intimacy was, how those who could not have children or live outwardly productive lives could show what true fruitfulness was.

From the vantage point of another 20 years' living and journeying Jean Vanier claimed that he would redo the book completely differently, in a more nuanced way, particularly in relation to homosexuality. In a world of increasing isolation and loneliness, he was not one to condemn two men who wished to live together in a deep relationship. For him the real question in relation to homosexuality, however, as in relation to morality in general, was: 'What happens when people become so immersed in one type of pleasure that it prevents them from discovering the pleasure of justice, contemplation and giving of oneself.' Too much was said in the debate on morality about what was or was not lawful, and not enough about where people put their energies and what was going to help them seek truth, struggle for justice and know God better. The principle behind so much moral teaching was that provided one abided by the law, the end was automatically achieved, but this was not necessarily so.

L'Arche remained firmly out of step with the school of thought which subscribed to sterilisation and the equation of the right to sexual pleasure with happiness. It was inconceivable in l'Arche that sexual relations should be encouraged without the enhancement of relationship and fidelity. The human heart was made for communion, that relationship first manifested between mother and child. So too was human sexuality. If, however, an individual cut him or herself off from his or her heart and the 'to-and-fro' of love, from the deep desire to give oneself in love, then his or sexuality too would be broken. The vital energies of that person's being were no longer orientated towards giving life to others but in some way turned in towards self. Self-centred hearts created self-centred sexuality, and sexual relations ceased to be an expression of life-giving tenderness but the selfish quest for fun and pleasure which ultimately proved empty. Only through true bonds with others in family, community and friendship did people begin to grow and become able to reach out ever more widely in love.

Even after Jean Vanier had stepped down both as international coordinator and director of the community at Trosly-Breuil, although the urge to write was often there the time in which to do it was not. Time had on one occasion been so short that he had been reduced to correcting proofs over the telephone from France to England. He wrote numerous booklets. He contributed regularly to the 'carnet de route', texts provided as a source of reflection for Faith and Light. Some books, such as the revision of *Community and Growth* were a matter of blood, sweat and tears; others were 'just given'. A case in point was *The Broken Body: Journey to Wholeness*, published in 1988.[7] A call to the reader to draw nearer to those who suffer, to follow Jesus on the path to wholeness and discover peace and joy by first accepting the reality of suffering, he wrote it in about ten days.

A Door of Hope – The Transformation of Pain[8] brought together texts indicating the philosophy behind l'Arche, more 'theoretical', contemplative passages on the spirituality of l'Arche and descriptive writings about daily life within the communities. In poetry and prose it pointed to a creator God who longed to transform people as they learned to live in true acceptance of each other's humanity. Other compilations extracted from Jean's talks and texts were assembled and translated into a growing number of languages, and often when he recognised the need for a message or was prompted by a publisher or someone else, he made the time to write more substantial works in his miniscule hand-writing, in French or in English, on paper supported on his lap. Those books which came from deepest within him were frequently structured in a somewhat unusual way, a fact which he felt irritated some, for he wrote as if in diminishing circles which spiralled down, trying to pick up threads and delving ever deeper. Yet it was through his books, rather than through direct personal contact, that a growing number of people had access to him and to the message of his life, and as if as a consequence of his awareness of this his writings became more personally revealing.

In 1997 *Our Journey Home*[9] which sought to highlight the common humanity shared by all, regardless of faith, gifts or handicaps, reflected on what it was to be human beyond the barriers separating strong and weak, races and nations, rich and poor. It was the fruit of his growing sense of anthropology. He had been asked to write something on the subject by the French publisher Plon. By then, he claimed, he was moving into the last stage of his life and chose to write very simply about what life had taught him, about what he believed and about his own jour-ney home. It went almost without saying that central to his thinking about human beings was communion, his understand-ing of which he attributed to Père Thomas, whose thinking was rooted in that of St Thomas Aquinas but who at the same time had great respect for the human sciences. This book, which was possibly the most autobiographical of any of his works to date, although by no means an autobiography, also reflected Jean Vanier's growing readiness to recount some of the experiences of his life in order to help others who were searching, suffering and seeking to love.

In it he wrote of how 'A bereavement is the loss of someone or something vital, who or which fills our spirit and heart, brings us alive and calls forth energies.' Their loss left an inner emptiness, disorientation and confusion when energies were no longer called forth. Emptiness or boredom turned into anguish. 'If we are to welcome the great bereavements of old age and death, we need to pass through stages, to have learnt to welcome all the little bereavements which begin early on in life and continue to occur throughout.' The process began with birth itself which was a moment of anguish and loss of security, but life urged the baby forward until the birth of a brother or sister meant the loss of his or her place as the centre of their parents' attention. Once again this was a point at which the child could be plunged into anguish, anger or rebellion, but it could also be a moment of growth, helping him or her to advance towards greater autonomy. And so the process of loss and potential anguish and growth went on.

Jean Vanier too had passed through times of grief, emptiness and inner pain. Obviously he was not exempt from the kind of grief which people suffered when 'Life is no longer before us, it is behind us. We discover that we cannot dream as we did before. Choices have been made, and the opportunities for change and for a new life have narrowed considerably.' There were other obvious losses. Neither Raphael nor Philippe, the two men with whom he had begun l'Arche, remained at Trosly-Breuil.

Philippe had been happy initially to be in the village because it represented such a change from the asylum, but he was a city man at heart. He loved to walk in congested streets, window-shop or go to the cinema and he found the lack of activity in Trosly hard to take. When therefore a community began in the nearby city of Compiègne he had been given the opportunity initially to try it for weekends and then to choose. He elected to leave and was happier in the busier atmosphere of Compiègne.

As the community grew larger Raphael in his advancing years found it hard to cope with the influx of new people. He was given the opportunity to go and spend weekends in other communities. In the smaller rural community of La Rose des Vents in Verpillières, half an hour's journey from Trosly-Breuil, he seemed to be more peaceful and so was given the option of living there. He chose to do so. It was a decision which was accepted with sadness on the part of those who from the beginning had felt so specially bonded to him, but it was accepted nonetheless. He retired in 1988 but continued to help out at home and to go to the occupational therapy workshop a few afternoons a week. His health declined and he was admitted to hospital in March 2003 where he died at the age of 74. His death occasioned in Jean Vanier a great sense of loss and also 'a little element of guilt' because life was such that he had not seen as much of him as he would have liked.

In January 1991 Père Thomas also chose to leave Trosly-Breuil. Jean Vanier was not entirely sure why but felt it might have had something to do with the fact that he could no longer cope with being surrounded by people in the way that he was at the Farm. His nature was such that he would never have been able to refuse those who called upon his energy and spiritual resources. He went instead to spend the last years of his life in the community founded by his brother, Père Marie-Dominique. The decision was in Jean Vanier's eyes 'painful but right'.

That same year saw the death of Madame Vanier. In *Our Journey Home* Jean Vanier mentioned having been privileged to be close to two people in their old age, his mother and Père Thomas. Both of them had been in many ways full of peace and serenity, welcoming reality and other people, and above all those who were distressed or lonely. 'But how both of them suffered, and how they were sometimes filled with anguish during the last months and years of their lives!' During his mother's final years her eye-sight had deteriorated to the point where she could no longer read, she had become weaker, had trouble walking and could not dress herself. She had continued to welcome and help assistants but in between visits time had hung heavily on her hands. Again, even in the pain Jean Vanier was able to perceive a certain grace. His mother's death was swift and almost unexpected despite her 92 years. Two days after medical tests revealed cancer of the intestine, she lost consciousness and very swiftly thereafter quite simply stopped breathing. For someone who had dreaded having to confront suffering and protracted illness, her departure was, in the words of her son, 'wonderful, if a bit too fast for us her children, and for the community'. Madame Vanier was buried beside her husband in the Citadelle, in Quebec. After her death the preparation of the necessary documents for a cause for her beatification was included with his.

Père Thomas died on 4 February 1993. Not long before his death Jean Vanier went to visit him. The priest who had had so profound an understanding of the pain of people with disabilities was himself in a state of anguish. Before Jean Vanier left, however, the two men were able to pray together peacefully. The loss of his spiritual father was an experience that touched Jean 'more deeply than he could ever have imagined'. L'Arche was given permission to bury him at the Farm and his funeral at Trosly, presided over by the Bishop of Compiègne and attended by 1,300 people, was in a sense a homecoming. Jean Vanier spoke then of how all Père Thomas's theology had been modified by the presence and message of the poor. He cited the stigmatist, Marthe Robin who had once said of Père Thomas that he was 'all heart', and called to mind the 'something' in the priest that had drawn people to God. Jean Vanier saw the mystery of his companion of so many years as that of a root, hidden, unseen, deep in the earth but essential and life-giving. In many respects the life of Père Thomas had epitomised the mystery of l'Arche itself. For some time afterwards Jean was unable to speak of him without weeping 'because it touched something where the union was so deep and yet the tensions were real'. In April that year he wrote:

> Even though Père Thomas had been absent from the community for the last two years, living close to his brother Père Marie-Dominique, his death touched me deeply. Perhaps I had the childish hope that he would live for ever! But the physical and spiritual pain I have felt with his death is important: it is calling me to greater maturity and responsibility, as well as to deeper humility and docility to the Holy Spirit. Père Thomas always encouraged me in all circumstances to ask Jesus to show me what to do.

In *Our Journey Home* he professed to have been able to cope with his sense of emptiness or vacuum or inner pain in times of grief because his energies had never been fixed on one thing. Bringing to birth and guiding the community had never been his only occupation. He had always maintained his intellectual interests. He had always kept up a life of prayer and communion with Jesus and he had continued to 'announce the Gospel' not only orally but also through the written word.

The confidence that l'Arche had a message the relevance of which extended beyond the boundaries of its small communities was growing. Others were writing too. In 1992 Thérèse Vanier, by then Chairperson of the Pastoral Ecumenical Committee for l'Arche in the UK, was inspired by the life and death of Nick Ellerker, a member of l'Arche Lambeth with Down's syndrome, who had a passion for reconciliation and unity, to write *Nick* –

Man of the Heart.[10] Nick, as the Right Reverend Lord Runcie wrote in his foreword, provided: 'a profile of hope for us all'. This was just one of several writings by Thérèse about l'Arche's spiritual journey to unity. A number of Henri Nouwen's books in which he wrote much about his own and others' weaknesses, fragility and need to be loved, were also written during the 11 years he spent in l'Arche, among them *The Road to Daybreak, Finding My Way Home, The Return of the Prodigal Son, The Inner Voice of Love* and *Adam: God's Beloved.*[11] Life in l'Arche evidently fed Henri's writings but there was a sense in which books were *the* work for him, whereas for Jean life in l'Arche was *the* work, of which his writings were one of the fruits.

It was as a consequence of Henri's writings that the two men came into contact with one another. Jean Vanier had first become aware of Henri when he found himself mentioned in one of his books. They actually met in the late 1970s when Jean invited him to join him at a silent retreat in Chicago. In the years that followed Henri made two visits to Trosly-Breuil, the second in 1984 being a 30-day retreat which he realised, as he wrote afterwards,[12] was part of a series of events 'in which Jesus was responding to my prayer to follow him more fully'. After much hesitation and inner debate, he left Harvard Divinity School and moved to France with the intention of spending at least a year with Jean Vanier and the community at Trosly-Breuil. He was to share Madame Vanier's house, Les Marroniers, and when on 13 August 1985 Pauline Vanier, at the age of 87, threw her arms round him in welcome, he felt as if he had come home. Henri Nouwen, though a man of great energy, vision and insight, suffered deep pain and terrible loneliness. He was one very much in search of a home. Jean was touched by the depth of his anguish, by his genius of the 'word', by his struggle in relation to his sexuality and the desire to do what was right. He was moved by his cry for love and unity and wholeness in himself and for others:

> Henri was a seeker of the word. The Word became flesh, and when it does it becomes an anguished, painful word. The Word became flesh so that the flesh can become word. I often felt how much the flesh of Henri revealed the word ... Some

people saw him as too traditional, and others saw him as too liberal, but in reality he was just a man searching and yearning to announce Jesus, an incredibly vulnerable lover. That is Jesus: a vulnerable, silent lover, who is waiting, yearning to be loved. Jesus' fundamental question to each one is: 'Do you love me? Do you really love me?'

Jean saw a mysterious relationship between Henri's cry for love, the cry of those in l'Arche who had been rejected and that fundamental question of Jesus. Yet Henri had an ability unintentionally to create chaos around him. Henri, who was so exposed and personal, was also very unlike the 'contained' Jean with his gift for forming community. He had a very different understanding of friendship which Jean found difficult. Whilst living at Trosly Henri expected to be able to knock on his door at any hour and spend an unlimited amount of time with him, while Jean Vanier's life had inevitably become one of pre-arranged and restricted appointments. By the time in June 1986 he returned after a period of absence, Henri Nouwen was aware that Trosly was not really his true home. In December of the previous year he had received a letter from the Daybreak community in Canada, inviting him to consider moving there:

> We truly feel that you have a gift to bring us. At the same time, our sense is that Daybreak would be a good place for you, too. We would want to support you in your important vocation of writing and speaking by providing you with a home and with a community that will love you and call you to grow.

He had been deeply moved by this letter. For the first time in his life he felt 'explicitly called', and in July 1986 took up the invitation. In Daybreak he lived with Adam and other people with disabilities who comforted him with their uninhibited love and brought him greater wholeness. He wrote a great deal about how life in l'Arche changed his attitudes and enriched his spiritual life, but much loved as he was and although he brought many people to l'Arche, difficulties arose at Daybreak. These were partly as a result of his extraordinary gift for announcing the word. He attracted a circle of followers with a strong emphasis on publicising or 'announcing' l'Arche in a way which could at times disrupt certain elements of the community. Furthermore, he did not share Jean Vanier's approach to ecumenism and the Church. Henri believed in intercommunion. Nor did he subscribe to Jean's sense of the importance of contact with local churches.

Henri Nouwen died in September 1996 of a heart attack. At his funeral in Utrecht Jean Vanier in his eulogy spoke not only of the mystery of Henri but also of his wounded humanity, of how Henri had found in l'Arche, a place founded on pain, the welcome of wounded healers:

> Henri was not particularly good at making breakfast! It was not really his gift and of course everything he tried to do in the house went wrong! That was Henri. He would laugh about it and get angry and excited, but somewhere living with Adam he found comfort. He discovered that Adam, Gordie and Laura were also wounded healers. They were beautiful healers because they were not ashamed to love. They threw themselves into the arms of Henri and kissed him. That was what he needed, and maybe that is what we all need but we do not know it.

L'Arche, Jean Vanier was at pains to emphasise, was a very human reality. By 1999 he was discovering more and more that an understanding of anthropology was important for a good understanding of a life of faith. *Becoming Human*[13] sprang more from Jean Vanier's experience of humanness and less directly from his life of faith. In it he quite deliberately avoided entering too fully through the door to spirituality in order to fix more clearly the human foundations of it. The book was once again based on a series of talks, on this occasion the prestigious Canadian Massey lectures. What astonished him at the time was that when he received the telephone call asking him to give the five talks on the Canadian Broadcasting Corporation radio programme *Ideas*, he knew immediately that they should be on: 'Loneliness', 'Belonging', 'From Exclusion to Inclusion', 'The Path of Healing' and 'Paths to Freedom and Forgiveness'. And yet in a way it was not astonishing for behind those titles lay the story of l'Arche: 'loneliness, belonging, then the movement from loneliness to belonging, healing and at the end of that you come to freedom and somewhere in freedom there is forgiveness.' Behind it also was the recognition that it was impossible to grow spiritually if humanness was ignored, just as it was impossible to become fully human if spirituality was ignored. His own growth had involved the recognition that the process of teaching and learning, of communication, involved movement back and forth:

> The one who is healed and the one who is healing constantly change places. As we begin to understand ourselves, we begin to understand others. It is part of the process of moving from idealism to reality, from the sky to the earth. We do not have to be perfect or deny our emotions.

Therein lay another profound truth:

> Understanding, as well as truth, comes not only from the intellect but also from the body. When we begin to listen to our bodies, we begin to listen to reality through our own experiences; we begin to trust out intuition, our hearts. The truth is also in the 'earth' of our own bodies. It is a question of moving from theories we have learned to listening to the reality that is in and around us. Truth flows from the earth. This is not to deny the truth that flows from teachers, from books, from tradition, from our ancestors, and from religious faith. But the two must come together. Truth from the sky must be confirmed and strengthened by truth from the earth. We must learn to listen and then to communicate.

In his own case his growing interest in anthropology, combined with all the 'living with' he had done over the years, seems to have tempered the exclusively Catholic vocabulary and imagery of his letters to his parents to a more universally accessible mode of expressing truths that were both spiritual and human.

Seeing Beyond Depression whilst reflecting his anthropological interest was more specifically[14] a response to the number of letters he had been receiving from people who were themselves experiencing depression or whose sons or daughters were. Depression was a painful reality, an illness from which an individual could not recover alone. Negative feelings surfaced, stemming from the wounds of childhood: the fear and anguish arising from what a child went through when he or she was mistreated, abused, unfairly rejected or witnessed unbearable conflicts for which he or she felt in some way responsible. At such times 'We need help to recover from it, and a friend to walk with us through the difficult times.' There might also come a point at which, with the help of a competent psychologist, an individual had to look more closely at the powers of darkness hidden within. 'So that was all part of anthropology, the conscious and the unconscious, the mess that is under it, which we hide and which explodes.' Jean was left feeling that he might like to write something else on anthropology but that he would need to do it in conjunction with someone who could demonstrate the connection with contemporary thought and authors in a way that he did not feel equipped to do. Despite an extraordinary depth and range of reading he felt the need for someone to give it 'a new type of certitude'.

There were times when he greatly appreciated collaboration:

> As I grow older I am discovering more and more the gift of my own poverty and weakness. When we are strong, we can often do it alone. When we feel weaker, when we live loss and anguish, we are more aware of our need for God, for others, for community.

In *Made for Happiness – Discovering the Meaning of Life with Aristotle*, discussion with Elise Corsini, a former journalist and teacher of philosophy, helped him to discover ways of presenting Aristotelian ethics to modern seekers after truth. Many people had no religious faith. It was important to be able to communicate with them at a rational level, to reflect upon things human and on human maturity. He had been 'pushed' into writing the book, 'and I was happy to do so because I found that my thesis on Aristotle was good but I was the only one who knew that ... Nobody else knew it and I've never really found anybody who has read it.' Only once, in a small village in Brazil, he had had occasion to stay in a priest's room and on the bookshelf he had found his thesis. *Made for Happiness*[15] drew not only on Jean Vanier's doctoral analysis of Aristotle's words and texts but also on his experience of life among fragile men and women wounded by illness and rejection whose desire, like anyone else's, was nonetheless to be happy. Jean Vanier had long ago realised that the gospel and Christianity could not be divorced from human, philosophical, and ethical thinking. Aristotle had loved all that was human. It was Aristotle who had made him pay attention not primarily to ideas but to reality and experience. Jean Vanier's aim here was to demonstrate the relevance of the wisdom of Aristotle and his profound sense of reality to those seeking the meaning of life and the truly human happiness for which we are all made, in the hurly-burly of the contemporary world.

The 1980s and 1990s had seen dreadful conflict and dramatic world crises and changes: the massacres in Rwanda, the fall of the Berlin Wall, the Gulf War and the decline of Communism, with all their attendant fears, hopes and renewed insecurities. In this context a number of new l'Arche communities were born: in Uganda, Japan, Jacksonville, Florida, Portland, Oregon, as well as in Austria, Hungary and Poland. Many more Faith and Light communities came into being, and Jean Vanier's journeys to visit them served increasingly to underline the extent to which they were founded on the Paschal mystery of crucifixion and resurrection. 'As I travel,' he wrote in the newsletter distributed ever more widely across the continents, 'as I listen to people and see different situations, I realise the immense suffering of our world: the pain of young people, of the unemployed, of refugees, of people who are marginalised or in impossible situations. A cry of pain rises up from our world.'

By the beginning of the new millennium that world seemed to be even more wracked by unresolved conflicts and wars, and the social dislocation caused by war or other political or economic changes was bringing much suffering. Few had more direct contact with such suffering than Jean Vanier. *Finding Peace*[16] was a small book that identified the desire for peace as another of our deepest human yearnings. Once again it was based on a talk, this time an hour-long programme for CBC. In response to such events as those of September 11, 2001, he identified those sources of conflict and fear within and among individuals, communities and nations that thwart the quest for peace. 'We might not all be called to work for peace on an international level,' he maintained, 'but we are all called to become men and women of peace wherever we may be – in our family, at work, in our parish, in our neighbourhood.' Those lighting the way to change were often 'little', unknown, unrecognised people.

Prophets of peace are those who in their person and attitudes do not awaken fear, but open people's hearts to understanding and compassion. They are those who are weak and who are crying out for relationship. In some mysterious way they are breaking down the barriers of fear in our hearts'.

Every year in August Jean Vanier would spend a month of rest, relaxation and prayer in a monastery in Orval, at the end of which he often wrote a circular letter to l'Arche and Faith and Light. Significantly perhaps, in August 1997 and 1998 he wrote of how he had spent time digging more deeply into the Gospel of John. In his 1997 letter he described how he always felt the need to be in direct contact with Scripture, the word of God, the words of Jesus:

Each day I discover more of the treasure. Sometimes I wonder how it is that I am discovering John's gospel in a new way when I am nearly 70! But each gift comes at the right time. Now is the time for me to enter more deeply into John's gospel and to discover Jesus in a new way, and dare I say, to discover more deeply the relationship between the spirituality of l'Arche and Faith and Light and the spirituality revealed by John, the beloved disciple of Jesus. John's gospel is a real catechesis; it is a path, a gentle revelation of Jesus and of what he came to give us. It is as if John is taking me by the hand and leading me into a deeper union with Jesus in order to discover more totally his message of love.

Although manifestly the fruits of many years of reflection, study, prayer and living in community, the catalyst for the actual writing of *Drawn into the Mystery of Jesus through the Gospel of John* was the invitation to make a television programme. In 1999 Dick Nielsen of Norflicks, with whom Jean Vanier had previously done a television series on l'Arche and its vision entitled *Images of Love and Hope*, suggested that they work together on a programme. Jean's response was a series of 25 talks on the Gospel of John for Vision TV. The television series, entitled *Knowing Eternity*, became the basis for a book which was perhaps closer than any other to his own heart, an interpretation of the gospel which reflected his own life's journey, written as so often in 'meditative prose' which he hoped would lead people to be drawn slowly and prayerfully into the mystery of Jesus.

Both the programme and the book evoked a very positive response. In general his books were appealing to a growing readership. What touched Jean greatly was that following the publication of *Drawn into the Mystery of Jesus through the Gospel of John* he was invited to speak to a group of exegetes at the Institute of Biblical Studies in Rome. The person who issued the invitation said he felt that they were giving undue emphasis to historical factors and had lost the sense of what the Word of God was about. 'I find that very beautiful. I would never have thought that an exegete would want to look at my book.'

The realisation that the Word he gave must be rooted in his experience of living in l'Arche provided the unifying strain through all his works. It was for this reason also that his books, if viewed chronologically reflected his personal path, a path not so much of change as of the kind of exploration T. S. Eliot referred to, the end of which 'is to arrive where we started and know that place for the first time'. There were those reviewers who claimed he was not saying anything new. In a sense it was true and yet the vision was widening and deepening. 'What I share in these pages' he wrote of *Drawn into the Mystery of Jesus through the Gospel of John*, 'is the music I have heard behind the words and the flow of the Gospel of John'. The invitation to others to look or listen beyond the words was implied.

He had come a long way since his thesis on 'Happiness as Principle and End of Aristotelian Ethics' and yet the influence of Aristotle was still there. It had been 'integrated'. In his foreword to *Drawn into the Mystery of Jesus through the Gospel of John*, he acknowledged asking 'many wise friends' to review the manuscript, echoing consciously or unconsciously the methods of Aristotle. In his seventies Jean Vanier was still quick to acknowledge that Aristotle had taught him to order his thoughts and distinguish what really mattered from what was less important. He differed from Aristotle with regard to certain aspects of anthropology, particularly over his definition of the human being as 'a rational animal', a definition which excluded people with mental disabilities from humanity. Jean himself would sooner define a human being as 'someone capable of love'. Yet there were more than superficial parallels to be drawn between the ethics Aristotle propounded in order to help people look more clearly into themselves and find their own fulfilment, and the process of being drawn into the mystery of Jesus through the Gospel of John. And perhaps friendship, truth and the 'logos' – that 'Word', vision and wisdom which has the power to change, create and transform – were somewhere at the heart of Aristotelian thought as at the heart of the Gospel of John.

TWELVE

PAIN AND UNION

THE PROCESS OF NURTURING 'friendships across difference' had continued. It was occurring on a number of levels, some more obvious than others. John, who waited at the garden gate in Norwood and chatted to anyone who happened to pass his way, promoted 'integration', goodwill and unity in his own particular and immeasurable way. The assistants who may have spent what represented only a brief interlude in their lives in a l'Arche community still often carried away with them into other corners of a broken world the vision that it offered.

For years Père André de Jaer brought a group of Jesuits from different countries to spend six months of their tertianship at Trosly-Breuil. They came to 'become more simple'. They came with their degrees in philosophy, theology and mathematics, and were obliged to leave them on the doorstep: 'Really we have to be ourselves and nothing more, we have to accept not having any social standing and the feeling that we are "wasting time".' Such acceptance did not come easily to all. One young Swiss graduate in theology about to start as chaplain to the university in Basel was convinced, after two weeks of working in the garden, that he was achieving nothing and would do better to go straight to his students. Advised to suspend his decision for a couple of weeks, by the end of that time he had completely changed his mind. Well organised, efficient and an intellectual, in l'Arche he discovered what it meant not to organise, but just to be with people and let them touch his heart and discover there a richness.

There was the Englishman who had read Greats at Oxford, a

highly cultured man with an extraordinary appreciation of music and history, for whom verbal communication was of great importance. He even had doubts about whether the severely disabled could really be considered people. Living with them brought a real discovery of another kind of communication, of deep communion through touch and being more completely present. It also brought a new sense of the cross, of the actuality of the passion and resurrection of Jesus in the contemporary world.

Another member of the Society of Jesus from Zaire was moved by all the young people he saw living a form of poverty with disabled people to examine his own conscience. He was a high school teacher who knew nothing of the extreme poverty in his own country. As the first black man to come to Trosly-Breuil, his time there was particularly difficult because some of the people with disabilities were slow to accept him. One woman would not even travel to work with him in the same car. After three months they were firm friends and when he left, he felt called to 'accompany' prisoners condemned to death.

Five Jesuits from Central America, from Salvador, Nicaragua and Panama where the poor were struggling for justice, had been drawn in their desperation to violence as a political solution. For them, l'Arche involved the discovery that the struggle should not only be for a just society but take into account the importance of every individual. In working for structures there was a danger of forgetting the person. Some people remained poor even when structures were changed, and the new rich too were liable to oppress others. Even for those with the best of intentions, there was a danger of 'working for' the poor and forgetting the value of 'being with' them. Some were afraid that an acceptance of l'Arche values would immobilise them. Père André maintained that it enabled them rather to return to the struggle with a new vision which was non-violent even when violence appeared more effective. It was founded instead upon a deep love primarily for the poor but also for the rich. The value of the tiny communities in Honduras, ostensibly nonsensical in a world of violence, must be upheld. In many Central American countries contemplative communities were not allowed by governments which accepted the Church only when it was manifestly useful. L'Arche communities could combine the contemplative with the 'useful' in a very significant way. In general, numerous gifted young priests were called upon in l'Arche to drop the barriers that their cassocks and status could create, acknowledge their own fragility and carry the message of their experience into their pastoral life. If Jean Vanier had his way, he acknowledged, he would have all priests spend time in l'Arche as part of their training.

Relations with Rome, which he had worked hard to maintain from the earliest days, had warmed and deepened. In the mid-1980s there had been a 'breakage' of about a year in the links with the Pontifical Council for the Laity, when Jean's lay contact there had required him to state clearly whether l'Arche was or was not a Roman Catholic community. Jean had stood firmly by the ecumenical and inter-faith direction in which l'Arche had been spontaneously drawn, and been informed that on that basis there could be no dialogue. In 1985, however, Cardinal Pironio, a man whom Jean credited with a great capacity for listening, and who saw in l'Arche something which he could personally value, took over as President of the Pontifical Council. Friendships had flourished once more and been further encouraged by a growing personal bond with Pope John Paul II. In October 1987 Jean had been invited to take part in a synod, the central theme of which was the vocation and mission of lay people within the Church. As a lay member of a lay community he strongly endorsed the spirit of the Second Vatican Council in relation to that vocation and mission. The opportunity for lay people to be present and address the assembly, even though they did not have a vote, was in his view a prophetic gesture. His reflections on the synod were full of words of welcome and appreciation for many aspects of it and for the fundamental message:

> We are all called to be holy as is the Father in heaven, according to our particular vocation. In our times, the thirst for holiness grows more and more in the hearts of the faithful, when they accept the call of God inviting them to live with Christ and to change the world.

They also included criticisms of the methodology of the wording of proposals to be given to the Pope which, he felt, allowed little space for the prophetic, the expressed regret that so little had been said about ecumenism, and a strong, characteristic call to see the poor and the fragile, who were often unable to assume responsibility or participate in decisions, as being at the very heart of the Church. By insisting on active participation and speaking of the place of lay people in terms of collaboration and corresponsibility, the synod was, he considered, overlooking the specific mystery of the gift of the poor to the Church, of those whose intangible contributions were those of giving life and awakening love. Of that occasion he had written also: 'John Paul II is at every session. I spend much of my time watching him, especially the way he listens to each speaker. He is truly a model for us.'

Doors had also opened in other directions. In the late spring of 1989 he gave a number of talks in Russia. The international vice coordinator of Faith and Light was Polish, and Jean had long harboured the idea of moving into Eastern bloc countries: 'Between him and me it could not not happen.' As the guest of the Canadian Ambassador in Moscow, he was able to meet not only Soviet people concerned with the care of disabled people but also Christians from the Orthodox Church, the Roman Catholic Church, Pentecostals and Baptists. The visit had left him with the conviction that something important was going to emerge from Soviet Russia:

> There is a thirst in the Russian people and something very deep coming up from the groundswell of their unconscious. Human nature is so beautiful. You can't keep it down. You can persecute it but it will always rise up again.

It had also left him with the conviction that there must still be a lot of prejudices in him: 'I found as I was going through the beautiful Moscow subway that I was amazed that I was actually there.' It had been a great liberation for him really to fall in love with the Russian people, and he had come away with the resolve to look more closely at the Orthodox tradition and at the works of Dostoevsky and Stravinsky to discover there the vision of people considered mad, who were in fact prophetic, saying things that others might know but did not dare to say.

As the Eastern bloc countries gradually opened their boundaries, Jean Vanier had made a number of visits not just to Russia but also to Lithuania, Romania, Hungary, Poland and Slovenia, to discover their needs and speak to them of the place of people with disabilities within the plan of God. In countries where such new communities were almost unheard of, he had found an obvious need for Faith and Light and l'Arche. The opportunity to work with members of the Orthodox Church had thus opened up a whole new area of potential ecumenical growth.

Pilgrimage in l'Arche was almost a process of making real, acting out what was happening in the daily journey of community. In 1991, to mark 20 years of the existence of Faith and Light, a pilgrimage to Lourdes was held. Its theme was 'Towards Unity': unity between countries, cultures and classes, unity between people with disabilities and their friends, unity between Christians of different traditions. The gathering was attended by 13,500 pilgrims from five continents, many of them from Poland, Hungary, Czechoslovakia, Russia, Lithuania and Romania. By then there were some 900 Faith and Light communities throughout the world providing support for people with disabilities, their families and their friends, and spreading a vision of new life and communion born of a relationship with the weak.

When Jean Vanier gave a retreat at the Orthodox Institute of Theology in Bucharest in 1992, it was open not only to members of the Protestant and Roman Catholic Churches but also to those of the Orthodox Church. The Orthodox Patriarch gave his authority for the Eucharist to be celebrated on alternate days in a local Orthodox church. It was the first time that such authority had been forthcoming. In his travels, Jean Vanier had encountered many such signs of friendship, recognition and closeness. In 1993, in the Ukraine, another ecumenical retreat brought together people from the Greek-Catholic, the Latin, the Independent Orthodox Church and the Orthodox Church attached to Moscow, as well as Baptists and Pentecostals. In Slovenia, as in many other former Communist countries, he had witnessed all the vitality and enthusiasm that stemmed from an initial taste of freedom after so many years, but he had seen too the economic difficulties which freedom brought with it, the discouragement and even a sort of nostalgia for Communism. The cry of the many broken, disabled people was not easily heard by those weighed down with the struggle to lead their countries to economic stability.

In a camp for refugees who had fled from Bosnia, he had heard homeless people insist that their lives were devoid of hope. 'Bosnia', he had afterwards asserted, 'is a sign of our helplessness. We do not know what to do in the face of all the horrors of war, of the thousands of refugees. Where are we going in this broken world?' At a time of widespread discouragement, worry about the future and disillusionment with the limitations and deceptions of those who exercised authority, he urged people to remember that if the quest for power rarely led to beauty of the human heart, the readiness to listen to the weak and vulnerable invariably did, and to look at the sense of helplessness in the face of so many world crises and discover there a mysterious potential.

In September 1997, together with the Faith and Light Coordinator for the Middle East and the Faith and Light leaders in Egypt, he had had some 'very moving encounters' with Pope Chenouda II, head of the Coptic Orthodox Church, the Orthodox Church with the largest membership in the Middle East. Pope Chenouda then invited Jean to speak to a large audience at the Orthodox Centre of Theology in Cairo. That same month he spoke to the Central Committee of the World Council of Churches in Geneva, attended by 250 delegates representing different Churches throughout the world. He had received a letter asking him to give a day's retreat to the various representatives and had thought quite simply, 'Why not?' He spoke at the Central Committee's session on Worship and Spirituality and his talk was followed by a liturgy of the washing of the feet. This liturgy, used at the Covenant retreats in l'Arche and previously celebrated at an ecumenical gathering and 'Festival for Peace', which Jean Vanier had attended in Northern Ireland in 1995, provided an increasingly helpful gesture of communion. It was an act of humility signifying the desire to serve one another, and an expression of the desire for unity and mutual forgiveness. Members of the World Council of Churches' Central Committee, advisers and staff, young and old, men and women, metropolitans and general secretaries, clergy and laity, some in suits, others in clerical garb, yet others in the traditional dress of many cultures from around the world, walked in procession to bowls on the floor of the Ecumenical Centre reception hall. They sat in chairs in small circles and removed their shoes and socks.

They dipped their feet into basins as others washed and dried them with small towels. They did it simply because Jesus had directed his followers to do so, and if many modern Christians were embarrassed by the rite, so too, Jean Vanier pointed out, were Jesus' disciples when he insisted on washing their feet.

Not long afterwards, at Pentecost 1998, John Paul II had invited him and three other founders of new lay communities to speak to a gathering of some 350,000 people over which the Pope presided, about the vision and spirituality of l'Arche and Faith and Light. Pascal, the son of a policeman, whose grief on the death of his father I had witnessed years previously in La Petite Source, was with him, and during the Sunday Mass celebrated by the Pope, took up the offerings to John Paul II who embraced him.

Then, in July that year, George Carey, Archbishop of Canterbury, invited Jean to take part in the Lambeth Conference for some 800 bishops of the Anglican Communion, more than half of whom came from Africa, Asia, Latin America and the Pacific Islands. Jean Vanier and Dr Carey had both previously spoken at an ecumenical gathering in Canada. The Archbishop stated afterwards that he knew then that Jean should come to Lambeth. When Jean Vanier responded that he needed more information, the Archbishop of Canterbury's chaplain, Roger Herft, who would subsequently develop a close, supporting relationship with l'Arche, was sent to discuss what was involved. Jean agreed to give a talk and suggested that once again the liturgy of the washing of the feet might be appropriate. He also stipulated that there should be no journalists present to detract from the sacred nature of the occasion. Roger Herft was not quite sure how to arrange for 800 hundred bishops to wash each other's feet. Nevertheless, after giving a talk on the call to holiness, which was followed by a mime prepared by the l'Arche community in Kent, Jean Vanier took part in an 'incredible liturgy' during which the bishops washed one another's feet at some twelve different stations. On a stage George Carey washed his wife's feet and Jean Vanier, deeply touched to be there because it was unusual for a Catholic layman to have received such an invitation, washed the feet of the leader of the Anglican Communion.

These four events, following as they did in rapid succession, had reinforced Jean's belief that l'Arche had a call to work for unity: unity on a social level by helping people with disabilities to be more included in the life of society and the Churches; unity between Christians belonging to different Churches, and unity with people of different religions or none. They had also convinced him that the Churches were discovering more and more that people with disabilities had a place at the heart of the Christian community. They were beginning to grasp the truth of St Paul's words: 'God has chosen the foolish and the weak in order to confound the wise and the strong' (1 Corinthians 1:27), and they were recognising the value and message of l'Arche and Faith and Light. These four major events had also made him feel that his was a voice 'a bit like John the Baptist's', the voice which pointed to Jesus hidden in the weak, and to the ability they had to transform if they were welcomed with compassion and truth.

In many respects the unity that l'Arche was living went far beyond what the Churches could as yet find, and l'Arche knew it. In the United Kingdom, with the passage of the years, the opening of a community in Scotland highlighting the need to listen to Presbyterian as well as Catholic and other sensitivities, and a growing need to support people from the Evangelical tradition, had meant that the Eucharist had ceased to be a source of pain in quite the way it once had been. It had become instead an instance for mature acceptance based on the knowledge that the covenant relationship that people were seeking to live with each other was in itself one of very real and deep communion. In India, the four Asha Niketans had been seeking ways to express words such as 'covenant' and 'metanoia' in ways that were as rich in meaning for Hindus or Muslims as they were for Christians. Appropriate writings of l'Arche had been translated into local languages. Globally, for the first time in 1993 it had become possible for Christian and non-Christian communities in the International Federation to subscribe to a single charter as 'communities of faith'. It was a step greeted as significant in the progress along l'Arche's own path to unity.

Yet the idea that l'Arche needed to be in touch with the priests, ministers, imams and others of the local churches and faith groups to which its members, especially its disabled members, belonged, continued to be important nationally and internationally. In France, once a year the Bishop of Beauvais would call together the priests 'accompanying' l'Arche communities. In Belgium, the Auxiliary Bishop of Brussels did the same. In the United Kingdom, appointed leaders from the Anglican, Roman Catholic and Protestant Churches were there to listen, advise and provide an element of accountability, but above all the purpose of these links was to establish 'a really friendly relationship with people' which, in the experience of Thérèse Vanier, was the way things had always worked best for l'Arche. An international group of Church leaders comprising a Roman Catholic Bishop from France delegated by the Vatican, an Anglican Bishop from Australia delegated by the Archbishop of Canterbury and a minister of the Church of Scotland delegated by the World Council of Churches to represent the Protestant element, provided similar possibilities at a global level.

L'Arche, Jean Vanier continued to maintain, must not become its own little church with its own little way of doing things. It must not reject the Church as obsolete and irrelevant. What Jean still saw as important was 'growth to wholeness within the Church, within the body of Christ'. 'To love one another you need spirituality and for spirituality you need something bigger than yourself – faith, the gospel, the Church.' L'Arche was in terrible need of the Word and the Body of Jesus which alone could give meaning to the lives of its people. The Church was what Jesus had wanted for the communication of the mystery. Jean was well aware of the human imperfections of the Christian Churches. 'I wonder how we in the modern Church would react if Jesus came to us and offered to wash the toilets?' he once enquired of a journalist alluding to the task Mahatma Gandhi assigned to himself in his ashram. All too often the Churches seemed to have lost their prophetic role and ability to speak out. All too often they were not seen as home to the 'good thief', to Mary Magdalene, caught up in prostitution. They were not a refuge for the weak and broken, the discouraged and those in pain, but rather for the comfortable and morally right. 'Where is hope?' Jean Vanier was inclined to ask. 'Where is Jesus?'

Time and time again his heart returned to the Gospel of Luke (10:29–37) and the parable of the Good Samaritan, told by Jesus as an illustration of what it means to love our neighbour: the Samaritan, who unlike the two men with important functions in Jewish society, did not pass by when he saw a Jew, attacked by bandits, lying in the road. Three things touched him particularly about this Samaritan, who saw the injured man first and foremost as a brother in humanity. Firstly, his love was unlimited: he not only rescued him but spent the night with him and committed himself to paying for his care. Secondly, he bridged the gap between the Jewish and Samaritan peoples, breaking through the barriers of his own culture, religion and ethnic group, not in order to convert another to his religion but out of love and compassion, trusting that such love would reveal the true face of God. Thirdly, the man from Samaria dared to walk the path of insecurity, risking the possibility that other Jews might accuse him of having committed the assault and other Samaritans see him as a traitor, collaborating with the enemy. Of two further things Jean was sure: that by daring to act out of love and compassion, the Samaritan became both poorer in his isolation, vulnerability and insecurity, and thereby richer in his increased awareness of the need for the help and presence of God; and that both men must have been changed by the experience, having discovered the presence of God in each other. They might feel isolated from or rejected by their respective groups, but they became a sign of peace and unity.

Jean Vanier so wanted, he had written in September 2000 on returning from a journey to Cuba, Mexico and Nicaragua, 'to be in a world where the signs of hope are flourishing, but I am not encouraged by all the strong, closed religious groups. And I do not have a sense that everything is advancing towards a world of peace and unity.' The people from whom he drew strength were the men and women he encountered who, whilst being rooted in their own culture and tradition, had open hearts; the men and women of compassion who reached out to the weak and broken from many backgrounds, listening to them and learning from them, accompanying them to the 'local inn', gently and humbly washing their wounds and seeing in them a brother or sister in humanity. 'We are in a world of war with flames popping up all over the place,' he protested, 'and we Christians can't come together to talk about the gospel? What is going on?' Yet l'Arche was not always understood when it welcomed people of different traditions into its communities. Some did not appreciate that members were not losing faith in their own tradition, but being called to go more deeply into it, to be more firmly rooted in it. At intervals he returned to Northern Ireland to give ecumenical retreats. There were pilgrimages to the Holy Land, talks in a multitude of other locations, often centres of Faith and Light communities, and in all of them he found people for whom ecumenism at very least was not an option but a common sense reality. Ecumenism, however, was not just a question of coming round the same table and having the Eucharist. What did it really mean? In his understanding it had to start from the vantage point of knowing what it really meant to be a Catholic or an Anglican, although it went without saying that he felt closer to an Anglican who understood people with disabilities than to a Roman Catholic who had no spiritual life. Jean Vanier was himself unequivocally a Roman Catholic, who recognised fully the importance of welcoming difference but remained wary of falling into syncretism. After all, the basic philosophy of l'Arche was to love uniqueness and difference.

In India the example of digging a well was cited to illustrate the point that for total inner transformation of the heart, one had to adopt one particular sadhana or path. To find water one needed to dig in one location until it emerged. Digging in one spot one day and another the next would keep a person digging, but no water would be found. Over the centuries different religions had developed specific methods for deep-level spiritual transformation. These methods demanded that they be practised wholeheartedly and faithfully over a long period of time. When Jean Vanier spoke of unity he did not imply everybody becoming the same but rather 'working together in the same direction', and the direction he had in mind was the recognition of the value of each person no matter what his or her limits, culture or religion might be. It meant working for peace by struggling against all forms of oppression, for greater love and compassion in our world, especially for those who were weak or marginalised, those in pain and living in misery, so that the God of love and the love of God might be better known and welcomed in the hearts of all.

In January 2004 he was invited to attend the international

symposium on the dignity and rights of the mentally disabled person organised by the Congregation for the Doctrine of the Faith in Rome. What Pope John Paul II said on that occasion had been another cause to hope:

> There is no doubt that in revealing the fundamental frailty of the human condition, the disabled person becomes an expression of the tragedy of pain. In this world of ours that approves hedonism and is charmed by ephemeral and deceptive beauty, the difficulties of the disabled are often perceived as a shame or a provocation and their problems as burdens to be removed or resolved as quickly as possible. Disabled people are, instead, living icons of the crucified Son. They reveal the mysterious beauty of the One who emptied himself for our sake and made himself obedient unto death. They show us, over and above all appearances, that the ultimate foundation of human existence is Jesus Christ. It is said, justifiably so, that disabled people are humanity's privileged witnesses. They can teach everyone about the love that saves us; they can become heralds of a new world, no longer dominated by force, violence and aggression, but by love, solidarity and acceptance, a new world transfigured by the light of Christ, the Son of God who became incarnate, who was crucified and rose for us.

On the basis of this and other statements made on such themes as communion, Jean Vanier was satisfied that Pope John Paul II was listening in a very particular way to the message of l'Arche and its fundamental acceptance of difference. It seemed to him significant that Cardinal Walter Kasper, president of the Pontifical Council for the Promotion of Christian Unity, had stated that a new spirituality of communion was needed which Pope John Paul II described as 'the ability to see what is positive in others, to welcome it and prize it as a gift from God; not only as a gift for the brother or sister who has received it directly, but also as a gift for me'. A spirituality of communion, Pope John Paul maintained, meant 'to know how to "make room" for our brothers and sisters bearing each other's burdens'.

In August 2004 Jean was invited to participate in the Pope's pilgrimage to Lourdes and to give short meditations on the luminous mysteries of the rosary: the Baptism of Jesus, the Wedding

Feast in Cana, Announcing the Kingdom, the Transfiguration of Jesus on Mount Thabor and the Eucharist. Whilst doing so he walked close to the 'popemobile'. Pope John Paul II was by that time 'living enormous poverty' and Jean found himself deeply moved by the seriousness of his disability and the desperate struggle he had to speak because of Parkinson's disease. Jean too was tired and weak with the heat and the Pope, clearly recognising his discomfort, called him to him, patted him on the cheek and gave him the rosary beads he had been using, as if to say 'I am part of your community now.' It was a moment of extraordinary communion.

September 2004 would see Jean Vanier at an International Council of Faith and Light not far from Damascus. In Damascus itself he visited the main Mosque and prayed at the tomb of John the Baptist, who was venerated by Muslims there, that 'the walls that separate cultures and religions might be lowered and that we, with all our differences, may learn how to dialogue with one another and live in communion'. The 38 Faith and Light communities in Syria were made up for the most part of a mixture of Catholics and Orthodox, encouraged by their bishops. They were 'full of life' and that unity which stemmed not necessarily from the top but from the bottom, through those who were humble and called to the heart. He gave two public talks in Damascus and in Alep, which brought together some seven hundred people – mainly Muslims – on each occasion. After his talk in Alep, the Mufti gave a testimony on how people with disabilities were a path to God. Jean Vanier was deeply touched by this as he was deeply touched by the fact that when they met for refreshments, the Grand Mufti picked up a small biscuit and placed it in Jean's mouth.

The fact that l'Arche had so swiftly become not only ecumenical but inter-religious had always been something which Jean Vanier welcomed as part of the mystery. Over the years his respect for and relationship with other denominations and faiths had grown. 'We're moving now,' he would say in 2004, 'to the position where what is important is to see the beauty of the other Church, and see the value of the presence of God in the other person.' In l'Arche what it came down to was:

Can we welcome Muslims and Baptists and treat them with the dignity they need, or can't we? And if we welcome them, they have a family … It is vital that we welcome people of other faiths not to make them Catholic or Christian but because they are in pain and need to grow humanly.

Yet his own constant point of reference was Jesus. If anything, he made more frequent reference now to Jesus as opposed to God, than earlier in the history of l'Arche. For him the meekness and fragility of Jesus was supremely important precisely because this was not the omnipotent God, the God of generosity, who gave from a position of control and superiority, but the God of compassion, vulnerability and powerlessness who sought relationship, the ultimate Good Samaritan. For Jean the vital question was,

> Do we accept the fragility of Jesus? Jesus is knocking at the door of our hearts and if somebody hears and opens the door, then he will come in and eat with them. And eating together in biblical language implies 'becoming a friend' so here we have something that is sometimes difficult to talk about even in Christian terms.

He had retained a strong sense of the importance of what he referred to increasingly as 'Church' without an article, essentially because of 'the mystery of Jesus, Jesus rendered present in a particular way through Sacrament and the real presence'. Moreover, as Pope John Paul II's health continued to deteriorate, it meant much to Jean and to l'Arche that at the heart and head of the Roman Catholic Church was a visibly suffering servant who conveyed a message to the world not so much through his encyclicals as through his body. There were those who felt he should retire – or die – soon. It was too hard to be a witness to his suffering. It was the kind of remark that Jean had often heard in relation to people with disabilities. Humanly speaking, such a reaction was understandable. When in St Mark's Gospel,[1] Peter protested in response to Jesus' prediction of his forthcoming suffering and death, Jesus rebuked him; 'Get behind me, Satan!'. Peter's words were human not divine: 'So there is something about being able to stand and be with suffering.'

For Jean Vanier the mystery of compassion was that it could not be divorced from the Paraclete, the comforter which takes away the anguish of loneliness and brings presence, security, peace and communion, as distinct from Spiritus, which implies movement, 'wind', the inner enthusiasm which made the prophets speak and do wonderful things. This, Jean Vanier felt, was distinctive to the Christian message: the link between the Spirit and pain. Through his physical poverty, humility and courage, the Pope was teaching the value of human life; he was showing the world a path to holiness, calling it to tenderness and goodness, and inspiring it to greater humanity. He, like l'Arche, was revealing the mystery of the presence of God in weakness, and he, like l'Arche, was a sign of the glory of God manifested through poverty and vulnerability.

THIRTEEN

OWNING THE STORY

It had not all been plain sailing. There had been times when things had not been handled as well as they might have been. The treatment of Monsieur Prat's son Jean-Pierre, for whom the Val Fleuri had originally been created, was a case in point. Although the contract for l'Arche's occupation of the Val Fleuri had been granted on condition that Jean-Pierre remain there for life, his mental state had deteriorated to the point where l'Arche, Trosly-Breuil had felt obliged to move him to an institution elsewhere. It had proved not to be a good one and Jean-Pierre's family had not been sufficiently involved in the decision-making process. The result had been tension and eventually l'Arche, Trosly-Breuil had been obliged to find the money to buy the Val Fleuri outright. Jean-Pierre had since died but there had been similar situations where parents had been unnecessarily distressed. The need for consultation in such circumstances with families and their elected psychiatrists was recognised. There had been other instances, Jean Vanier acknowledged, of naïvety on his part and on the part of others, a lack of wisdom, setbacks, crises and shortcomings, but in all these there had been potential for learning and those graces which only frailty could allow.

A number of l'Arche communities had at one stage or another come near to closure. Some, particularly in the earlier days, had found themselves too isolated and without enough support. In Uganda the community, whose director had previously been imprisoned and tortured, had been through a very difficult period and was, like Zimbabwe, still struggling financially. Communities elsewhere had suffered from lack of good direction. The 'incul-turation' begun in the 1970s and 1980s and consequent gradual withdrawal of European and North American founder/leaders meant that all the communities in India, Africa and the Latin American zone now had local leaders, but the handover had not always been instantly to good effect. In the case of one of the Honduran communities the quality of care had declined dramati-cally. In Bethany, by contrast, the community had been too dependant on Europeans who had been unable to stay when the Gulf War broke out. The people with mental disabilities had to be returned to hospital or their families. At the time it had been a terrible experience for all concerned but something positive had been salvaged. One of the community members subsequently returned to visit and support them, and started a workshop based on l'Arche values. Her presence in Bethany, especially in the hospital, had a transforming effect on attitudes and behaviour: people with disabilities were now bathed instead of being hosed down.

If there had been a major change over the years, it had been in the way in which communities were founded. Whereas once it had been a case of individuals going out from Europe to places such as Haiti, now it was a much slower and more structured process undergone in cooperation with local people. The inter-national coordinators saw it as their role to identify people with the potential, desire and motivation to do something within their own country, and then support them through the International Federation. The lesson of not 'implanting' from outside had been learnt the hard way.

A number of communities in the Federation had existed for some years before joining l'Arche. There, as in Japan, the problem was potentially the difficulty of reconciling the vision of the founder with that of l'Arche. Communities near Ottawa, in Montana and in Norway, originally formed independently of l'Arche, had joined the Federation but subsequently left. At the time of joining they had not fully appreciated the requirements of belonging. Their leaving had highlighted the need for founding-directors and teams to spend time in an existing l'Arche community before giving birth to a new one. Even then, how-ever, it had on occasions been a mistake for potential founders to come and spend time in a French community. The tendency then was to try to transplant what worked in France.

For some within l'Arche the failure to develop more in the former Eastern bloc countries such as Romania, despite the extremity of the need and Jean Vanier's commitment to them, was a source of embarrassment. L'Arche seemed to have reached a point, however, where expansion had in some measure to be sacrificed to deal with the growth and life within existing communities. From the early days of the all-too-swift acquisition of the honey-coloured houses in Trosly-Breuil, it had rarely been possible to be certain that when the disabled people arrived there would be the necessary assistants to look after them. The problem of finding people prepared to make a long-term commitment was still a world-wide one. In general the opening up of the world and greater possibilities of travel might have meant that in many European communities the range and diversity of assistants had broadened, but as one United Kingdom community leader acknowledged, 'Put together people with disabilities, faith, and all the freedoms you have to give up in order to live in community, and that does not make a sexy package for a modern 21-year-old.' The tendency was still to come for a year or two and then move on to other things. The constructive consequences of such intervals might be immeasurable. When Thierry died in one *foyer*, his body was subsequently placed in the chapel. An assistant went to pay her last respects and was moved to find another, a Muslim in his prayer robes, reciting prayers for the dead from the Koran. When, following the events of September 11 disparaging remarks were being made about Muslims in general, she could not be a party to them. L'Arche did not fail to recognise the ripple effect of this and a multitude of other experiences of discovering respect for difference.

The fact remained, however, that for the disabled people the rate of change in their lives was very demanding. Young assistants came, formed deep relationships with them for a year or so, then moved on and were replaced by others before people had really had time to grieve the loss of their predecessors. A certain amount of flow was healthy and normal: families changed, friendships changed, people moved on, and on the whole the disabled people coped extraordinarily well. It was part of the pain and the

gift they carried that they continued, despite the many departures, to welcome new people into their lives. There were nevertheless those who coped by cutting themselves off from entering
too deeply into relationships too quickly, because each time an
assistant left them it triggered the pain of a multitude of other
departures. Assistant turnover affected everything from the quality
of community that could be built to the quality of care provided
and because the problem of the shortage of assistants persisted,
assistants had been welcomed whose vocation was obviously not
really to l'Arche. Power struggles and open conflict had ensued in
a way which had made it all too clear that l'Arche must be wiser
in its discernment of whom it should welcome. The circumstances of some incidents and departures had caused pain and
suffering, but then l'Arche was founded upon suffering, and pain
was a necessary part of growth.

There was scope for criticism of l'Arche. Those concerned
with the struggle to change social structures sometimes saw it as
personalist and inclined towards conservative reactionary positions based on the idea that social structures were in some way
out of reach, could not be changed, and the only thing that
mattered was the individual. Those who, through relationship
with people with disabilities, became more sympathetic in their
criticism, could still hold on with some justification to the idea
that not all communities were sufficiently concerned with the
social reality encompassing them. In the larger communities,
l'Arche life, like any organisational or institutional life, tended to
become the total universe and there were those who saw this fact
as a grave short-coming. There were also criticisms associated
with the inbuilt dilemma between the essential focus on the
disabled people on the one hand, and care for the life of the assistants on the other. As one priest at Trosly-Breuil put it, 'The
insight about the disabled people has been tried and tested and is
clearly of the spirit and solidly in place. The same cannot be said
of the assistants.' Ultimately perhaps it was a problem of structure.
To a Jesuit coming from an order which, according to its own
criteria, was well structured and had been for a long time, l'Arche
in its desire not to reproduce tired structures from the past had
put together a system which was unnecessarily cumbersome and
in which responsibilities were not well defined and clearly

located. In such circumstances painful decisions tended to fall between the cracks.

Professional carers might envy the conditions in which those in l'Arche could encourage the growth and development of people with disabilities: the fact, for instance, that an assistant might have the opportunity to spend the greater part of his day with one disabled person. In one respect l'Arche had had a flying start in relation to health authorities and social service departments. In terms of the idea of shared life and disabled people being brought out of hospitals and institutions, l'Arche, when it began in 1964, had been somewhat in advance of its time. Its convictions about professional practice or the appropriate circumstances for mentally disabled people within and not outside the wider community had subsequently proved to be in the forefront of a widespread movement which continued to gain momentum. On the other hand, l'Arche's strong emphasis on family life, with all the mutual support that entailed, did not always meet with the approval of those who believed in promoting maximum independence.

By the end of the twentieth century in some Western countries people with disabilities were coming to l'Arche from a very different vantage point from those welcomed in its early history. When l'Arche began in Lambeth it was offering something different, in particular the belief in engaged relationship, when there was little else. By the turn of the millennium it was offering something different when there were many other options. People with disabilities had more of a say in their own lives and l'Arche was placing greater emphasis on supporting them in their own choices. On the whole the people who came to l'Arche still tended to be those seeking a supportive family life, epitomised by the sizeable dining table round which quite a number could be seated with space for one or two newcomers. There were some professionals, however, who maintained that not many people in the West were in fact now living in this way and that 'normalisation' should not mean the creation of conditions for disabled people which were different from the lifestyle of the majority of the remainder of the population. L'Arche on the other hand wanted to show that 'normalisation' did not mean exclusively conforming to what was the 'norm', that human beings were not necessarily fulfilled in independence and loneliness. It believed that human fulfilment came through bonds of love, of family and of city, and that it was from this source of love, this network of relationships that each one could grow in his or her capacity to serve, work, accomplish works of art and discover communion with God.

All the same, it encouraged those who wanted complete independence to try and achieve it. In the United Kingdom it was now possible for any person, no matter how severe their disabilities, to live alone, if that was what they wanted. It might take 24-hour care with a team of four people and much persuasion of the social services. But it was still possible. Disabled people in England tended to arrive with an established quality of life and the question was then what their next step should be. Did they aspire to living on their own, getting married, having a job or driving a car? The choice was theirs. L'Arche would endeavour to help them achieve it. One member of the Lambeth community had recently moved into her own flat nearby. Elsewhere, in France, two disabled people had married and were managing to live a reasonably autonomous life in Compiègne. And in those cases where the gulf between the disabled person's ideal and the reality of their life was too great, l'Arche was there to support them in their pain.

As the pressure from local authorities to conform to regulations with regard to housing and living conditions for people with disabilities grew, some people in l'Arche had found themselves moving further and further away from the original idea of the simple *foyer* and questioning what precisely that concept meant. The French idea of a shared life in a home was being recognised as more of a tool, a method, than the essence of l'Arche. As Australia had discovered fairly early on in its history, the charism could well express itself in different forms in different countries and cultures. This might mean a presence through workshops and support of families rather than an actual home. The idea of life together in a big house forming the core of the community, with a cluster of married and other external members, including more autonomous people with disabilities, living on the fringes but coming together in the shared physical space for different activities and purposes, had become a conceivable model for the future.

There were obvious areas for potential questioning associated with the very idea of untrained people living with the disabled, and linked also to them the whole issue of the space and distance between the carer and the cared for, the detachment which most professionals would consider crucial. In Western countries regulations ensured that the professional element present in l'Arche from the very beginning was a constant and demanding consideration. In England, for example, there were 42 detailed standards with which l'Arche, like any other care home, had to comply, and houses were inspected to those standards twice a year. The question of how members of the community could marry what was labelled a 'professional' approach to commitment to another person in the spirit of l'Arche remained a burning one.

L'Arche had on occasions been attacked for allegedly driving vulnerable people into religion: 'There has been a feeling that we make disabled people feel like Jesus when they don't want to be Jesus. It is easy to attack on those grounds. It is easy to deform religious language.' In the view of Patrick Mathias, the psychiatrist at Trosly who professed to be an atheist, there was far too much independent and critical thought in l'Arche for there to be any danger of the kind of religious coercion found in sects. Trosly-Breuil was a Roman Catholic community and made no secret of that fact. What mattered was the space afforded to the individual to have his or her say. That had to be constantly watched and safeguarded, but then l'Arche was made up of 'marginals'. Jean Vanier himself was in a sense a marginal. Marginals were needed in order to move society on, but among marginalised people it was rare to find ten people who thought the same way.

Other criticisms had arisen in connection with the spiritual and ecumenical life of the communities. From l'Arche's own point of view a central question remained: what constituted an appropriate shared spiritual life in the houses? Quite a spectrum of spiritual life existed in the various communities, ranging from the essentially Roman Catholic intensity of the Farm at Trosly-Breuil, to the prayers to the Creator God before or during sunrise and the silence and other sacred moments observed at Asha Niketan, Kolkata, to much less obviously shared and regular worship. Whilst Jean Vanier fully recognised that it would be madness to try and reproduce the Farm everywhere, the question persisted nevertheless as to whether communities were 'living l'Arche' if there was no shared spiritual life within the houses.

By failing to conform to the usual prescribed definitions of either State-recognised institution or Christian community, l'Arche had been a sign of contradiction since its very inception. Yet it wanted to be both a centre accepted according to the norms of the State and a Christian community firmly anchored in the values of the gospel. Furthermore, even whilst finding unity in communion with God and communion with the poorest and weakest, it had recognised that its communities were non-homogeneous and must take into account the great diversity of its members, their vocation and way of expressing their faith. It was small wonder then that these ambiguities had at times disconcerted both State and Church. Government representatives did not always fully appreciate that when 'the growth of people' was paramount, efficiency was sometimes sacrificed. They did not necessarily understand, for example, when Daybreak needed a number of vehicles because the ten houses there, though geographically some distance apart, were connected, and their occupants needed to come together for meetings and celebrations. Other organisations with ten houses similarly situated tended not to require that sort of bonding. In France, the social security representatives had reacted strongly to the policy of assistants not receiving normal salaries. There was no provision in French law for centres to have volunteer workers or assistants with lower wages. It had taken l'Arche several years to negotiate an agreement with government officials by which an assistant could be considered under training for the first two years, and so receive simply a stipend and social security benefits. Only after two years did he or she receive the minimum legal wage.

Jean Vanier was fully appreciative of the number of men and women in administration who did recognise the values of l'Arche. One head of the Department of Social Welfare in Beauvais, France, in particular had understood and summarised most clearly the position, questions and concerns of people in government authority. When, in 1977, Jean explained the aims and life in l'Arche to her, she had responded:

I admire what you are doing. It is surely the best thing for people with a handicap, but if something goes wrong … If, for example, assistants accepting small salaries and your lifestyle no longer come, what can I do to help you? If I give you subsidies, what guarantee do I have that l'Arche will continue?

She was, Jean Vanier acknowledged, pointing out the folly of l'Arche.

Similarly, although there were those who found Jean Vanier not revolutionary enough, too spiritual and too ready to identify himself with the Church, there were ongoing difficulties associated with the question of specific religious identity, not just in the relationship of a lay community to the Church but also with the role of the priest within l'Arche. The importance of priests in the spiritual and mystical growth of community members might have been increasingly recognised, but there had always been a tension, an element of power in l'Arche, as in the Church, between clergy and lay people. Jean Vanier maintained his belief in the importance of priests in l'Arche, not least because people with disabilities were deeply attracted to priests and the mystery they represented. Nevertheless, the idea of priests following naturally in the footsteps of Père Thomas remained for the most part an ideal. For some it was difficult to discover that they really had no obviously important position and that their role was simply to 'live the Eucharist, befriend people and through that friendship lead them to Jesus'. Some had become priests precisely because they wanted a clearly acknowledged role. It was vital that they did not see themselves as all-important, but equally important that directors did not confine them to the sacristy. It came back to the vision of the Church as communion in which each person's gifts were honoured.

Politically and economically l'Arche had encountered difficult seasons. Whereas at one point in certain parts of the world the deinstitutionalisation, decentralisation and reintegration of people with disabilities had been high on the list of social and government priorities, as the struggle to provide places and care for people with AIDS/HIV and battered women and children became more pressing, disabled people had become more marginal amongst the marginals. L'Arche had at times had trouble with finance. Financiers in France had revealed that, whereas at one time it had been best to ask for money for India or Africa, now the prevalent attitude not just in France but in many other countries was that of looking after one's own people first. People had tended to close in on themselves, yet the need in poorer countries such as Zimbabwe, Uganda, and even Poland was so great. Nor was it easy in an apparently increasingly threatened world to attract people in the materialistic West into communities which appeared insecure. People were looking for more institutionalisation and human security, and possibly needed it before they could accept the insecurity of the gospels.

Jean Vanier had a gift for transforming limitations, criticisms and blockages into challenges to be viewed with excitement and a certain peace: 'It is peace giving when we discover that we don't have to succeed but just to let Jesus work in and through us.' Jean, however, was in his seventies and, as the fortieth anniversary of the founding of l'Arche approached, was soon to retire from the International Board. There was a feeling within l'Arche that a crossroads had been reached. As part of its enormous growth over those 40 years, it was being subjected to all kinds of pressure to change in shape and organisation, and be more professionally and transparently run. Furthermore, even though Jean had long since ceased to hold an official leadership role and was generally applauded for being very good about not interfering, the reality was that he still held a moral authority that no one else possessed. His vision had founded and sustained l'Arche members to date, but the need for each member now to take real responsibility for l'Arche and its future must be addressed, as must other areas of difficulty such as the reality that long-term assistants in l'Arche were not as young as they once were and younger assistants, particularly in the West, needed somehow to be shown that among the many choices open to them, giving their lives to l'Arche was a viable option even if they had not yet 'sniffed all the other flowers'. Where there was no shortage of long-term assistants the challenge was to remain open to new blood. The reality also had to be faced that the original generation of assistants and people with disabilities, those who had been close to the founders, were entering old age, and among those coming up behind them were many who felt unclear about the real nature of what they were living.

In 1999 Jean-Christophe Pascal and Christine McGrievy were elected international co-ordinator and vice-co-ordinator of the International Federation of l'Arche. Each region within the Federation had its own specific problems but the international coordinators identified a consistent shortage of assistants combined with an increased turnover, a lack of leaders and, possibly most seriously of all, increasing confusion in naming the identity of l'Arche, as difficulties affecting them all. There was by this time so much diversity within the l'Arche Federation that some found it difficult to see a unifying identity.

With a view to finding greater unity and clarity of identity for the future, on a bleak October day in Chicago that year a meeting of the International Council of l'Arche was held. Jean Vanier was there. Also present was Gerald Arbuckle SM, a priest and consultant anthropologist and an expert on Refounding and Pastoral Development, who had been asked to give an objective analysis of how the founding story of l'Arche might be faithfully carried forward. Part of Gerry Arbuckle's thesis, as it emerged on that occasion and in the course of other subsequent conversations was that 'The most powerful myth[1] in every culture is its creation myth, since it provides people with their primary source of identity as a distinct group.' Myths could change in various ways. Perhaps the one potentially most relevant to l'Arche at this stage was what he referred to as 'Myth Drift', which occurred when 'myths change, degenerate or disappear without deliberate planning'. This was a common process, unless a proactive stand was taken to retain the integrity of the original founding story.

In the high-growth early stage of any organisational culture there was a strong sense of shared purpose in the group; people did not question the legitimacy of the founder to lead, and followers saw in his articulation of the founding myth something that gave deep meaning to their own lives. At this stage the group remained small enough to allow ready access to him and the authority structure remained tied to the founder who governed by virtue of his personal qualities. His personality or charisma was sufficient to inspire people to follow his vision. There was potentially a grave weakness here, however, that if not addressed would lead to major tensions in the movement later. The longer the leader failed to develop independent authority structures, the less likely it was that appropriate authority roles would be clarified throughout the movement. Everything would be centred – implicitly or explicitly – on the founder. What was really needed was authority related to the task and not authority that had its source in relationship.

With the rapid growth in size and complexity of any movement or organisation people found themselves increasingly distanced from access to the founder. They felt removed from his charismatic inspirational power, and with this came a decline in understanding of the founding experience which the founder had invariably not had time to articulate fully in written or verbal form. In any case, the founder himself might still be developing an understanding of the founding experience or myth. Nevertheless, if the sense of common purpose and direction was not to decline, and future chaos and even schism was to be avoided, it was vital that he or she was able to share the founding charism, the 'faith shock', or experience of the chasm that existed between the gospel and the world around him that had so pained him as to impel him, by God's grace, to do something about it. It was vital too that the founding story was told not in so sanitised a fashion that it failed to evoke a radical response. Sharing the founding story meant far more than a recital of historical developments of the group. Above all, would-be followers must be able to identify with the founder's faith shock and recognise in it something of their own personal experience. If they could not 'own', for example as in the case of l'Arche, the pain of the gulf between people with disabilities and the contemporary world, the founding experience would remain remote and non-transforming and their following would be unreflective; theirs would be a dependency relationship not strong enough to sustain them and the movement in the future.

These insights were general ones drawn from the lessons of history. They were not without a certain relevance to l'Arche, however, and Jean Vanier's early attempts to hand over authority were not the only indications that he recognised that fact. He himself had written in 1993 in *The Founding Myth and the Evolution of Community*[2] of how 'the original founder has to know when to disappear and let go so that he or she does not prevent the "refounders" from accomplishing their mission'. In the same paper he emphasised the need for the clarification and purification of the vision of community:

> A community must move from the necessary idealistic certitude of its uniqueness and goodness to a wider knowledge and acceptance of the body of the Church and of humanity. It must evolve from the myth of the 'perfect founder who does everything inspired by God', to a more collective ownership of the founding story, purified of the non-essentials.

If l'Arche members were to be able to 'own' the founding story, it must be told as an experience of the spirit, without accidental historical details becoming integral to the charism itself; without the charism being reduced to an inflexible, history-bound object. Furthermore, it must emerge with all its suffering, difficult though that might be, because otherwise the story might not be fully grasped. Those who followed on behind must know when they too experienced suffering, when they, like the people more overtly labelled disabled experienced the gulf between their ideals and the reality of their lives, that this too was part of 'living l'Arche'.

On that bleak October afternoon in a Dominican Conference centre in Chicago, Gerry Arbuckle also pointed out that through the mystery of God, history showed that every founding story incorporated a Gethsemane experience. In the Garden of Gethsemane the physical sufferings that Jesus was to experience evoked in him dreadful fear, loneliness and the need for people to feel his inner pain, the yearning for compassion and companionship. Instead his disciples avoided responding by sleeping, leaving him alone, personally alive to the enormity of the gap between the mission given him by the Father and the frailty inherent in his human nature. Mark the evangelist explained this lack of compassion: 'They did not know what to say to Jesus.' This was because they had not yet owned up to their own inner need for understanding and compassion. For this reason they refused the gift of mutuality with Jesus that would have consoled him in his loneliness. It was not the three disciples but the Father who heard the anguish of Jesus and consoled him. And Jesus was so transformed by this that he took up his role of messiah with renewed energy (Mark 14:42).

There was something about the sacred that should not be flaunted. It was moreover not always right that what was private should become public. There was a danger of people believing that if only their questions relating to the story were answered all current problems would be resolved, or of seizing too rigidly upon a fragment of the whole, or of taking what was particular to a specific set of circumstances and assuming its general appropriateness and truth. Jean Vanier too, however, must 'own' the story as he came to understand it better: the roots; the structuring of his personality; his own marginalisation and renunciation; the gentle questions and promptings of Père Thomas; his experience of the gulf between the gospel message and the needs of people with disabilities; the balancing of competence and practical efficiency with spirituality, of earth and sky; the discovery of the inner pain of his own 'disabilities', the desire to control others, his own proneness to hidden anger and violence; the sense of alienation from his spiritual father; the gap between his ideals and the reality of his life that was his personal Gethsemane; the inner healing of communion; the compassion that led to inner transformation – all of which pointed to the active designs of a loving God. 'It has taken me a long time to accept that I am a founder!' he wrote in August 2004 on the 40th anniversary of l'Arche.

> Founders generally know what they want from the very beginning. I did not. I only knew that I wanted to live the gospel and to share my life in community with those who were poor, and in this shared life together to be a sign of love in the world ... I had energy, a sense of authority and organisation, and was open and ready to take risks. But above all, I wanted to follow the 'wind' or 'breath' of the Holy Spirit ... I realise now how everything had been prepared in the heart of God. God made use of the deep union, the communion between Père Thomas and myself, and of our poverty and our openness, to create something new and beautiful.

By then a process of clarifying the real nature of the 'something new and beautiful' that had been created, and of looking to the future of l'Arche and its development, was well under way. Jean Vanier had long believed in the importance of good theology. Since 1993 a series of meetings had been going on at Trosly with theologians from various traditions and members of l'Arche and other communities. Among those theologians were Frances Young, a Methodist minister who had been for some years Cadbury Professor of Theology at the University of Birmingham and who was herself the mother of Arthur, a man with severe mental disabilities, Canon A. M. Allchin, an honorary Professor of the University of Wales in Bangor and David Ford, Regius Professor of Divinity and Fellow of Selwyn College, Cambridge. Part of the purpose of these gatherings had been to try and put the spirituality of l'Arche into more theological language and to bounce Jean Vanier's ideas and vision against external theological thought. In the earlier meetings, some of them attended by Dr Rowan Williams, Thérèse Vanier had also contributed her extensive experience of the ecumenical situation in the United Kingdom and her habitual valued tendency to 'earth the otherwise great and glorious vision of beautiful relationships'.

This process of 'seeking the wisdom' of l'Arche was extended in 2002 to the whole International Federation. Following the advice and input of Gerry Arbuckle and a Jesuit, Franck Janin, who designed the method, it was proposed that a three-year process of discernment through prayer, reflection and sharing – of listening to the Holy Spirit – be established. A similar process had previously been used in North America but this time it was to be extended across the Federation and every member would be invited to contribute.

The aim of this 'Identity and Mission' process was 'to understand and respond to God's call for l'Arche today'. In the first year members were invited to look at what they had lived since the beginning of l'Arche and to say what they felt it had all been about. The main objective was, through the sharing of people's 'sacred stories' to establish those aspects of l'Arche that were essential to the life of communities throughout the Federation. It proved to be an extremely positive experience, giving members the opportunity, in some cases for the first time, to express their reasons for being in l'Arche. The reports were conspicuously consistent: l'Arche was about relationships, its desire was to be a 'sign' for the world, a sign that peace was possible, that people of different ages, religions, sexes and nationalities could live together in unity. There was nothing perhaps surprising about this in that both 'relationships' and the aspiration to be a 'sign' were existing ingredients of the Charter of l'Arche. Another recurrent message, however, was that relationships with people with disabilities had been *transforming*, and this was something hitherto not so overtly articulated. The process of developing an identity statement remained unfinished but the essential elements were identified:

- People with developmental disabilities and others sharing life together
- Relationships that are a source of mutual transformation
- Faith, life and trust in God
- Acceptance of weakness and vulnerability
- Competence and quality of care
- Cultural and religious diversity
- Members of an International Federation open to and engaged with the world

The second year's reflection invited members to name their failures, the pitfalls and obstacles that had kept them from fully living l'Arche and to accept personal responsibility, to ascertain what they had done or failed to do. It was an emotional experience for many in that it was a time for owning their weakness. At the same time the opportunity to be honest allowed participants to discover greater maturity. The International Reflecting Group, which met in Belgium to discern the findings of the second stage, identified as a major obstacle difficulty in recognising and naming God as central to community life. Faith tended to remain personal and private. L'Arche's structures did not effectively develop or sustain commitment, vocation and membership. The role of authority in l'Arche was not clear. There was also ambivalence about giving real authority to those in leadership roles. People had difficulty in recognising their limits. Too often there was a lack of honest communication resulting in hurt and broken relationships. It was, moreover, felt that there was not sufficient clarity and understanding of the founding story of l'Arche, and that this limited members' flexibility, creativity, vision, sense of identity, and the story's potential power to challenge and transform.

The object of the third stage of the Identity and Mission process was to define 'for today' the essential elements of the mission of l'Arche; how was its identity to be incarnated in contemporary reality? In March 2005 the International Reflecting Group met again in Belgium, this time with members of the International Board and a mission statement was agreed upon for the Federation:

- To make known the gifts of people with developmental disabilities revealed through mutually transforming relationships.
- To engage in our diverse cultures, working together to build a more human society.
- To foster an environment in communities that is inspired by the core values of our founding story, and responds to the changing needs of our members.

The three-year Identity and Mission process was pronounced a gift. Many people spoke of personal and community renewal and many groups had taken fuller responsibility for some of the questions l'Arche was currently facing, but much depended on continuing commitment to the actions suggested to help implement this Mission Statement.

Jean Vanier welcomed the process. In fact he found it very moving in that it had underlined the sense that 'we are part of a family'. He was also the first to acknowledge that 'we can fall into a sort of vision that is good' but forget the problems. He was glad that Jean-Christophe was international coordinator because of his capacity to bring together the spiritual and the human, for listening and not proceeding too quickly, and because of his ability to see the negative. Jean Vanier himself would see it but not want to admit it. He knew there was a strong tendency towards idealism in him but then it was this very idealism which had helped to bring about the extraordinary growth of the founding years. Even the human uncertainty created by the shortage of assistants could be viewed in a positive light as a form of poverty at a time when l'Arche in many countries was in other respects not as poor as it once was. What remained important for him was that Identity and Mission and what followed it should incorporate an awakening of the heart, the desire to follow that 'wind' or 'breath' of the Spirit.

'Spiritual masters in sacred scripture often tell stories', he wrote in *Becoming Human*,[3] to reveal truths and awaken hearts:

Jesus spoke in parables; Hasidic Jews and Sufi teachers tell tales; Hindu scripture is full of stories. Stories seem to awaken energies of love; they tell us great truths in simple personal terms and make us long for light. Stories have a strange power of attraction. When we tell stories, we touch hearts. If we talk about theories or speak about ideas, the mind may assimilate them but the heart remains untouched.

Sacred stories should be told and heard and 'owned' in this spirit. Similarly whilst he welcomed the fact that 'transformation' had been cited by many as a consequence of life in l'Arche, what was important was what was meant by transformation. As one community leader put it: 'Transformation can be about "my life", a change which enables me to exercise greater choice in the future of my life, not the transformation of the gospels.' Most who came to l'Arche would say that their experience of faith was more positive on their way out than on their way in. L'Arche was very undogmatic; religion within it was very non-threatening. 'Most would say that they had experienced something which made them a different person on leaving from the person who arrived but that could just mean that they were better equipped for the job market, with better people skills etc.'

In May 2005 at the conclusion of the Identity and Mission process a meeting of 350 members of the International Federation of l'Arche was held in Assisi. Archbishop Rowan Williams and Cardinal Walter Kasper joined the gathering for the last day. Not surprisingly, Jean Vanier's address in Assisi related the experience of l'Arche to the founding vision of St Francis and St Clare. He referred to the appeal of God to St Francis to rebuild his ruined church, a call to which Francis responded both literally by rebuilding the dilapidated church of San Damiano, and more generally and profoundly by attempting to reconstruct the Church at a time when it was racked with scandal and the quest for wealth and power. Was that not also part of the vocation of l'Arche? asked Jean Vanier. 'Are we not also called by God to repair the breakages of our world, the breakage between the powerful and the weak, between the healthy and the disabled, between religions and Churches?'

He also referred to St Francis' own account of how whilst he was still in sin the sight of lepers, those whom society regarded as horrible, dirty and to be rejected, had been unbearable to him. But after he had been led by God to be present to them and care for them, what had previously seemed bitter became sweet for him in body and spirit. Was this not an experience of transformation, of the reality of the gospel?

Transformation for Jean Vanier was the message of Jesus. It was closely linked to 'wonder'. Mother Teresa had spoken of how her initial response to the dying destitutes on the streets of Kolkata was fear and revulsion. She had gone on to explain that when she touched the broken body of an apparently repellent person, tended him and gave him a bath, she felt compassion and this compassion could then lead to a real encounter which she described as 'wonder'. Through relationship with the poor person she had seen the face of God. Generosity, according to Jean Vanier, should lead to an encounter with the weak person and beyond it to wonder:

> You tell me your story. I listen to you. I come to know your name and your suffering. It is at this point that a communion of hearts occurs, when I become vulnerable to you. There is no more superior and inferior. We are bound together in a covenant. My heart is transformed. This is a moment of wonder.

If Jean Vanier was concerned about assistants it was in relation to whether they were identifying what they were living in this light. Many he encountered now lacked what might be called 'structure'. Some had no previous experience of the conditions that helped to nurture relationships, of the 'family' meals for example over which people took time to talk and share, and which had always been central to life in l'Arche. Those who had come in the early years had in many instances been reacting against authority and the Church's understanding of religion, but there was a whole group of assistants now who knew nothing about religious faith. In some ways they were much more open for that reason but it meant that l'Arche was called to assist them towards a good understanding of anthropology and theology.

How could assistants be helped to discover the mystery of what it meant to be united to Jesus on a spiritual level and to people on a social level, to discover the freedom of living simply this friendship with Jesus in the Spirit?

Reviewing his own life Jean could see that following the structuring of the personality and the mind, he had been able to grow a little further, not contradicting the past with its clearly defined understanding of right and wrong but integrating it. For Aristotle being human did not mean simply obeying laws that came from outside, but attaining maturity. In the Gospel of John there was:

> ... the gradual discovery that Jesus was bringing a new truth and that he was going to liberate the Jewish people, but then the realisation that he was going to do it in a way that was completely unexpected. It is not a case of the Jews being right and the Romans being wrong. Jesus' message was that it was not just the Jews who were precious but everyone. There is a love that takes people to the very end and eventually the only answer is to give one's life.

There had been stages of growth in his life and even stages of truth in that growth. What had been important was discovering truth as he went along. The danger lay in remaining adolescent because for the adolescent there was necessarily right and wrong. Too much importance could be placed on obedience which could crush, and not enough on helping people to develop conscience through which the Holy Spirit operated. It was important that structures were established in the first place. Law was necessary because every society needed rules but over and above the society or the group were personal encounters that transcended regulation. The relationship between structure, obedience, law and freedom of conscience was a subtle and complex one. Education for Jean was a matter of teaching people how to grow in conscience rather than in obedience.

In Jean's own case Père Thomas, who had, despite his orthodoxy, in specific circumstances responded to the call of the Holy Spirit to go beyond ecclesial norms, had given him the freedom to think and to let the Spirit do what it had to do. Like Jesus in the gospels, Père Thomas had known how not to tell the young Jean Vanier what to do but rather to ask first 'What are you look-

ing for?' What is your desire, your conscience?' He had communicated something precious that had flowered while the priest
was still alive and had continued to do so even after his death. The
perspective then from which so many things were viewed was
not that of swift categorisation as 'right' or 'wrong' but of
whether something was giving birth to something new and true,
whether it was leading to the deepening of personality, whether
it was moving towards greater union with Jesus.

In 1999 a system of three cycles of formation known as the
'Ecole de Vie' had been introduced. Those who had been in
l'Arche for between two and four years came together for three
fortnights a year for two years, during which Jean gave instruction in anthropology and Elise Corsini, with whose help he had
written his book on happiness in the ethics of Aristotle, spoke on
philosophy. The third cycle consisted of three weeks a year for
assistants who had been in l'Arche for ten years at which Jean
Vanier spoke on, among other themes, St John's Gospel. In
between the two, a second cycle was held to reflect on the meaning and nature of life in l'Arche. Additional retreats were
conducted annually for assistants. Despite this and despite the
process of accompaniment, the weakness of l'Arche might be that
people were not being fed the mystical meaning of what they
were living. He was still not sure that assistants were helped
adequately to realise that their experience was an experience of
God, and that the message of that experience of God had a
relevance far beyond 'doing good things for disabled people' who
were potentially a source of illumination for the Church and
beyond.

FOURTEEN

NEW LIFE IN GOD

At the age of 76, seated in a small room in his stone-built house in Trosly, surrounded by books and the papers that formed his 'less than perfect' filing system, and watched over from the mantelpiece by photographs of Raphael and Philippe, Pope John Paul II, Aung San Suu Kyi and an early picture of himself with Père Thomas, Jean Vanier admitted: 'I sense that my vocation today is more about the message than community.' The message had been revealed in community but the message was about the value of the person with disabilities in society and in the Church, which obviously surpassed community. So what was really important was the message and not its institutionalisation or 'concretisation'. The 'concretisation' might well change. 'Institutionalisation' was necessary because clear rules had to be established with regard to the community's goal and the way in which it was governed, but if the form was found not to work then other forms could be created.

L'Arche's strength lay in its openness to change and its recognition of the value of growth. Already Jean Vanier could discern a shift of emphasis in its story: from the accent being on the group to the 'liberation of the person'. What remained important was listening to the voice of the poor. It was the experience of l'Arche that 'if we listen to people in depth, truth comes from them'. As another community leader put it:

> The history of l'Arche has a truth and a wisdom to it which is not by coincidence. What Jean listened to was the needs of

people with disabilities. Some in my community now are saying they want to live in a big house and share their home with people and some are saying absolutely the opposite. If we are true to the call to listen to what people want, we have to go with it and trust that we would not have been given a mission that was just about one model. Relationship, transformation, sign, faith are not referring to houses and living together, although it is a particularly good way of doing it. The physical model is not where truth lies. It is something much deeper.

As far as Jean was concerned, it would be wrong even to think that only l'Arche could deliver that truth, propagate that message. The message might be better revealed in parishes or through the parents of people with disabilities. He was nonetheless happy to use the last years of his life to announce the vision of Jesus: his love for the weak and the poor.

It was not that he no longer had a role in community. Only recently Francis, his neighbour in the adjoining end-of-terrace house, had told Patrick Mathias, the psychiatrist, that the knowledge that Jean was there on the other side of the wall made him feel safe. For people who were mentally ill or had problems of insecurity it was vital that there were 'centres of stability'. 'Stability' was not quite the right word but Jean thought that his role was to provide a presence which made people feel safe. It was not entirely true, of course, but the important thing was that they believed it. There was a girl who would come up to him after Mass. She was a bit disturbed but was attracted to him in some way. He would take her face in his hands and she would talk to him about her mum, and he would have nothing to say, but that did not matter. Once again it was a question of touch and presence.

He was still very much part of his own *foyer*, the Val Fleuri. In August 2004, while the men of the Val Fleuri had been away on their annual holiday, a fire had badly damaged the building. During the period of refurbishment accommodation had had to be found for its occupants in different *foyers* in the village. It had been a difficult time for them all but they had carried each other through and 'normality' had now been restored. He loved spending time there. Whereas once he had carried the responsibility for it, taking care of its members, now he was touched by the way in which they all took care of him, giving him the best chair in the room, suggesting he rest or read the newspaper instead of doing the dishes. He was, he knew, the daily recipient of a thousand small gestures, each one a gesture of love, the kind of small gestures which he saw as part of a 'trickle of peace'.

L'Arche, with its more than 125 communities now divided into eight zones, had come of age, and there was much to celebrate. Notwithstanding the difficulties, Jean Vanier could give thanks for years of amazing, surprising, unexpected and unhoped for gifts and fruits, for the evolution of l'Arche was the story of men and women and an increasing number of children who had come from asylums, psychiatric institutions and other situations of rejection and abandonment and had 'made the passage from death to resurrection, from anguish, loneliness and despair to trust, community and hope, and had been able to do so because many extraordinary assistants were there to accompany them'. An immense amount of attention was given to each person with disabilities in l'Arche and on the whole he felt that things were done well.

Faith and Sharing had spread all over North America, and Faith and Light had become a 'phenomenal reality'. At the beginning of the twenty-first century there were some 1,500 communities and it was a source of joy to see this mysterious growth. A parent would hear about it, or a priest would realise that he had a number of people with disabilities in his area, and a new community would be initiated. In places such as Syria and Lebanon young people sometimes met every week. Parents gave each other mutual support and there were mimes, games, celebration, prayer and theological reflection on themes provided by Jean Vanier in the 'carnet de route'. Elsewhere, in places like Paris where there was more for people in general, and even for people with disabilities, to do, Faith and Light members met less frequently. It was all still very fragile. The more time he spent with parents the more he realised how many were still desperate and ashamed of their children with disabilities. The tendency then was to close up. As in l'Arche, people in Faith and Light could become too preoccupied with paperwork and similar considerations when what really mattered was relationships. As in l'Arche, there was a need for good formation because it could all too easily become just a place where parents could get rid of their son or daughter on a Wednesday afternoon, but it remained an extraordinary source of support to many. He had recently accepted a position of authority in relation to the administration of the Farm. New government regulations had meant that the old farm buildings with their limited bathrooms and kitchen facilities could not be used for accommodating guests in the way they had previously. A process of total modernisation had been undertaken, preserving the external walls but providing modern bedrooms with en suite showers and toilets, and kitchens that complied with government standards. The Farm had remained very much the spiritual home of Père Thomas and a handful of people who sought to spread his message, and some of the longstanding tensions persisted. Because it had a different if complementary role as a place of prayer, formation and welcome, earning money as a place of hospitality and a retreat centre, it had been set up as a separate charitable foundation. Jean Vanier, having renounced all other administrative positions, had agreed to be its chairperson to ensure it remained part of l'Arche, and at the service of all the communities. It was, according to some close to him, an act of loyalty and love for his spiritual father which could not have been easy, in that it had entailed his once more confronting the complexities of the history of l'Arche and the relationship between the founder and the 'inspirer'. If anything Jean's fidelity to Père Thomas had grown in the period since his death.

Jean Vanier was continuing to occupy his mind with a vision of anthropology rooted in the weakness of the child, which led to the weakness of the old person, 'passing through a time of strength and the development of our capacities, which should be at the service of unity and peace, within each person, and then in family, community and society'. He was still publishing books. *Befriending the Stranger*[1] began life as a series of talks he gave in the Dominican Republic for people in l'Arche in Latin America and the Caribbean. In it he reflected on how communities were built, and asked in particular whether it was possible to be compassionate with others if one was not compassionate with oneself. He was continuing his work with assistants who wanted to grow in

New Life in God   269

their understanding of and commitment to l'Arche through such retreats and through the different sessions of 'Ecole de Vie'.

He felt called continually to talk about the vulnerability of God hidden in the weak and in his own weakness, to announce the beauty and the pain of people with disabilities and the joy of living in community with them, and to speak also about the pain of parents. He received many despairing letters from parents with disabled children, some of them to the effect that they could see the beauty in the child but he or she still drove them to distraction. His message in such circumstances now was that parents should be as compassionate with themselves as they would like to be with their child, and talk honestly with each other and members of their family. Often he would telephone the writers of letters of this kind. A telephone call enabled him to respond more sensitively to the person in pain, and touched them in a way that a letter possibly did not.

As a layman he had trodden paths outside the community of l'Arche which would not have been open to him, and spoken out not just to religious audiences but also to professionals in the human services field in a way which might not have been possible had he been a priest, and he would continue to do so. He had long pursued his insights on a large scale. His movements attracted attention in the press, his books were widely read and reviewed, and he appeared not infrequently on television in connection with ethical issues. The Kennedy Foundation Award that he had received together with Mother Teresa was by no means the only honour he had been afforded. In 1997 Pope John Paul II had given him the Paul VI Award for Peace and Development. The Knights of Columbus in Canada had presented him with the Gaudium et Spes Award, but recognition had come from much further afield than the Roman Catholic Church. The Order of Canada, the Bank of Canada Award, the Légion d'Honneur and the Community of Christ International Peace Award in the USA were just some of the tokens of appreciation he had received, not to mention the numerous honorary degrees that he had been offered but declined.

In the late 1980s the community at Trosly-Breuil had been thrown into frenzied activity to find him suitable clothes to wear for lunch with Queen Elizabeth II at Buckingham Palace. His scant regard for clothes had meant that he did not possess a suit and one of his late father's had had to be altered for the occasion. Much more recently in 2005 he had been on CBC's shortlist of 'Greatest Canadians'. There were times when Jean Vanier felt quite French but his accent betrayed him. He liked being Canadian and felt a certain satisfaction when the Canadians beat the Russians at hockey. In truth, however, he felt more 'Archian' than anything. His culture was l'Arche, his thinking was l'Arche and if he accepted international recognition it was in order to carry the message of l'Arche to the world.

As to the easy entrée he had to Church leaders, he had endeavoured to ensure its continuance by encouraging links between them and the two international coordinators. It was one of the insights that he shared with Jean-Christophe Pascal and Christine McGrievy that if the l'Arche communities were to continue, it must be under the umbrella of Church, and so much depended on individual friendships. Asked what he thought Jesus had in mind when he founded the Church, Jean Vanier, ever tentative and exploratory, wondered whether Jesus in his humility had envisaged anything. The fact that Jesus had stated that he said nothing of his own will, that it was the Father who told him what to say, suggested that in this communion Jesus did the Father's will in choosing Peter but did not know how, with the need to adapt to changing situations and individuals, things would evolve. This was the incredible humility of God who would nonetheless 'be with you to the end'. Of one thing Jean was sure: Jesus would have wanted a compassionate Church. He felt too that what he wanted was a union of on the one hand the 'announcing' Church, through which the Spiritus operated, and on the other a praying Church through the 'whole mystery of Mary', Mary who because of the Paraclete had been able to stand at the foot of the cross, without understanding but trusting and believing.

At the gathering in Assisi in June 2005 Jean Vanier had reminded l'Arche members how during his lifetime Francis had been supported in his mission by the presence and prayer of Claire, who also cared for him when he was sick. After his death in 1226 she had suffered for many years. The woman who had been so strong became poor, dependant and apparently 'useless', offering up her life with the crucified Jesus. Prayer was vital in l'Arche. In order to give affection to other people one must first receive. L'Arche was often poor and bereft in the face of the challenges of the world. It needed the prayerful support of others and had long been sustained by it.

If there were times when Jean Vanier still needed 'confirmation', he was still receiving it. For him one of the most beautiful stories of l'Arche was that of the foundation in Argentina. As long ago as the early 1970s Jean had been asked to take part in a pilgrimage to Chartres. Another speaker on that occasion had been an Argentinian lady by the name of Margarita Moyana. The theme had been 'Who is God for you?' Thereafter Margarita had visited the l'Arche communities on a number of occasions and talked about the poor in Latin America. At a time when the two tendencies in many Latin American countries had been either towards arch conservativism or towards Liberation Theology, she felt that l'Arche had the gifts of both. Many years later in 2003, after Jean with her help had begun developing relationships with people with disabilities, their families and others in Argentina, he was due to speak and meet people there with a view possibly to initiating a community. When he landed at the airport he was informed that the woman who had laid the foundations for this visit and planned his schedule had died on the previous day. That evening he was due to give his talk at the University of Buenos Aires. When he walked into the hall an audience of 1,300 people was waiting for him. Never before had he had such a huge response to a first talk in a country. Afterwards there was a question and answer session. The first of the written questions that he opened was: 'Who is God for you?' Afterwards he realised it had been written by Margarita before her death.

A little house had already been bought under Margarita's guidance. Jean was introduced to mothers who were deeply distressed because they no longer knew what would happen to their children if the community was not begun. A short time later Jean-Christophe visited Argentina and was struck by the abundance of talents and gifts he encountered, and the number of friends who had gathered round a young lawyer, Paulina, who had been coming to the *barrio* to give free legal advice and had absorbed from Margarita the spirit of l'Arche. To him it was a clear sign of the Holy Spirit. He suggested that someone must be praying for l'Arche in Argentina. It was only then that Padre Oscar, a local priest, told him about Sister Laetitia, a Carmelite nun who had given her life for l'Arche. An appointment was made for him to meet her but when Jean-Christophe arrived at the convent the whole community wanted to see him. He spent two or three hours with the Sisters. By 2005 Paulina was living with one person with disabilities in the tiny house Jean had originally seen, and additional accommodation was being built in order that others might follow.

As long ago as 1949 Jean had been introduced by his mother to Mother Thérèse of Jesus in a Carmelite convent in Nogent, where later he also came to know Sister Marie-Madeleine, a cousin and spiritual daughter of Père Thomas. Contemplatives, constantly in the presence of Jesus, they had prayed for him and then for l'Arche. There were other Carmelites in Cognac who held l'Arche in their prayers. In the early days of the community Odile Ceyrac had brought Jean Vanier into touch with Marthe Robin. He had visited her and, physically disabled as she herself was, she had been moved in a special way to pray for l'Arche. The community in Tegucigalpa was carried by the prayers of the Jesuits. In the asylum in the Honduran capital where once Marcia had been kept, I had met a friend of hers, too physically disabled even to alter the position of her limbs in bed. Her frail life was given up to praying for Marcia and her 'family' in Casa Nazaret. There were numerous other examples. Only in heaven, Jean Vanier maintained, would the extent to which the offering of many hidden prayerful people had wrought 'miracles' be known.

Since 1970 Jean had been going twice a year for two or three days to speak to the contemplatives in one Carmelite convent. He would give as many as five or six talks during his stay. The 26 Sisters hung on his words because this was in many ways their only nourishment, and he found that they drew something exceptional out of him. He had discovered that he could speak there in a way that he could not in l'Arche, partly because what he said would go no further than the confines of their walls; partly because he could give greater emphasis with them on what would bring them to intimacy with Jesus.

Within l'Arche there was something contemplative about the 'strange ambience of silence', precisely because on the whole people with disabilities were people of presence and spirit and not many words. In the evenings as they gathered in the *foyers* to pray it was essentially a silent, listening experience. The quiet passing of a picture book, reflection punctuated by the painfully articulated but manifestly heartfelt words of the 'crazy' and 'weak': 'Visited home. Amen.' 'Papa well. Amen.' 'New curtains. Amen.' It was important too that assistants prayed. In *Befriending the Stranger* Jean Vanier referred to the fact that when accompanying assistants he often asked them whether they prayed.

> I am not asking if they *say* prayers
> but if they have 'quiet times',
> times of nourishment with the Word of God,
> time alone to rest in God,
> time to deepen their personal relationship with God.

Frequently the response was that they did not have time even on their days off. Jean could understand this – pressure and fatigue were persistent if more recognised problems by this time – but he suspected also that it had something to do with the notion many people had of a God who obliged, demanded sacrifices, condemned and punished rather than one of communion, revelation and love. And yet a contemplative, mystical perspective rooted in prayer was essential if they were to see the face of the crucified but risen Jesus in their own disability, in those more obviously labelled 'disabled', in the disabled Church and the divided world; and approach them all with compassion.

Among the many with whom he had maintained contact over the years was Pedro Arrupé, a Spanish priest of great intellect and vision who had been Father General of the Jesuits. When some of the l'Arche members went to Rome on pilgrimage in 1980 they had visited him. Some years later, after he had suffered a stroke, Jean had called on him again. 'I offered him a book *I Meet Jesus,* with drawings, designed for children. He looked at the pictures and his eyes shone like the eyes of a child.' Pedro Arrupé lived for another ten years, growing weaker, becoming incontinent and needing to be fed and bathed, unable to do anything unaided. 'We may not all live and die as Pedro Arrupé did, but each one of our lives is leading to that same weakness and decline', Jean Vanier reminded his readers in *Befriending the Stranger*, 'We need to learn how to accept that fragility, and how to enter into the mystery of growth through weakness.' To grow in maturity was to grow in tenderness. It was also to grow in acceptance of reality.

Consciously, at least, Jean had reached the point of peaceful acceptance of his own story. He could see that he had made mistakes but that was all right. At the conscious level he did not feel guilt. He did not believe that Jesus wanted guilt or was pondering upon all the things he had not done well. What Jesus was concerned with was relationship now. Jean Vanier was not aware of any fear of death but that was because it was hidden: 'I would say that I have fear of anguish, fear of pain, but of death in the sense that we can talk about today, I have no fear.' He could not answer for the day that fine line between the conscious and the unconscious was broken. 'People have said that I can talk about tragic stories with a smile on my face so perhaps still somewhere in me there is not real compassion, that state of total identification and yet total separation.' He thought he had integrated his past but what anguish lay beneath he could not say. But then that was something we would all have to go through: 'The only thing we can die with is the feeling that we need Jesus.' And somewhere in him was the belief in mercy, on which the whole of l'Arche was founded.

There was a sense of a whole generation of the original assistants and people with disabilities drawing nearer to this point, or at least to retirement and old age with the accompanying increase in illness and weakness. Retirement arrangements for people with disabilities had been in place in many l'Arche communities for some time. In retirement support groups, while others went out to work, the older people with disabilities chatted and knitted, went for trips and did very much what other retired people did. Declining health posed much more complex problems.

❋

One thing Jean Vanier would like to have done that he had not was to found a religious order or something of that nature for old people. In a world which sought the elimination of the weak, it still took very little to create an ambience of friendliness for the elderly. It was relatively easy to make old people dance; far less so to make the powerful and the intellectual join in. It was Jacqueline d'Halluin's condition that had introduced him to the world of old people's homes. She had for some time been suffering from Parkinson's disease. She had also fallen and subsequently had to be hospitalised. When she was fit to leave the hospital Jean had found her a place in an old people's home in Compiègne but it was too far away from Trosly-Breuil. For a while she had returned to a small house in Trosly but it had not been possible to look after her properly. It was she who had decided she must leave. She had found a place run by Sisters nearby, from which she could return regularly to Trosly, and was enduring what she described as the 'last kiss of Jesus' with great fortitude. Jean found her an excellent example: 'She will always say that she is getting weaker and that she is not happy but then she smiles and accepts it as the cross she has to live.' What, however, would happen in the future when there were more people like her? The whole question of ageing disabled people and assistants requiring more medical care than l'Arche could provide was one of those with which the community was still 'walking'.

For some time now Jean himself had suffered from an irregular heartbeat. He had recently also experienced several painful blows. The death of Pope John Paul II had affected him more than he expected. He had also been deeply saddened by the effects of another fire, this time at La Vigne in 2005, in which two much-loved l'Arche members lost their lives. There were times when he lacked stamina and his legs felt like cotton wool. He knew he had to be more careful, but it did not stop him travelling that year to among other places, Chile, Madagascar, Portugal and Lebanon. In July he also went to Jordan to visit institutions for Muslim children who had been on the street or were in rehabilitation. He had shared with educators, psychologists and others – some Christian but for the most part Muslim – his beliefs about what such young people needed in order to come to know themselves better. Afterwards Roy Moussali, the vice international coordinator of Faith and Light, wrote about the extraordinary effect of the spiritual realities of which Jean spoke on this mixed audience: 'We are thirsty for prophets with this vision, charism and way of touching those who have been alienated by our Christian language and our narrowness of mind.'

If Père Thomas' insight had been that the mystical life lay at the beginning of our existence and not just at its end, it had also been that[2] its characteristic was that the more we discover unity with God, the more we emerge from ourselves and become aware and awakened. It was a truth to which Jean Vanier's own life bore witness. He might well be pleased to have 'more time for prayer and to work on myself, so that I may grow in love, patience and truth', but the schedule of his days seemed as full as ever. His secret, he maintained was a body well-formed by the Navy, a high level of motivation and the fact that his energy was not dissipated on trivial and disparate things. As to the future of l'Arche without him, temperamentally he was one who was able, perhaps sometimes too readily, to accept things as they were. '*C'est ainsi*' ('That's how it is') was an attitude which came spontaneously to him. Nor was he one to concern himself unduly with those things over which he had no control. He still met regularly with Jean-Christophe Pascal, Christine McGrievy and other community leaders, and he sensed, trusted and believed that l'Arche was in good hands.

The joy of human beings was to leave this earth having given life to others, who in turn were called to give life to another generation. Jean Vanier was undoubtedly still giving life to many. We had talked in his or my car, on the telephone, as we walked together through the village of Trosly-Breuil, at my home or in his room. We had shared many words, much laughter, a few tears, innumerable cups of tea, and we had shared the silence. His vision, I sensed, had deepened considerably since first we had worked on a book about l'Arche. He had, he acknowledged, reached greater maturity. What was more, the television series on the Gospel of John, the retreats and his contributions to the 'Ecole de Vie' had obliged him to give it expression. He was not someone who could give what he had always given. He was constantly seeking to offer something new and that had impelled him forward, as had the encouragement of people like theologians David Ford, Frances Young and Donald Allchin. There was also the absence of Père Thomas, that good and holy priest by whom he had been blessed to be shepherded. His death had brought Jean sadness, the sense of loss … and liberation.

In *Drawn into the Mystery of Jesus through the Gospel of John* Jean Vanier had written of how, after kneeling down and washing his disciples' feet in John 14 Jesus said goodbye, and at the same time promised to see them again soon:

> Announcing his departure and proclaiming his return
> seems to have another meaning too:
> about the growth of each one of us in love.
> This growth takes a lifetime
> and implies times of presence and absence, encounters and
> departures.
> What is true in regards to human friendship
> is particularly true in the friendship that bonds us to God.
> The presence of someone we love brings joy.
> We savour their presence.
> But their absence requires trust, hope and fidelity;
> it deepens the 'well' of our being.
> Absence hurts
> but as the pain increases, the desire is strengthened,
> so that the presence that will come will be even fuller and
> more total.
> In order to live more deeply this friendship with God,
> other desires that have taken up too much room
> in our hearts and lives may have to be pruned or cut away.
> But their loss can also be the prelude
> to being filled in a new and deeper way with God.

NOTES

***Chapter 1*: Reading the Miracle**
1. Jean Vanier, *Drawn into the Mystery of Jesus through the Gospel of John* (Darton, Longman and Todd, 2004/Paulist Press, 2004/Novalis, 2004).
2. For Jean Vanier 'Logos' has a much wider meaning than the 'Word', referring not only to the spoken word, but also to the *idea* and *thought* behind the spoken word, the *vision*, the *plan* and the *wisdom* that inspire it.
3. Vanier, *Drawn into the Mystery of Jesus.*
4. Vanier, *Drawn into the Mystery of Jesus.*

***Chapter 2*: 'The Life Is in the Roots'**
1. Jean Vanier, *In Weakness, Strength* (Griffin Press, 1970).
2. Jean Vanier, *A Door of Hope – The Transformation of Pain* (Hodder and Stoughton, 1996).
3. Jean Vanier, *Drawn into the Mystery of Jesus through the Gospel of John* (Darton, Longman and Todd, 2004/Paulist Press, 2004/Novalis, 2004).
4. Vanier, *Drawn into the Mystery of Jesus.*

***Chapter 5*: Sharing the Word**
1. *Préfet*: local administrator for the region.
2. Jean Vanier, *Drawn into the Mystery of Jesus through the Gospel of John* (Darton, Longman and Todd, 2004/Paulist Press, 2004/Novalis, 2004).
3. Jean Vanier, *Community and Growth* (Darton, Longman and Todd, 1989/Paulist Press, 1991).

Chapter 6: Between Two Worlds

1. Expression meaning 'children of God' used by Gandhi to refer to those who in traditional Indian society were the 'untouchables', people of low caste or outside the caste system.
2. Jean Vanier, *A Network of Friends* (Lancelot Press, 1992). Letter from Bangalore, India, 22 October 1970.

Chapter 7: Towards Communion

1. Jean Vanier, *Our Inner Journey* (l'Arche publication, 1974),
2. 'Decree on the Ministry and Life of Priests', *Documents of Vatican II* (Geoffrey Chapman, 1966).
3. Thérèse Vanier, *An Ecumenical Journey – l'Arche in the UK* (l'Arche publication, December 1989).
4. Thérèse Vanier, *One Bread, One Body* (Gracewing, 1997/ Novalis, 1997).

Chapter 8: Servants of Communion

1. Jean Vanier, *Drawn into the Mystery of Jesus through the Gospel of John* (Darton Longman and Todd, 2004/Paulist Press, 2004/Novalis, 2004).

Chapter 9: More Earthy and More Heavenly

1. Stephen Verney, *Into the New Age* (Fontana/Collins, 1976).
2. Jean Vanier, *Our Inner Journey* (l'Arche publication).
3. Jean Vanier, *Community and Growth*, (Darton, Longman and Todd, 1989/Paulist Press, 1991).

Chapter 11: The Music Beyond the Words

1. Jean Vanier, *In Weakness, Strength* (Griffin Press, 1970).
2. Jean Vanier, *Tears of Silence* (Darton, Longman and Todd, revised edition, 1991).
3. Jean Vanier, *Followers of Jesus* (Gill and Macmillan, 1993/Paulist Press, 1976).
4. Jean Vanier, *Be Not Afraid* (Gill and Macmillan, 1976/Paulist Press, 1975).
5. Jean Vanier, *Community and Growth* (Darton, Longman and Todd, 1989/Paulist Press, 1991).
6. Jean Vanier, *Man and Woman He Made Them* (Darton, Longman and Todd, 1988/Paulist Press, 1986).
7. Jean Vanier, *The Broken Body: Journey to Wholeness* (Darton, Longman and Todd, 1988/Paulist Press, 1988).

8. Jean Vanier, *A Door of Hope – The Transformation of Pain* (Hodder and Stoughton, 1996).

9. Jean Vanier, *Our Journey Home* (Hodder and Stoughton, 1997/Orbis, 1977).

10. Thérèse Vanier, *Nick – Man of the Heart* (Gill and Macmillan, 1992).

11. Henri Nouwen: *The Road to Daybreak* (Darton, Longman and Todd, 1989/Doubleday, 1990); *Finding My Way Home* (Darton, Longman and Todd, 2001/Crossroad, 2001); *The Return of the Prodigal Son* (Darton, Longman and Todd 1994/Doubleday, 1994); *The Inner Voice of Love* (Darton, Longman and Todd, 1997/Doubleday, 1999); *Adam: God's Beloved* (Darton, Longman and Todd, 1997/Orbis, 1997).

12. Nouwen, *The Road to Daybreak*.

13. Jean Vanier, *Becoming Human* (Darton, Longman and Todd, 1999/Paulist Press, 1999).

14. Jean Vanier, *Seeing Beyond Depression* (SPCK, 2001/Paulist Press, 2001).

15. Jean Vanier, *Made for Happiness* (Darton, Longman and Todd, 2001/House of Anansi Press, 2001).

16. Jean Vanier, *Finding Peace* (Continuum, 2005/House of Anansi Press, 2003).

Chapter 12: Pain and Union
1. Mark 8:31–3.

Chapter 13: Owning the Story
1. Defined as 'a set of narrative symbols, a story or tradition that claims to reveal to people, in an imaginative way, a fundamental truth about the world, themselves, their lives.'

2. Jean Vanier, *The Founding Myth and the Evolution of Community:* 2nd Prophetic Paper, 1993.

3. Jean Vanier, *Becoming Human* (Darton, Longman and Todd, 1999/Paulist, 1999).

Chapter 14: New Life in God
1. Jean Vanier, *Befriending the Stranger* (Darton, Longman and Todd, 2005/Novalis, 2005).

2. P. Thomas Philippe OP, 'Les ages de la vie: I L'enfance', *Les Chemins de l'Arche* (La Ferme, 1996).

BIBLIOGRAPHY

BIBLIOGRAPHY

Books by Jean Vanier
In Weakness, Strength (Griffin Press, 1970)
Be Not Afraid (Gill and Macmillan, 1976/Paulist Press, 1975)
Followers of Jesus (Gill and Macmillan, 1993/Paulist Press, 1976)
Man and Woman He Made Them (Darton, Longman and Todd, 1988/Paulist Press, 1986)
The Broken Body: Journey to Wholeness (Darton, Longman and Todd, 1988/Paulist Press, 1988)
Community and Growth (Darton, Longman and Todd, 1989/Paulist Press, 1991)
Tears of Silence (Darton, Longman and Todd, revised edition, 1991)
A Network of Friends (Lancelot Press, 1992)
A Door of Hope – The Transformation of Pain (Hodder and Stoughton, 1996)
Our Journey Home (Hodder and Stoughton, 1997/Orbis, 1977)
Becoming Human (Darton, Longman and Todd, 1999/Paulist Press, 1999)
Seeing Beyond Depression (SPCK, 2001/Paulist Press, 2001)
Made for Happiness – Discovering the Meaning of Life with Aristotle (Darton, Longman and Todd, 2001/House of Anansi Press, 2001)
Finding Peace (Continuum, 2005/House of Anansi Press, 2003)
Drawn into the Mystery of Jesus through the Gospel of John (Darton, Longman and Todd, 2004/Paulist Press, 2004/Novalis 2004)

Befriending the Stranger (Darton, Longman and Todd, 2005/Novalis, 2005)

Books by Thérèse Vanier

An Ecumenical Journey – l'Arche in the UK (l'Arche publication, December 1989)
Nick – Man of the Heart (Gill and Macmillan, 1993)
One Bread, One Body (Gracewing, 1997/Novalis, 1997)

Others

Buell, John, *Travelling Light – The Way and Life of Tony Walsh* (Novalis, 2004)
Coady, Mary Francis, *The Hidden Way – The Life and Influence of Almire Pichon* (Novalis, 1998)
Clarke, Bill, SJ, *The Face of Friendship* (Novalis, 2004)
—*Room Enough for Joy* (Darton, Longman and Todd, 1974, revised edition Novalis, 2006)
Nouwen, Henri, *Adam: God's Beloved* (Darton, Longman and Todd, 1977/Orbis, 1997)
—*Our Greatest Gift – a Meditation on Dying and Caring* (Hodder and Stoughton, 1994)
—*The Inner Voice of Love* (Darton, Longman and Todd, 1997/Doubleday, 1999)
—*The Return of the Prodigal Son* (Darton, Longman and Todd, 1994/Doubleday, 1994)
—*The Road to Daybreak* (Darton, Longman and Todd, 1989/Doubleday, 1990)
Philippe, Pére Thomas, OP, *Les Ages de la Vie: 1 l'Enfance* (Les Chemins de l'Arche, 1996)
Reid Thomas, Helen, *L'Arche Communities – New Movements and Communities in the Life of the Church* (Catholic Truth Society, 2002)
Verney, Stephen, *Into the New Age* (Fontana/Collins, 1976)
Wilson, Hilary, *My Life Together – L'Arche Communities and the Challenge of Unity* (Darton, Longman and Todd, 2004)

ADDRESSES OF

L'ARCHE COMMUNITIES

ARGENTINA

El Arca Buenos Aires
Juncal 871, 5è piso (1061)
Buenos Aires
mlgowland@fibertel.com.ar

AUSTRALIA

www.larche.org.au

Beni Abbès

PO Box 132
Moonah TAS. 7009
T/F: 61-36-228-39-20
Beni-
Abbes.Community@tassie.net.au

Brisbane

PO Box 260
The Gap
4061 Queensland
T. (61) 7.32.17.30.11
F. (61) 7.32.17.30.44
larchebrisbane@comcen.com.au

L'Arche Genesaret

PO Box 734
Woden, ACT. 2606
T/F: 61-26-295-2627 (O)
T: 61-26-282-4206(H)
larche@austarmetro.com.au

L'Arche Sydney

PO Box 312
Burnwood 1805 NSW
T. 61-29-747-5858
T. 61-29-715-6567
larcheoffice@iprimus.com.au

BELGIUM

www.larche.be

De Ark Antwerpen

Frans Segerstraat 46
BE 2530 – Boechout
T. 00 (32) 3-454-34-02
F. 00 (32) 3-454-32-75
ark.antwerpen@moso.be

De Ark Moerkerke

Vissersstraat 71/1
BE-8340 Moerkerke
T/F: 00 (32) 50-50-18-84
info@arkmoerkerke.be

L'Arche Aywailles

Rue Mathieu Carpentier 50
BE-4920
T/F: 00 (32) 43-84-31-43
aywaille.larche@ticali.be

L'Arche Bierges

Rue St Pierre 14

BE-1301 Bierges
T. 00 (32) 10-40-14-53
F. 00 (32) 10-40-15-58
arche.bierges@belgacom.net

L'Arche Bruxelles
Avenue Eudore Pirmez 36
BE-1040 Bruxelles
T. 00 (32) 2-733-76-68
F. 00 (32) 2-649-08-54
arche.bruxelles1@yucom.be

L'Arche Namur
Chaussée de Charleroi 145
BE-5000 Namur
T/F: 00 (32) 81-22-13-22
namur@larche.be

BRAZIL

Arca do Brazil
Rua Manoel Aquilino dos Santos
163
Jardin Eliza Maria
Cep 02873-520 Sao Paulo SP
T. 00-55-11-38-51-34-59
F. 00-55-11-39-85-33-04
arcadobrasil@bol.com.br

BURKINA FASO

L'Arche Nongr Maasem
01 BP 1492
Ouagadougou 01
T. 00-226-31-04-35
F. 00-226-30-57-38
arche.nongremassem@fasonet.bf

CANADA
www.larchecanada.org

L'Arche Agapé
19 Rue Front
Hull, PQ J8Y 3M4
T. (819) 770-2000

F. (819) 770-3907
arche.agape@qc.aira.com

L'Arche Antigonish
97 Church Street
Antigonish, NS B2G 2E2
902-863-50-00
902-863-82-24
larche.antigonish@ns.sympatico.ca

L'Arche Arnprior
16 Edward Street South
Suite 103
Arnprior, ON K7S 3W4
T. (613) 623-7323
F. (613) 62-9629
larche@arnprior.com

L'Arche Beloeil
221 Rue Bernard Pilon
Beloeil, QC J3G1V2
T. (450) 446 10 61
F. (450) 446 23 96
archebelo@qc.aira.com

L'Arche Calgary
307-57 ave SW
Calgary, ALB T2H 2T6
T. (403) 571-01-55
F. (403) 255-13-54
office@larchecalgary.com

L'Arche Cape Breton
Whycocomagh
NS BOE 3M
T. (902) 756-31-62
F. (902) 756-33-81
office@larchecapebreton.org

L'Arche Comox
Sile 336, RR3 C16
Courtenay, BC V9N 5M8
T. (250) 334-8320
F. (250) 334-8321
lrm@island.bet

L'Arche Daybreak
11339 Yonge Street
Richmond Hill, ON L4S 1L1
T. (905) 884-3454 (O)
F. (905) 884-0580
office@larchedaybreak.com

L'Arche Daybreak Toronto
1190 Danforth
Toronto, ON M4J 1M6
T. (416) 406-2869 ext 22
F. (905) 884-0580
toronto@larchedaybreak.com

L'Arche l'Etoile
617 Christophe Colomb Ouest
Québec, PQ G1N 2K54
T. (418) 527-88394
F. (418) 527-8738
larcheletoile@videotron.ca

L'Arche Hamilton
116 Holton Avenue South
Hamilton, ON L8M 2L5
T. (905) 312-0162
F. (905) 312-0165
larchehamltn@idirect.com

L'Arche Homefires
10 Gapereau Avenue
Wolfville, NS B4P 2C2
T. (902) 542-3520
F. (902) 542-7686
larchehomefires@ns.sympatico.ca

L'Arche Joliette
879 Rue St Louis
Joliette, PQ J6E 3A3
T. (450) 759-0408
sophiecote31@hotmail.com

L'Arche de Lethbridge
239-12B Street North
Lethbridge, ALB T1H 2K8
T. (403) 328-37-35

F. (403) 320-67-37
larche@telusplanet.net

L'Arche London
225 Whisperwood Ave
London, ON N6B 4E8
T. (519) 641-2262
F. (519) 641-8823
Larche_london@bellnet.ca

L'Arche Mauricie
570 Rue St Paul
Trois-Rivières PQ G9A 1H8
T. (819) 373-8781
F. (819) 373-1910
archemauricie@qc.aira.com

L'Arche Montréal
6646 Blvd Monk
Montréal, PQ H4E 3J1
T. (514) 761-7307
F. (514) 761-0823
larche-montreal@qc.aira.com

L'Arche North Bay
Suite 233-101 Worthington St
East
North Bay, ON P1B 1G5
T. (705) 474-00-81
F. (705) 497-34-47
larchenorthbay@on.aibn.com

L'Arche Ottawa
102-119 Ross Avenue
Ottawa, ON K1Y 0N6
T. (613) 729-16-01
F. (613) 729-45-39
larcheottawa@on.aibn.com

L'Arche le Printemps
1375 Principale, CP68
St Malachie, PQ GOR 3N0
T. (418) 642-5785
F. (418) 642-57-99
archeleprintemps@globetrotter.net

L'Arche le Saule Fragile
CP 33
Amos, PQ J9T 3A5
T. (819) 732-12-65
F. (819) 732-03-67
archeamos@sympatico.ca

L'Arche Shalom
7708-83rd Street
Edmonton, ALB T6C 2Y8
T. (780) 465-06-18
F. (780) 465-80-91
edmoffice@larcheedmonton.org

L'Arche Shiloah
7401 Sussex Avenue
Burnaby, BC V5J 3V6
T. (604) 435-95-44
F. (604) 435-95-60
Office@larchevancouver.org

L'Arche Stratford
PO Box 522, Stn Main
Stratford, ON N5A 6T7
T. (519) 271-9751
F. (519) 271-1861
info@larche.stratford.on.cainfoca

L'Arche Sudbury
1173 Rideau St
Sudbury, ON P3A 3A5
T. (705) 525-10-15
F. (705) 525-44-48
larchesudbury@attcanada.net

L'Arche Winnipeg
109 Bond St
Winnipeg, MB R2C 2L1
T. (204) 237-03-00
F. (204) 237-03-16
larchwpg@mts.net

COTE D'IVOIRE

L'Arche Ivory Coast
BP 304

Bonoua
T. 00-225-21-31-01-32
houphouetalain@yahoo.fr

DENMARK

Niels Steensens Hus
Nygade 4a3000 Helsingør
T. 45-49-21-21-39
F. 45-49-20-11-76
jhviid@get2net.dk

DOMINICAN REPUBLIC

**El Arca de la Republica
Dominicana**
Apartado 2-8
Calle les Cayenas #4
Buenos Aires de Herrera
Santo Domingo
T. 00-809-561-00-97
F. 00-809-472-68-23
elarcard@tricom.net

FRANCE

Aigrefoin
Chemin Rural No. 3
78470 St Rémy les Chevreuses
T. 33 (0)1-30-52-89-89
F. 33 (0)1-30-52-89-90
archeaig@club-internet.fr

L'Arche
29 Rue d'Orléans
BP 35
60350 Trosly-Breuil
T. 33 (0)3-44-85-56-00
F. 33 (0)3-44-85-65-51
dir.trosly@archoise.org

L'Arche à Agen
24 Rue des Vertus
47220 Astaffort
T/F. 33 (0)5-53-47-53-17
arche-en-agenais@wanadoo.fr

L'Arche à Cognac
3a Rue de L'anisserie
16100 Château Bernard
T. 33 (0)5-45-36-15-00
F. 33 (0)5-45-32-19-85
arche.cognac@wanadoo.fr

L'Arche de Cuise
122 Rue Domaine
BP 4
60350 Cuise la Motte
T. 33 (0)3-44-85-44-44
F. 33 (0)3-44-85-75-22
arche.cuise@archoise.org

L'Arche à Dijon
16 Rue de l'Est
21000 Dijon
T/F: 33 (0)3-80-36-26-96
arche.dijon@wanadoo.fr

L'Arche à Lyon (la Croisée)
73 Rue Henri Legay
69100 Villeurbanne
T. 33 (0)4-78-41-16-90
F. 33 (0)4-78-26-92-46
arche-lyon@libertysurf.fr

L'Arche au Carmel
88 bis bd Clémenceau
29480 Le Relecq Kerhuon
Tel : (33) 02.98.30.54.05
Fax : (33) 02.98.30.41.67
larcheaucarmel@larchefrance.org

L'Horizon
Arche de Jean Vanier en
Languedoc
158 Rue du Pioch de Boutonnet
34090 Montpellier
T. (0)4-67-72-69-00
F. (0)4-67-72-59-52
arche.horizon@libertysurf.fr

L'Arche à Paris
10 Rue Fenoux

75015 Paris
T. 33 (0)1-42-50-06-48
F. 33 (0)1-48-28-71-62
arche.paris@wanadoo.fr

Arche de la Vallée
Quartier Piache
26390 Hauterives
T. 33 (0)4-75-68-81-84
F. 33 (0)4-75-68-74-41
archevallee@wanadoo.fr

L'Atre
21 Rue des Châteaux
59118 Wambrechies
T. 33 (0)3-20-78-81-52
F. 33 (0)3-20-78-81-40
arche.wambrechies@free.fr

Le Caillou Blanc
5 route du Drennec
29950 Clohars-Fouesnant
T/F: 33(0)2-98-54-60-05
arche-lecailloublanc@wanadoo.fr

Ecorchebeuf
Hameau d'Ecorchebeuf
76590 Anneville-sur-Scie
T/F: 33(0)2-35-04-40-31
arche.ecorchebeuf@free.fr

L'Espérance
1 Rue du Bourg
60350 Pierrefonds
T: 33(0)3-44-95-33-40
F: 33 (0)3-44-95-33-46
esperance.pierrefonds@archoise.org

Le Levain
1 Place St Clément
B.P. 10 733
60207 Compiègne
T. 33 (0)3-44-86-25-03
F. 33 (0)3-44-20-99-83
arche.levain@net-up.com

La Merci
16200 Courbillac
T. 33 (0)5-45-21-74-16
F. 33 (0)5-45-96-50-85
accueil@larche-lamerci.com

Le Moulin de L'Auro
Chemin de la Muscadelle
84800 l'Isle sur Sorgue
T. 33 (0)4-90-20-61-51
F. 33 (0)4-90-20-70-57
lemoulindelauro@wanadoo.fr

L'Olivier
30 Rue de la Noë
35170 Bruz
T. 33 (0)2-99-52-72-74
F. 33 (0)2-99-52-56-17
larche.lolivier@wanadoo.fr

La Rebellerie
49560 Nueil sur Layon
T. 33 (0)2-41-59-53-51
F. 33 (0)2-41-59-99-89
la-rebellerie@wanadoo.fr

La Rose des Vents
12 Grande Rue
80700 Verpillières
T. 33(0)3-22-87-22-57
F. 33(0)3-22-87-14-52
j.jrobin@wanadoo.fr

La Ruisselée
13 Rue du 8 Mai
72220 St Mars d'Outille
T. 33 (0)2-43-42-70-96
F. 33 (0)2-43-42-77-95
arche.la.ruisselee@wanadoo.fr

Les Sapins
Domaine des Abels
16130 Lignières Sonneville
T. 33 (0)5-45-80-50-66
F. 33 (0)5-45-80-55-88
arche.lessapins@wanadoo.fr

Le Sénevé
'La Carizière'
44690 La Haye Fouassière
T. 33 (0)2-40-36-98-39
F. 33 (0)2-40-36-78-70
seneve@club-internet.fr

Le Sycomore
73800 Myans
T. 33 (0)4-79-71-51-66
F. 33 (0)4-79-71-56-25
arche.sycomore@wanadoo.fr

Les Trois Fontaines
6 Rue de l'Ecluse
62164 Ambleteuse
T. 33(0)3-21-99-92-99
F. 33(0)3-21-33-39-63
arche3fontaines@netinfo.fr

GERMANY
www.arche-deutschland.de

L'Arche Ravensburg
Eisenbanstrasse 38
88212 Ravensburg
T. 49-751-35-24-672
ravensburg@arche-deutschland.de

L'Arche Regenbogen
Apfelallee 23
49545 Tecklenburg
T. 49-54-82-77-00
F. 49-54-82-97-40-24
tecklenburg@arche-deutschland.de

L'Arche Volksdorf
Farmsener Landstr.198
22359 Hambourg
T. 49-40-603-55-34
F. 49-40-603-15-363
volksdorf@arche-deutschland.de

HAITI

L'Arche de Carrefour
BP 11075
Port-au-Prince
T/F: 00-509-234-42-55
archecarrefour@hotmail.com

L'Arche de Chantal
C.P 63 Les Cayes
T. 00-509-286-14-27
F. 00-509-286-14-28

HONDURAS

El Arca de Choluteca
Apartado 241
Choluteca
T/F: 00-504-8-80-20-94
archolut@hondutel.hn

El Arca de Tegucigalpa
Apartado 1273
Tegucigalpa DF
T. 00-504-232-56-18 (O)
T. 00-504-222-42-41 (H)
arcal.c@datum.hn

HUNGARY

www.larche-europesud.org

Barka
Arany JU 45
2330 Dunaharasti
T. (36) 24-46-18-37
T/F: (36) 24-46-18-38
larche@freemail.hu

INDIA

Asha Niketan Bangalore
CA7 80 Feet Road
20th Main, 6th Block,
Koramangala
Bangalore 560095

T. 0091-80-552-4584
F. 0091-80-227-7489
anbangalore@rediffmail.com

Asha Niketan Calcutta
37 Tangra Road – Kolkata
700015
T. 0091-33-2329-12-49 (O)
T. 0091-33-2328-29-74 (H)
F. 0091-33-2329-20-02
larcheawpzon@onlysmart.com

Asha Niketan Madras
1/194 East Cost Road
Kottivakkam, Thiruvanmiyur PO
Chennai 600 041
T. 0091-44-492-77-98
F. 0091-44-442-16-58
anchennai@sify.com

Asha Niketan Nandi Bazaar
Nandi Bazaar
Katalur PO – Calcut Dt
Kerala 673531
T. 0091-496-602-620
F. 0091-496-620-725
ashaclt@eth.net

IRELAND

www.larche.ie

L'Arche Belfast
The Ember
c/o 563 Ormeau Road
Belfast BT7 3JA
T. 44 (0)28 90 87 29 77 (H)
T. 44 (028) 90.22.13.37 (O)
F. 44 (028) 90.872.992
belfast@larche.ie

L'Arche Cork
'Le Cheile' – Togher, Cork 4
T. (353) 214-31-88-80
F. (353) 214-31-88-83
niall.h@larche.ie

L'Arche Dublin
Seolta, Warrenhouse Road
Baldoyle, Dublin 13
T. (353) 18-39-43-56
F. (353) 18-39-54-60
dublin@larche.ie

L'Arche Kilkenny
'Cluain Aoibhinn'
Fairgreen Lane, Callan
Co Kilkenny
T. (353) 56-25-628
F. (353) 56-25-946
kilkenny@larche.ie

ITALY
www.larche-europesud.org

Arcobaleno
Via Badini 4
40050 Quarto Inferiore
Italia
T/F +(39) 05-17-67-300
arcabologna@libero.it

Il Chicco
Via Ancona 1
00043 Ciampino, Roma
T/F: (39) 06-79-62-104
arcachicco@libero.it

JAPAN

Kana-No-Ie
Ashikubokuchigumi 1255
421 2124 Shizuoka-Shi
T. (81) 54-29-61-116
F. (81) 54-29-66-433
larchehayashi@yahoo.co.jp

MEXICO

El Arca de Mexico
Apartado 112-100
Colonia Santa Marta

Acatitla, Mexico DF 09 510
T/F: (52) 55-57-32-8391(O)
T/F: (52) 55-57-32-1642 (H)
ideales8@prodigy.net.mx

El Arca de Querétaro
Plaza de la Conchita n°2
Colonia las Plazas
Querétaro, 76180
T/F: (52) 442-216-9056
regine_arca@yahoo.com

NETHERLANDS

De Ark Gouda
Wethouder Venteweg 224
NL-2805 J.V Gouda
T. 00 (31) 182-54-80-24
F. 00 (31) 182-54-81-22
ark.gouda@planet.nl

NEW ZEALAND

L'Arche Kapiti
13 Redwood Close
Paraparumu 6010
T. (64) 904-9793
F. (64) 904-0635
larche@larche.org.nz

PHILIPPINES

Punla
118 Camia Street
Bayanihan Village
Cainta Rizal 1900
T. (63) 2-655-1482 (O)
F. (63) 2-655-1481
larchepunla@edsamail.com.ph

POLAND

L'Arche Poznan
Wspolnota w Poznaniu
Ul. Polanska 13A

61-614 Poznan
T/F: (48) 61-82-56-200
Larche.Sledziejowice@poczta.fm

L'Arche Sledziejowice
Sledziejowice 83
32-020 Wieliczka
T/F: (48) 12-27-86-958
baska.pestka@poszta.fm

L'Arche Wroclaw
Ul. Jutrosinska 29
51-124 Wroclaw
T/F +(48) 713.25.68.23
wroclaw@larche.org.pl

SLOVENIA
www.larche-europesud.org

Skupnost Barka
Zbilje 66
1215 Medvode
T/F: (386) 13-61-36-17
barka.skup@guest.arnes.si

SPAIN
www.larche-europesud.org

El Rusc
Veïnat de Saint Ponç 12
08490 Tordera
T/F: 34-937-640-150
associacioelrusc@wanadoo.es

Els Avets
Carrer Calders S/N
08180 Moiá
T/F: 34-93-830-13-62
elsavets@wanadoo.es

SWITZERLAND
www.arche-helvetia.ch

La Corolle
24 chemin d'Ecogia

1290 Versoix-Genève
T: (41) 22-755-51-82
F: (41) 22-779-29-18
corolle@arche-helvetia.ch

La Grotte
28 Av. Jean Gambach
1700 Fribourg
T. (41) 26-323-15-85
F. (41) 26-323-14-35
lagrotte@arche-helvetia.ch

Im Nauen
Oberdorfstr.9 – Postfach 34
4146 Hochwald
T. (41) 61-751-49-33 (B)
T. (41) 61-751-49-34 (H)
F. (41) 61-753-93-34
imnauen@arche-helvetia.ch

SYRIA

L'Arche Al Safina
Vieille Ville
BP 22639, Bab
Touma/Kaymariyeh – Damas
T/F (963) 11.542.41.15
alsafina@mail.sy

UGANDA

L'Arche Uganda
PO Box 14095
Mengo, Kampala
T. (256) 41-270-579 (H)
T/F (256) 41-270-234
larcheug@utlonline.co.ug

UNITED KINGDOM
www.larche.org.uk

L'Arche Bognor Regis
Bradbury House
51A Aldewick Road
Bognor Regis

West Sussex PO21 2NJ
T. 44-12-43-86-34-26
F. 44-12-43-84-03-83
bognor@larche.org.uk

L'Arche Brecon
Steeple House, Steeple Lane
Brecon, Powys LD3 7DJ
WALES
T. 44-18-74-62-44-83 (O)
F. 44-18-74-61-00-46
brecon@larche.org.uk

L'Arche Edinburgh
132 Constitution Street
Leith, Edinburgh EH6 6AJ
T. 44-13-15-53-34-78
F. 44-131-554-32-36
edinburgh@larche.org.uk

L'Arche Inverness
Braerannoch, 13 Drumond Cres.
Inverness 1V2 4QR
T. 44-14-63-23-96-15
F. 44-14-63-71-10-89
inverness@larche.org.uk

L'Arche Kent
Little Ewell
Barfrestone, Dover
Kent CT15 7JJ
T. 44-13-04-83-09-30
F. 44-13-04-83-23-93
kent@larche.org.uk

L'Arche Lambeth
15 Norwood High Street
London SE27 9JU
T. 44-20-86-70-67-14
F. 44-20-86-70-08-18
lambeth@larche.org.uk

L'Arche Liverpool
Lockerby Road
Liverpool L7 OHG

T. 44-15-12-60-04-22
F. 44-15-12-63-22-60
liverpool@larche.org.uk

L'Arche Preston
3 Moor Park Avenue
Preston PR1 6AS
T/F: 44-17-72-25-11-13
preston@larche.org.uk

UNITED STATES
www.larcheusa.org

The Arch
PO Box 0278
Clinton, IA 52732
T/F: 563-243-9035
larchia@clinton.net

L'Arche Chicago
1049 S. Austin Blvd
Chicago, IL 60644
T/F: 773-287-8249
larchechicago@hotmail.com

L'Arche Cleveland
PO Box 20450
Cleveland, OH 44 120
T. 216-721-2614
F. 216-229-2311
rebecca_larchecleveland@juno.com

L'Arche Erie (The Earth)
1101 Peach St 2 Floor
Erie, PA 16501
T. 814-452-2065
F. 814-452-4188
office@larcheerie.org

L'Arche Harbor House
700 Arlington Road
Jacksonville, FL 32211-7306
T. 904-721-5992
F. 904-721-7143
larchfl@aol.com

L'Arche Hearthland
PO Box 40493
KS 66204
T. 913-341-2265
F. 913-648-6764
LARCHKC@juno.com

L'Arche Irenicon
PO Box 5034
Bradford, MA 01835
T. 978-374-6928
F. 978-373-9097
office@larcheirenicon.org

L'Arche Mobile (Hope)
151 South Ann Street
Mobile, AL 36604
T/F: 251-438-2094
larchmob@hotmail.com

L'Arche Nehalem
8501 SE Stephens
Portland, OR 97216
T. 503-251-6901
F. 503-251-6952
mail@larche-portland.org

L'Arche Noah Sealth
PO Box 22023
Seattle, WA 98122-0023
T. 206-325-9434
F. 206-568-0367
Gerry@larcheseattle.org

L'Arche Spokane
703 E Nora, Spokane

WA 99207
T. 509-483-0438
F. 509-483-0460
larchespokane@earthlink.net

L'Arche Syracuse
1232 Teall Avenue
Syracuse, NY 13206
T. 315-479-8088
F. 315-479-8118
larchesyracuse@aol.com

L'Arche Tahoma Hope
12303-36th Ave East
Tacoma, WA 98446
T. 253-535-3178
F. 253-539-9208
tahomahope@larchethc.org

L'Arche Washington
2474 Ontarion Road NW
Washington, DC 20009
T. 202-232-4539
F. 202-387-0963
Larchedc@worldnet.att.net

ZIMBABWE

L'Arche Zimbabwe
PO Box CY2730
Causeway, Harare
T. 00-263-4-614-295 (foyer)
wicosaru@internet.co.zw

INDEX